'Imagine a peasant woman, paralysed, with no exceptionable education, (Julie Billiart) and an aristocratic woman (Francoise Blin de Bourdon), thrown together in the terror and persecution of the French Revolution and you will have some idea of the inspiration of the founding of Myra Poole's congregation. This book – both thrilling narrative and creative spirituality! – is a most unusual blend of the history and spirituality of the founding of the Notre Dame congregation looked at in the light of its relevance for contemporary challenges by one of its loyal members. What makes it unique is the way the original mystical charism, prophetic role and suffering of Julie Billiart are encountered in the light of contemporary Christian feminist spiritually, and shown to present fresh inspiration not only for the life of her own followers, but for all believers. The book is both the personal testimony of one of Julie's present day disciples exploring her own prophetic and pioneering role and , more significantly, it is a trail-blazer in that the mystical charism of someone from an entirely different historical context is re-interpreted as showing a way forward in response to contemporary challenges.'

Mary Grey
D.J. James Professor of Pastoral Theology
University of Wales

'*Prayer, Protest, Power* by Myra Poole is a rare piece of literature. It takes a topic that would, under ordinary treatment, have very little interest to very many people today and turns it into a work of unusual contemporary value, especially to women everywhere.

It is one woman's explanation of how, as a feminist, she not only can but must remain in religious life if she wants to be true to the feminist values she holds. Poole traces the work of Julie Billiart, the foundress of the Sisters of Notre Dame de Namur, and finds that it is the feminist spirit of this woman that feeds the well of her own feminism. Most important of all, she shows us all how mysticism, the spirituality of the time drove Billiart to confront both church and society.'

Joan Chittister OSB

'Remember the past, to enrich your future.' Myra Poole's book illustrates the truth of that dictum. What could you have been a sterile account of the life of an eighteenth-century foundress, has become a source of refection on the challenges facing women in today's Church. Graphic descriptions of historical scene alternate with penetrating analyses of deeper implications and their application to modern times.

Myra Poole has successfully identified and probed the structural elements in Julie Billiart's life – protest, vision, friendship, freedom, service of the poor and readiness for reform. This approach allows her to transcend the limitations of her French heroine, focussing instead on overriding values such as the ability to initiate change, the gift to inspire, the duty of religious women to face the real spiritual needs of their time.'

John Wijngaards

Myra Poole SND has been a member of the Sisters of Notre Dame de Namur for more than forty years and for much of that time was a teacher of history and a head teacher at Notre Dame High School, Southwark. Taking early retirement she studied theology in the USA, Holland and in London.

Her particular interest in women's spirituality and theology has led to active involvement with groups such as the Catholic Women's Network, Catholic Women's Ordination and the British and Irish School of Feminist Theology.

She lives in London.

Prayer, Protest, Power

The Spirituality of
Julie Billiart
Today

Myra Poole SND

CANTERBURY
PRESS
Norwich

© Myra Poole 2001

First published in 2001 by The Canterbury Press Norwich
(a publishing imprint of Hymns Ancient & Modern Limited
a registered charity)
St Mary's Works, St Mary's Plain
Norwich, Norfolk, NR3 3BH

British Library Cataloguing in Publication Data

A catalogue record for this book is available
from the British Library

Bible quotations are taken from the Revised Standard
Version Catholic Edition, Thomas Nelson and Sons Ltd,
London, 1966

Myra Poole has asserted her right under the
Copyright, Design and Patents Act, 1988, to be
identified as the Author of this Work

ISBN 1-85311-427-8

Typeset by Rowland Phototypesetting,
Bury St Edmunds, Suffolk
Printed in Great Britain by
Biddles Ltd, Guildford and King's Lynn

Que votre coeur soit vaste comme le monde
Your heart must be as wide as the world
– Julie Billiart

Contents

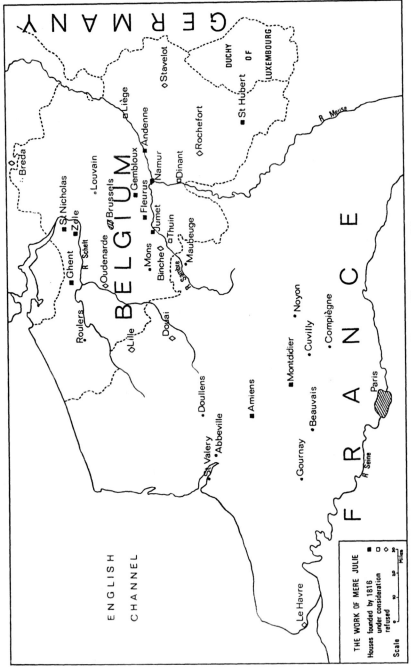

ENGLISH
CHANNEL

GERMANY

◇ Breda

◇Stavelot

DUCHY OF

St Hubert ■

LUXEMBOURG

Liège
Andenne
◇Rochefort

■S. Nicholas
•Louvain
Gembloux
■Zele
Brussels ◇
Namur
BELGIUM
Fleurus
R Meuse
Ghent ■
Oudenarde◇
Jumet◇
Dinant
R Schelt
Mons•
Binche◇□Thuin
Roulers•
◇Lille
•Maubeuge
R Sambre

◇Douai
•Noyon

•Montdidier
•Cuvilly
•Beauvais
•Compiègne

•Doullens
•Amiens

FRANCE

St Valery•
•Abbeville

Paris

•Gournay

R Seine

Le Havre ◇

THE WORK OF MÈRE JULIE
Houses founded by 1816   ■
under consideration   □
refused   ◇
Scale   Miles

First published in *Quiet Revolution*, by Mary Linscott s ND, Burns: Glasgow, 1966, p. 22.

Acknowledgements

I dedicate this book to four very special people. First, to Jennifer Worrall SND, for her unfailing support, inspiration, encouragement, humour and practical assistance during the long birth of this book. Secondly, to Barbara Ravenscroft SND, who, with Jennifer, understands so well the cost of physical suffering. Thirdly, Marie Therese Coleman SND who has been a constant companion throughout my religious life. Fourthly, my mother who died in March, 1991, at eighty-four years of age, after a long, fruitful, but hard life as a widow with three children; a life lived through two world wars. She personifies, for me, the strength of women in adversity.

I have so many other people to thank in the writing of this book. The Sisters of Notre Dame de Namur in Britain, particularly Srs Margaret Foley, Magdalene Randall, Magdalen Lawler and Margaret Mulholland, as well as Sisters in other parts of the world, for their friendship, financial assistance and encouragement to write. My family and friends for keeping me down to earth and sane. All my former colleagues in education, particularly the staff and pupils of Notre Dame High School, Southwark, 1975–1986, who helped in the birthing of my 'feminist' consciousness and with whom I shared many happy years.

The people in the women's movement, national and international, especially those who have nurtured me in friendship, as well as in my spiritual and academic growth, in the past ten years – June Boyce-Tillman, Dorothea McEwan, Alexina Murphy, Ianthe Pratt (who, with her late husband Oliver, made their home and the Women's Resource Centre so freely available

to me), Veronica Seddon, Lala Winkley and all members of
Catholic Women's Network, Catholic Women's Ordination,
and Women's Ordination Worldwide, who have been so supportive and such good friends, but who are too numerous to
mention by individual names. All these are people with whom
I now weave change.

Catherine Walsh for her patient belief and invaluable help in
the process of drafting and writing this book. Professor Mary
Grey, who guided me in my first early steps in Nijmegen, Holland, and who has been continually supportive of me; members
of the Titus Brandsma Institute in Nijmegen, for sharing their
methodology; Dr Sue O'Brien, for her historical research on
women religious in the nineteenth and early twentieth centuries;
Pat Pinsent for her proofreading of the manuscript, Jean
Bunn SND and Anne Burke SND for their archival knowledge,
Hannah Ward for her early comments in the initial stage of the
writing, Mary Hayes SND for sharing her new research on the
life of Julie, and Mary Ann Recker SND for sharing her work
on the meaning of friendship. Many thanks also go to Jo
Chambers for her artistic skills in providing the illustrations for
the book.

Joan Bond and Brothers Gerard and Alexander, Franciscan
Friars of the Atonement, at the then Catholic Library at Victoria,
for making the books so available to me in spite of the fines I
logged up. A special thanks to Joan who never tired of assisting
with any book query and who has struggled so hard to ensure
the Catholic Library is not lost to the use of ordinary readers.
Ecumenically, the Revd Jean Mayland, the Revd Katherine
Rumens, the Revd Nikki Arthy and the Revd Janet Wootton,
all ministers in other churches, who have shared so many of
their experiences of ministering with me. Not forgetting my
parish priest, Father Colin McLean, and all the Sisters with
whom I have lived during the writing of this book. To all these
and so many unnamed with whom I have shared my life so far,
a big thank you.

Introduction

The incredible story of courage and determination of the nineteenth-century crippled and paralysed French woman, Julie Billiart, is little known to the general public, or even to the many pupils who have been a part of the educational system of the Sisters of Notre Dame de Namur for many generations. However, my love for Julie's spirituality and its influence on my growth to Christian feminism have inspired me to write a book about her spirituality rather than a straightforward biography. In the process I discovered how the structure of Julie's spirituality, her mysticism, has transformed my Christian feminism and has enabled me to stay within religious life. To help the reader understand my quest the following is a short account of the main milestones in my story which explain the experiences which lie behind this book.

It has been my past fifteen-year involvement with those in the women's spirituality and theological movement that has brought the charism – that is, the particular characteristics – of Julie Billiart's spirituality alive, in most unexpected ways. In the women's movement, secular and religious, we have learnt together new insights and new ways of thinking. We have developed liturgies, out of our own experience, and have questioned profoundly the inherent sexism and racism that pervade much of inherited and 'received' theology.

The women's movement is international. It is made up of thousands of groups both secular and religious. From this networking a number of religious initiatives have begun in Britain in the last twenty years: in 1984, the Catholic Women's Network

(CWN) was founded, to provide a safe space for women to exchange views and develop theology and liturgies based on their experience of the Christian message. In 1993, the Catholic Women's Ordination (CWO) was born, as a result of the Anglican vote in favour of women priests on 11 November 1992 – an organisation which is a direct challenge to the all-male priesthood of the Roman Catholic tradition. This was followed in July 1996 by Women's Ordination Worldwide (WOW), which came into being by the public acclamation of over a thousand women at the First European Women's Synod in Gmunden, Austria. Other more ecumenical organisations which have been founded include The British and Irish School of Feminist Theology (BISFT), in 1992; the Ecumenical European Women's Synod movement (1996); and the first Women's Synod, Wales, Ireland, Scotland and England (WISE), which took place at Liverpool Hope University in July 1999. All these new developments are connected in some way to other international organisations that have sprung up over the past few years, such as the international movement We Are Church (IMWAC), the European Network of the Church on the Move, the Eighth of May, in Holland, and Call To Action, in the USA. And these are only a few of the 4,000 reform groups which not only realise the urgent need for change, but work continually for a renewed, more relevant and healthy Roman Catholic Church for the twenty-first century.

In the 1980s, I was one of a group which went regularly to support the women at Greenham Common. It was here, even more than by visiting developing countries such as Sri Lanka, Nigeria, Zimbabwe and South Africa, that I learnt the meaning of moving from 'notional' to 'real' assent. Although I had been a religious Sister for many years nothing changed me as much as the action at Greenham Common. Here it seemed we did lay down our lives on the line, to be laughed at or scorned. And I have found through experience the cost, as well as the joy, of moving to 'real' assent: we felt like suffragettes on the Wednesday evening that we first raised our banner proclaiming Catholic Women's Ordination, on the piazza of Westminster Cathedral.

It is experiences such as these that have sustained me and helped me grow, spiritually and theologically, in the last fifteen years. Ironically, my experiences have not led me away from the spirituality of Julie Billiart, which has been a part of my life for so long, but into the very heart of its power and meaning.

My story

My spiritual inheritance from my parents' side was Anglicanism, but as a family we were not strict in our practice of the faith. However, from my family, especially my mother, I inherited a deep sense of spirituality. At the age of six, during the Second World War, with my two older sisters I was sent to the local Holy Family Convent School, Tooting, London. The school did not have a sixth form of its own and it was my mother who fought for me to go to Notre Dame High School, Southwark. At the school it was the custom to take all the sixth form to the Novitiate of the Sisters of Notre Dame, in Ashdown Forest, the seat of training for women who wished to become Sisters of Notre Dame de Namur. My friend Marion and I went for the day. Marion was terrified, as she thought she might get a vocation, while I, who was not even a Catholic at the time, went along for the day out! Marion ended up married with four children and ten years later I was to end up in the very Novitiate we visited that day!

It was while I was at university that I became a Catholic, and a short way into my first teaching job at Loreto, Manchester, my vocation to join the Sisters of Notre Dame de Namur hit me like a thunderbolt. I had in fact almost decided to get married but I could not resist this other call. My vocation came one Sunday night. I had just returned from speaking on a soap box for the Catholic Evidence Guild, in Manchester, and I went to wash my hands. As I did I was totally overcome with the certainty that I was to be a Sister of Notre Dame de Namur. Yet I had not given them a thought since I left school, in fact I could not even remember what they wore. The next day I went into school and looked up where these Sisters could be contacted.

On 8 September 1959 I took the train from Victoria to the novitiate at Ashdown Park, with twenty-five other hopefuls, most of whom spent the journey having their last cigarettes, or so they thought at the time. I began my religious life a few years before Vatican II and from the beginning I felt there was something deeply wrong with the way this life was lived. I found it very strange and rigid; but my calling was so strong I knew I had been called to this life for some reason beyond my understanding. The past forty years have gone very quickly and have seen enormous changes, at least enormous external changes, the giving up of the habit and living in small groups or alone being the most obvious. Nearly thirty years of my life as a Sister were spent in the education of girls between the ages of 11 and 18 years, as a history teacher and later as a headteacher. I ended this part of my life as Headteacher of Notre Dame, Southwark, a multi-cultural comprehensive school in the heart of the inner city – the very school I had attended as a sixth-form pupil.

It was while I was here that major shifts began to occur in my life. The Inner London Education Authority, ILEA, began its initiatives of raising awareness of classism, racism and sexism. From that moment something came alive in me and a new vocation was born. Notre Dame High School never looked back from those days. The staff tackled the new initiatives with great gusto and soon many of the girls would say 'Why are we all feminist here, Sister?' and 'Go on Sister, you say Mass – why wait for a man to come?' Then in 1983, another turning point came in my life. I went to a weekend conference at King's College, London, given by Rosemary Radford Ruether. I saw the many books that had been written on women's theology and I was hooked on the developing women's issues and concerns. This was followed by my attendance at the Second International Conference on Women, at Groningen University, Holland, in 1984, and my new future began to open out to me. I wanted to study not just theology, but women's theology.

This led me to taking early retirement (1986) from my position as headteacher and I began my journey into a very insecure and unknown future. The next few years took me to the

Women's Theology Centre, Boston, USA, where I had the privilege of attending lectures and seminars given by, among others, Elisabeth Schüssler Fiorenza, the scripture scholar; Katie Canon, a well-known black woman theologian, and Carter Heyward, known for her theology of redemption. Coupled with this I felt the great need to go away and pray for a while and I found my way to Guelph, Canada, to make the forty-day Ignatian Exercises.[1] On my return to Britain I attended Heythrop College to gain a necessary academic qualification, as MTh in Pastoral Theology. But the question within me was still unanswered: how had I become a Christian feminist out of a nineteenth-century charism?

This book is the fruit of my search. Thanks to Dr Mary Grey I was led to Nijmegen University, Holland, to attend her courses on 'Feminism in Christendom', and through her I was led to the Carmelite Titus Brandsma Institute at Nijmegen. I enrolled for a PhD but realised my subject was too broad for a narrow academic approach. However, I owe a great deal to the work of this Institute because their methodology for the study of spiritual texts, namely the 'structural dynamic' approach, was the lynchpin which opened up a way to unlock the question which continually worried me.[2] It supplied, for me, what I always felt was missing from the understanding of Julie Billiart's spirituality. By using this methodology the structure and charism, the unique gift, of her spirituality have become clear.[3] And to enable the dynamic aspect of Julie's spirituality to be more fully understood, at the end of each chapter I have reflected on its relevance for the twenty-first century. A deeper understanding of religious life emerged naturally from a study of her spirituality, even to the point of being able to rename this life in a more meaningful way.

The structure of the book

This book is based on the methodology of the Titus Brandsma Institute, summed up in the following words of Professor Kees Waaijman in the Institute's journal *Pharos*: 'A structural approach looks at things as a whole, and not at the parts

themselves' (Waaijman 1991:27). He illustrates this methodology by comparing these spiritualities to Gothic architecture:
'Gothic architecture, for instance, does not only consist of
pointed arches, crossed vaults and multicoloured stained glass.
On the contrary, these characteristics and forms give expression
to a particular spirit. It is the spirit that defines the *entirety* of
a cathedral or other forms of art' (ibid.:26). The spirituality is
dynamised by the mystical element within the spirituality, in
Julie's case her charism. The present grows out of the past and
the past is brought to life and re-interpreted by present experience. The Titus Brandsma Institute calls this the 'structural
dynamic' approach to spirituality, which aims to reveal the mystical dynamism within all classical spiritualities.[4]

To allow the structure and the dynamic of the spirituality of
Julie Billiart to emerge, the following chapters have been
arranged around the core elements without which her spirituality cannot exist. The structure of her spirituality is written into
the chapter headings: the pillars of her spirituality are vision,
friendship, the cross and the poor, but the spirit which gives life
to all these elements is her charism, her special gift, the 'liberty
of the children of God'.

In the first chapter the reader is introduced to the 'Women of
Protest' of the French Revolution: first, Julie Billiart, the crippled
and paralysed artisan/peasant woman ('peasant' being a term to
include all citizens of France except the clergy and the nobility);
secondly, her close friend, Françoise Blin de Bourdon, an aristocrat, a member of the nobility, destined to become the co-
foundress of the new congregation; thirdly, the three groups
into which the women of the revolution predominantly fall –
the *enragées*, or angry crowd of Parisian market women, the
clubistes, a small group of educated women who supported
political rights for women, and the counter-revolutionary
women who wanted to restore the Catholic religion to France.
This last was by far the largest group, and the one to which
Julie and Françoise belonged. This chapter, like those following,
ends with a reflection on the present-day importance of the
aspect of spirituality under consideration.

Chapter 2, 'Women of Vision', opens with an introduction to the 'social construction' of the mystical tradition. This is followed by a discussion of the role of visions in the lives of medieval women mystics. The second half of the chapter gives an account of Julie's founding vision at Compiègne in 1792. The chapter ends with reflections on the importance of Julie's vision in the life of her congregation in the light of women's visionary experiences.

Chapter 3, 'Women of Friendship', focuses on the friendship between Julie Billiart and Françoise Blin de Bourdon as it unfolds in the letters of Julie. This friendship is compared and contrasted with both the classical, mainly male, tradition of friendship and the developing theological insights into the role of friendship in women's lives.

Chapter 4, 'Women of a Mystical Text', introduces the reader to the Letters of Julie Billiart as a mystical text. The chapter includes an introduction to reading a mystical text; an understanding of the spirituality of the French School of Spirituality and others that underpinned the development of Julie Billiart's own spirituality; and an introduction to the style and content of her letters.

Chapter 5, 'Women of Freedom', is based on the first thirty-three Letters of Julie and brings her charism, 'the liberty of the children of God', into the full light of day. These Letters were written as spiritual guidance to Françoise in the early days of their friendship. It is a key chapter on the study of the charism and spirituality of Julie, especially her teaching on contemplative prayer, as the way to spiritual freedom. The question asked in this chapter is, what is spiritual freedom?

Chapter 6, 'Women of the Poor', traces the situation of general and female poverty in the eighteenth century, with an account of Julie's establishment of schools for the poor, her educational principles, and her concept of personal and congregational poverty – Julie's 'rapture of action'. The chapter ends with a reflection on the growing understanding of the theological underpinnings of women's poverty.

Chapter 7, 'Women of the Cross', identifies her charism of

liberty as central to Julie's understanding of the cross. A short introduction to the dominant Anselmian cross theology of the atonement is followed by a full account of Julie's difficulties with church authorities and some of her Sisters. As the place of the cross in Christian life has become a stumbling block, especially to many women, the chapter introduces the reader to the important contribution of the theologies of women of colour, as well as that of Feminist Theology, to a renewed understanding of the cross. The chapter concludes with reference to the likeness between Julie's experience of the cross and some of these insights.

Chapter 8, the concluding chapter, 'Women on the Threshold of Change', draws together the fruits of Julie's spirituality and charism. The first part of the chapter is a critical-historical reflection on the growth of the congregation, based on an unpublished paper written by Dr Susan O'Brien (1994). Then the reader is introduced to the understanding of the meaning of 'liminal' groups as threshold groups. The resulting concept of the role and purpose of these groups is discussed in full. The chapter concludes with an explanation on the interdependence of the 'official' liminal groups, those of monastic/religious life, and the newly forming *ad hoc* liminal groups.

This book can be understood at many levels but my overriding purpose has been to capture Julie Billiart's spirituality in its entirety and show its relevance for today. Hence there is a personal reflection at the end of each chapter. Releasing Julie Billiart's spirituality from its present narrow confines of women's religious life enables it to be shared by men and women of all ages and all times. But it is not a cosy spirituality for the fainthearted. It is one full of challenge and daring. In fact, I have found that 'we must work hard for a spirituality that embraces change rather than denies it' (Ward and Wild 1995:5).

I

Women of Protest

'There is no democracy to equal that of the starving.'
(Miles 1989:187)

Julie Billiart (1751–1816) and Françoise Blin de Bourdon (1756–1838), her great friend and co-foundress, lived during one of the most tempestuous times known to history – the French Revolution followed by the Napoleonic Empire. It was out of this turmoil that Julie's spirituality of protest emerged, which she shaped into a spirituality unique to her, and which has been passed on, for nearly two hundred years, to others who have followed her.

The ideas of the *philosophes*, especially the *Social Contract* of Jean Jacques Rousseau (1712–78) – although how far he was one of the *philosophes* is disputed – were the ideological springboard, not only of the Revolution itself, but of the formation of the modern state in many parts of the world. The words *liberté, égalité, fraternité* rang round the world and became the bedrock of any demands for human freedom. Yet in France little was outwardly changed in the life of the majority of people by the Revolution. Those who had little before 1789 still had little in 1799 when the *coup d'état*, which led to the eventual rise of Napoleon, took place. Thanks to authors such as Charles Dickens in *The Tale of Two Cities*, both the horrors and the heroism of the Revolution are well known. Madame Defarge, knitting while the tumbrils passed and heads rolled at the guillotine, is an image deeply imprinted on the human psyche. On the other hand, we have Sydney Carton who offered his life for another. Public horrors and sheer brutality, on this scale, were

unknown to history, and yet this was a revolution which claimed
to be that of the people.

It was the French Revolution that changed the meaning of
'revolution' for ever. Before the nineteenth century a revolution
was deemed to be 'putting the clock back' to a better past; from
this time on it became a metaphor to describe the irresistibility
of a violent transformation for radical change of the political,
religious and all supporting arrangements of a country. The
Revolution paved the way for change to a French Republic in
the next century and accelerated the decline, which had already
begun, of the Roman Catholic Church over the minds and hearts
of the French nation.

Pre-Revolution France

The 'will or the sovereignty of the people' became the underlying
cry of the modern state, not the medieval cry of the 'divine right
of Kings'. That had entailed privileges of birth and honours
bestowed by the monarchy, a form of government known to
French history as the *ancien régime*. It was a relic of feudal
medieval government, where the monarchy looked to the nobility and the clergy to maintain its authority. Eighteenth-century
society was still largely qualified by Estates or Orders – the First
Estate, the nobility, the Second Estate, the clergy, and the Third
Estate, sometimes split into burghers (merchants) and peasantry.
The first two Estates paid lower taxes and in many cases were
exempt completely. The image of fat bishops living off the
wealth of the land was as prevalent as that of the nobility. The
Church, as an integral part of the *ancien régime*, mirrored the
same inequalities between wealthy and poor clergy. The latter
tended to be the humble parish priest, known as the *curé*, a figure
well loved at this time. In the same manner most monasteries and
convents were deemed far too wealthy and the Revolution was
to destroy much of what was then known as religious life.

The system of dividing people up by class was alien to the
ancien régime. In fact the word 'peasant' covered the majority
of people; only about two to three per cent were in the wealthy

'noble' class. Although Julie Billiart is often referred to as a peasant woman, in today's language, especially that of the developing countries, her family would be called 'traders'. That is, she came from working-class people who made an adequate living, partly by farming but more and more by trading cloth in the local markets on a regular basis. The fact that the local peasants fired a bullet through her father's window shows that her family were deemed by the rioters to be of some standing in the village of Cuvilly, where she lived.

The causes of the French Revolution

The initial causes of the French Revolution are many and the relative importance of certain events over others is disputed by historians. However, there is general agreement on the overall causes that precipitated this event. The country was on the verge of bankruptcy, due to the crippling wars fought by France in Europe, as well as her intervention in the American Revolution. These wars increased the terrible burdens of taxation on the people, who were already overloaded with debt. To this can be added the gradual transformation of France by a growing industrialisation and the rise of a merchant class. This precipitated the move of many of the poor from the countryside to the towns, and their experience of this dislocation, from rural to industrial poverty, led to increasing violence of desperation. Add to this that drought had caused poor harvests in the 1770s and 1780s, and the cry for bread began to reverberate around France, especially in Paris among the market women. The privileged existence of the few crumbled, opening the way for the implementation of the ideas of the *philosophes* – ideas that had been finely honed in the *salons* of the eighteenth century, places of literary and political discussion presided over by women of wealth and education.[1] *Les Citoyens* demanded not just bread but the right to citizenship, to new ways of governing which would reflect the 'sovereignty' of the people not the 'sovereignty' of the King.

The 'Bible' of the Revolution was Rousseau's *Social Contract*. It was published thirteen times between 1792 and 1795, even in pocket size for soldiers to carry during war. The ideas extolled by Rousseau in this theoretical pamphlet filled the vacuum left by the decline of the *ancien régime*. He extolled human goodness – *la vertu* – to take the place of the old God of the churches; the nation – 'the general will' – took the place of the King. Thus the ideas of 'virtue, nature and the nation became so closely associated that they almost became synonymous' (Best 1989:28). Another important aspect of Rousseau's influence was his belief that people were naturally good when they were not corrupted by institutions.

Events

The key events of the early days of the Revolution in Paris are well known. The most decisive step was taken when the States-General were replaced by something wholly new: the National Assembly, in June 1789. The assertion and acceptance of the name 'National' stripped, by implication, the Church, the monarchy, and the nobility of all legitimate authority or privilege, except what might be delegated to them by the representatives of an all-powerful nation. Thus began the idea of the nation state, an ideology that was to boost the morale of the French army throughout the French Revolutionary and Napoleonic wars. The storming of the Bastille, the symbol of political prisoners, in July 1789 was quickly followed by the Declaration of the Rights of Man and the Citizen, the confiscation of all Church property to the State, and the suppression of all religious orders (unless engaged in teaching or other charitable work) and of monastic vows. In April 1792 France declared war on the Austro-Hungarian Empire 'for the just defence of a free people against the aggression of a king' (Best 1989:31). By September 1792, the monarchy had been abolished and France was declared a Republic, to be dated year 1. On 21 January 1793 the King was executed, followed by Queen Marie Antoinette the following October.

The Girondins, so called because several of their prominent speakers represented a department of France of that name, were in the ascendant and responsible for the declaration of war, which proved disastrous to their fortunes. These events precipitated the rise to power of an extreme group who had always favoured the deposition of the monarchy: the Jacobins, named after the club at which they gathered. With the Jacobins in the ascendant the government of France was now centralised under the Committee of Public Safety and the Revolutionary Tribunal. Maximilien Robespierre, an ardent disciple of Rousseau, became the leading political figure and the scene was set for the 'reign of terror' of July 1793–July 1794.

The dechristianisation of the Church escalated during this time, even to the horror of Robespierre who was essentially a deist. However, one of the most important and durable measures, although less anti-clerical in intent, had already been passed in September 1792 – the secularisation of all births, deaths and marriages. This removed, at a stroke, a major source of influence of the parish priest over the life of the individual. This later period saw the inauguration of the 'worship of reason' and the festival of the Supreme Being. A month before the downfall of Robespierre, on 8 June 1794, Paris witnessed, as a part of his moral regeneration of France, the most extraordinary spectacle of the 'reign of terror'. While tumbrils rolled at one end of the street, at the other end the inauguration of the worship of the Supreme Being was celebrated. Robespierre, who was the main instigator of these proceedings, as president played a central role. He had commissioned a hymn to the Supreme Being, and had nature declared the high priest of the new religion. It was his most politically ambitious production and his final attack on the dechristianisers. But Robespierre's glory and his new religion were brought to a swift end. He had made many enemies, and on 28 July he was viciously executed, swiftly followed by 115 other Jacobins. And all this was done in the name of *liberty, equality and fraternity!*

By 1794 the 'terror' gradually subsided and in 1795 a Directory of Five was appointed and freedom to worship according to any form of religion was restored as a political expedient. In 1799, as a result of failures in war, France underwent a *coup*

d'état which brought the parliamentary system to an end; the
final outcome was the installation in power of a 'Consulate' of
three, whose outstanding figure was a young general, Napoleon
Bonaparte. In 1800 he had outmanoeuvred his rivals to a position of power and was declared the First Consul. In 1801 he
restored Roman Catholicism as the state religion and in 1804
he was declared Emperor of France. The scene was set for the
realisation of his dynastic desires, to set up an Empire to equal
that of Charlemagne.[2]

The background to all these political changes was the failures
and successes of the wars which France continued to wage, wars
which encompassed 22 years of some of the most brutal, as well
as fruitful, times of French history. The French Revolution also
inaugurated a revolution in warfare. The *philosophes* understood warfare as a necessary outcome of constitutional changes.
Rousseau recognised the principle of universal military service
as deriving from service to the state from which citizens gained
so much and to which they therefore owed allegiance. The concept of fighting for the nation was one of the main reasons for
the early successes of the French, especially during the early days
of the Napoleonic Empire. The origins of the war of 1792 arose
from the emergence of this 'national' pride in supporting any
country that wished to follow the lead of the French in revolution. But the desire to regain the 'natural' borders of France
grew and soon France was at war with most of the countries
by which it was surrounded – Austria, Belgium, Prussia, Italy,
Spain, England, the Dutch Republic. During the Napoleonic
Empire of 1804–15 the *Grande Armée* of France was the main
weapon by which Napoleon imposed and extended his dynastic
desires to preside over a great Empire which stretched from the
river Rhône to the Volga.

Women, known as the 'engine of the revolution' (Miles
1989:172–95), played a crucial role before, during and after the
Revolution. Their attitudes towards the state and the Church
image the diversity of views throughout France, and the successes and failures of the Revolution and the Napoleonic era
had a great impact of women's lives. Julie Billiart and her great

friend Françoise Blin de Bourdon were a part of this enormous upheaval; it is out of these unprecedented circumstances that Julie's charism, of contemplative freedom and love of the very poor, 'the poor of the most abandoned places', was born. However, before introducing the reader more fully into the early life of these two women, it is necessary to have a greater understanding of the Church of their time on which their ecclesiology and love of the Church was based.

The Church before the Revolution

Although in the eighteenth century the vast majority of French men and women were Catholic from the moment of birth, during the second half of this century a steady decline in religious practice began, especially among men. There was something profound happening in France to the Tridentine model of French Catholicism which had emerged out of the reforming Council of Trent in the sixteenth century. Although France was nominally a Catholic country, by the middle of the eighteenth century many differentiating factors emerged in the practice of religion. The reasons are unclear why religious fervour differed from place to place both in towns and countryside (Gibson 1989:10). One thing, however, is certain from the *cahiers* (the written journals of the times): the parochial clergy were greatly respected because of their work, whereas, because of its vast wealth, the image of the monastic way of life was in serious decline. Hence, a notable feature of the Church in France on the eve of the Revolution was the vitality of most parochial communities in both towns and country. The Revolution was far more influential in the towns than the country, and the Church lost its grip there. The strength of the Church passed to the parish communities of the countryside, a reversal of the situation in the earlier part of the century. This phenomenon was guaranteed by the fact that the Church was a vital expression of the two loyalties paramount in peasant psychology: the family and the parish. The parish was the centre of all the major celebrations and sorrows of family life, as well as a social centre for all to meet.

Although the image of the Tridentine form of Catholicism is one of rules and the inducement of fear, it was, ironically, a good thing for women at this time. The reasons lie in the support and help the Church gave women, in the communal life of the parish, against the grossest forms of immorality inflicted upon them. The origin of this shift can be traced back to the zeal of the reformed Tridentine clergy, who were charged with a centralised thoroughgoing reform and control over the morality of people's personal lives. Men were the chief target of this new sexual ethic and 'it was male organisations and customs that were under attack: youth groups, festivals, confraternities of the Holy Spirit' (Gibson 1989:11). The youth groups had exercised immense power over women and they were specially singled out along with all riotous male behaviour. Married men were also faced with new obligations towards women imposed by the new ethics. Women, then, enjoyed considerable gains from the Catholic Reformation. Not only were they given new outlets for sociability in Rosary confraternities[3] and parish charities, but the clergy did its best to liberate them from the grosser forms of sexual oppression, 'protecting them from abandonment in pregnancy, from rejection by their husbands, even on occasion from ritual gang rape' (ibid.). The parishes also provided them with the only social outlet they had, in their busy and hard lives. It is not surprising, therefore, that women emerged during the Revolution as the great supporters of religion and the Church. No state had ever protected or looked after the welfare of women and their families as had the Church.

For the majority of men the Catholic Tridentine Church was a massive exercise in spiritual alienation, to the extent that the eighteenth century saw a 'feminization of catholicism' (Gibson 1989:10) not apparent in the century before. The greater appeal of Catholicism to women was a relatively new development, for the Catholic Reformation in France, in the seventeenth century, had been inspired not only by the clergy but by a militant male laity. It was left to the women to provide the largest and strongest force of opposition to the new régime in their support for the Catholic faith.

The Civil Constitution of the Clergy and dechristianisation

The confiscation of all Church property to the State in 1789 was swiftly followed by increasing State control over the Church, in the passing of the Civil Constitution of the Clergy on 12 July 1790. Attitudes towards the Civil Constitution became the defining factor in religious attitudes towards the Revolution. In essence the principle of the sovereignty of the people was to be applied to the Church; that is, the Church was to come under lay, state control rather than being governed from Rome. The tithe to the Church was to be abolished, Church property nationalised, and all clergy paid by the state. Moreover, all bishops and clergy were to be elected by 'active' citizens, that is, those who paid taxes to the value of at least three days' labour (Gibson 1989:37) Although the curés of the Third Estate welcomed the lessening of the overweening power of many of the rich bishops, they wanted 'a synodal solution, whereby the bishops were elected by the *curés* themselves' (ibid.). The Constitution, therefore, initiated a public and fundamental clash over the source of authority in the Church. The Pope delayed its condemnation till 10 March 1791, and when he did it was unfortunate that he also condemned the fundamental tenets of the Revolution.

All priests were required to take an oath of allegiance to the state. Those who took the oath were legally known as *jureurs*, those who did not as *non-jureurs* or *réfractaires*. As many women wished to re-establish the Roman-centred Tridentine Church in France, it was totally consistent that they became the supporters and harbourers of the non-juring priests – many to the point of death. The underlying tension was between different understandings of church; one a Gallican church independent of Rome in appointments and finance and controlled by the French State; the other the Ultramontane church, whose central power and organisation was based in Rome. The women who fervently wished to restore the Catholic faith to France and who opposed the Civil Constitution of the Clergy became known as the counter-revolutionary women. Julie and Françoise belonged to this group, a group destined to become the largest in France which opposed the Revolution.

The early life of Julie Billiart

Marie Rose Julie Billiart was born in Cuvilly, a small village in France, a few miles north of Paris, in the southern part of the Province of Picardy. Her father, Jean François Billiart, was the son of the 'Lieutenant de Justice' of the village, and in 1739, at 22 years of age, had married Marie Louise Antoinette de Braine, 24, from Maignelay. Jean François's family had lived in Cuvilly for generations, as merchants, bakers, thatchers, stonecutters and farmers, and the newly married couple moved into the Rue Lataule, where they were to remain for the rest of their lives. Jean François not only farmed the land which he had inherited, but also opened a draper's shop where he sold cloth and lace, as well as the produce from his land. Julie, therefore, came not only from peasant stock, but from the artisan class of small shopkeepers, and developed early in life a strong commercial orientation.[4] The circumstances of her life mirrored outwardly the social, cultural and economic circumstances of the lives of many French women and families of the time: a time of much disease and economic and social unrest.

Julie was the sixth of seven children. Three died before the age of eight, and one in her first year of marriage, probably from giving birth. Her sister Madeleine was blind almost from birth, and her brother Louis a cripple. Julie was exceptionally lucky for her time as she had robust health until her teens. In the early years of the eighteenth century something like a quarter of all babies died before reaching their first birthday, and another quarter before reaching the age of eight: 'Of every 1,000 infants, only 200 would go on to the age of fifty, and only a 100 to the age of seventy, and this is a description of the average!' (McManners 1981:5) Julie was lucky that her parents both lived into their seventies, but her own health broke in her teens and by the age of eighteen she was partially blind and suffered from neuralgia. From her early twenties till her fifties her life was

marked by an almost total paralysis, including loss of speech.
Outwardly, Julie's life was undistinguished. She went to the
local village school, which was run by her uncle, Thibault Guil-
bert, a school for both boys and girls, as the poverty of the
village did not allow the luxury of the single-sex school preferred
by the rich. Julie's early good health enabled her to assist her
father in the fields, and to travel alone on a donkey to Compiègne to sell cloth to augment the family income. In appearance
Julie was a dark-haired, short, stocky French woman not unlike
many a young woman who could be seen at market most days
of the week.

The paralysis that Julie was to suffer for the greater part of
her adult life (until she was 53) was a direct result of the social
unrest of the 1770s. The textile industry was in decline and
when Julie was sixteen her father was robbed of lace and other
materials leaving the family in great poverty. One night in 1774,
rioters threw a rock through the window of her father's house
and fired a gunshot. No one was hit, but Julie, who believed
the shot was intended for her father, as he was the owner of
what was deemed to be a thriving business, never recovered
from the shock of this attack. Her health had begun to weaken
and in 1782 she succumbed to a violent attack of fever for
which the remedy of 'bleeding' was applied. Bleeding, often with
leeches, sucking out the person's blood, was the main cure of
the age for all ills, but the reduction of blood often succeeded
only in weakening the invalid concerned. Julie was no exception,
and she was lucky not to die. She became so weak that at the
end of six months of this treatment, she was left with a paralysis
so complete that for long periods of time her speech was greatly
affected. Julie refers to the ill effects of this treatment in her
later correspondence: 'Tell the doctor I have learned from my
experience that blood-letting is terrible for these kinds of nerve
disease ... I can assure you of that without being mistaken'
(Letter 171:457).

In matters of the spirit, however, she was not so typical. She
seemed to be on a fast learning track. At the age of eight she
was fortunate to have as her parish priest the Abbé Dangicourt,

a learned and holy man who had been trained at the Sorbonne, in Paris, and was 'the counsellor and director of the most fervent priests of the whole area around Cuvilly' (Roseanne Murphy 1995:9). He was amazed at her spiritual precocity. Not only did she know the catechism by heart, but she had an understanding of it beyond her years. It was this priest who introduced her to meditation, and from him she learnt in her early days how to curb her natural impetuosity. He schooled her well both academically and spiritually and all sources on her life testify to a remarkable sensitivity to the Holy Spirit which began to manifest itself at an early age. She acquired from the local people a title of great honour which was normally reserved for those much older: 'La Dévote'. In using this title the people evoked the original meaning of the word, to denote a person of great inner strength and wisdom, someone people implicitly trust and go to for advice and help. Moreover, in spite of the fact that Julie was comparatively unlearned – although her education was far better than that of most of her class at this time – the Jesuits at Namur were later to refer to her as a 'doctor of theology' (Linscott 1966:21).

Her later letters reveal not only the unusual extent of her scripture knowledge but also her familiarity with the great spiritual classics of the day: *The Imitation of Christ*, by Thomas à Kempis, which was to become another Bible to her; the works of devotion of Teresa of Avila, the great sixteenth-century Carmelite; and the seventeenth-century writings of St Francis de Sales, all of which she was to use to full advantage for the rest of her life. The wisdom of the Abbé Dangicourt can also be recognised in his freedom in permitting her to receive her first communion at the then early age of nine, as well as allowing her to commit herself entirely to God, at the age of fourteen, by taking a vow of chastity. Julie must have understood at an unconscious level at this early age the constraints that marriage and family impose on women, especially in times of great poverty, and the freedom which celibacy allowed (Ruether 1974). Julie's later life was never free of illness, nor of other trials and tribulations, but throughout all this, her sense of the goodness of God never left her. In the saying for which she is most famous she declares, 'How good is the good God, who tries us.'

For Julie, as for many women of her time, there were few barriers between pious peasant women and pious women of noble birth.[5] This is reflected in her life's work and friendships. Amongst her friends she counted many of the rich who owned châteaux around Cuvilly. Many of them came to her for help in times of trouble when she was paralysed. She was so popular that one of her friends, Madame Pont l'Abbé, built an outside door to her room so that Julie's many visitors would not disturb the other members of the family.

But her time in Cuvilly was limited and in 1791 she was forced to flee to Compiègne to escape the anger of the revolutionaries because she was accused of harbouring non-juring priests, who included her beloved Père Dangicourt, and of inciting others to do likewise. Julie remained hidden from the revolutionaries in Compiègne for three years. At the end of the 'reign of terror', when the worst horrors of the Revolution seemed to have abated and France was under the government of a new Directory of Five, she was persuaded to leave Compiègne for Amiens by her great friend and benefactor from her Cuvilly days, Madame Baudoin. It was while Julie was in Amiens that the fateful meeting took place between Françoise Blin de Bourdon and Julie. The cementing of their friendship was to be the foundation stone of the religious congregation that Julie, through her vision at Compiègne in 1792 (see chapter 2), felt called upon to establish: a new congregation of religious women, to go all over the world, to educate the poorest in society.

The early years of Françoise Blin de Bourdon

Françoise Blin de Bourdon was born in 1756 of wealthy landed aristocratic parents whose ancestry dated back to the eleventh century. She was the daughter of Pierre-Louis de Blin, Viscount de Domart-en-Pontieu, and Marie Louise Claudine, daughter of the Baron of Fouquesolles, Viscount of Doullens. The family was part of the lesser nobility, but they were important enough to enable Françoise to have been presented at the court of Louis XVI in 1775 at the age of eighteen, with the hope of her making a good marriage: a prospect that Françoise was never drawn to with much enthusiasm.

Françoise was the youngest of three children, reflecting the decline in family size in wealthy families in France. Hers was one of the good aristocratic Catholic families, who acted responsibly towards the poor around them. The giving of alms was the major form of Catholic charity in the eighteenth century, but few families it seems were as generous as the Blins. A saying about the family was well known in the region: 'Bon comme un Blin'.

Françoise's early upbringing was left in the hands of her grandmother. She spent the best part of her first sixteen years at Gézaincourt, her grandmother's home, about twenty miles from her family home at Bourdon. This arrangement of the extended family was not unusual for the time. Françoise was a normal, healthy, lively child with a mind, will and temper of her own. Her education followed that of the wealthy Catholic aristocracy and she attended an expensive girls' boarding school at Doullens, run by Benedictine Sisters.

Like Julie's, Françoise's life was greatly dislocated by the French Revolution. As a member of the aristocracy her life was always endangered, but while Julie fled from the revolutionaries successfully to Compiègne, Françoise was taken prisoner in a night raid on her grandmother's home. The tenants of the area surrounded the castle of Gézaincourt, carrying farmyard weapons with which they threatened the revolutionaries and defended Françoise and her grandmother. Françoise, however, offered herself to the revolutionaries in place of her grandmother, who was in her eighties, agreeing to go with the soldiers only if they spared her grandmother. They did not give in to her demand until after two long hours of discussion. Françoise then dismissed the tenants, thanking them for their support. The revolutionaries did not allow her to re-enter the castle for any of her belongings, or to say goodbye to her grandmother. It was the middle of a February night in 1794. Françoise was then 38 years of age (SND 1964:36–7).

Françoise found herself imprisoned along with many other aristocrats, in very cramped and damp conditions in 'la Providence' prison in Amiens. On arrival she quickly learnt that a similar fate had befallen her father and brother. When Madame de Fouquesolles, Françoise's grandmother, heard what had happened, the shock was so great that she refused to eat, and died on 18 March 1794. Françoise was her sole heir, and she regretted to her death that she had not been able to be there to console her grandmother in her last moments.

The prison authorities, fearing the outbreak of riots and disease due to the overcrowded conditions, offered the women prisoners the option of staying at the nearby Carmel. Françoise jumped at this chance. She had felt an attraction to the Carmelite way of life for a long time, but had been prevented from following her calling by the need to care for her grandmother, after the death of her own mother in 1783 from injuries sustained in an accident in her carriage. While there she heard that her father and brother were to be guillotined, and she knew that she would follow. Françoise was saved at the eleventh hour by the fall of Robespierre on 27 July 1794. The worst of the Reign of Terror was over, but traces lingered on for others who, like Julie, continued to harbour priests.

The first meeting of Julie and Françoise in Amiens did not take place until 1795 when the worst part of the Revolution was over. Later chapters in the book deal with the unfolding of their friendship, as well as the later course of their lives in establishing a religious congregation for women. But in order to understand the importance of the stance taken by Julie and Françoise, and other counter-revolutionary women, it is important to situate them within the broader context of the part women played as the 'engine' of the Revolution.

Women and the French Revolution: 'The Third Estate of the Third Estate'

It was not till George Rudé (1959) undertook research on the 'crowd' in the French Revolution and the later 'gendered' approach to history that the rôle of women as the 'engine' of the revolution in its early stages became clear. They had this rôle despite the fact that the French Revolution was a predominantly male event, and the watchwords of the revolution, *'liberté, égalité et fraternité'*, were never meant to apply directly to women. There is a long history of women and protest before the French Revolution. Bread riots were a well-known feature of both the seventeenth and the eighteenth centuries, coupled with occasional riots in support of religion when it was deemed to be under attack. Both forms of riots were an extension of the main rôle given to women by society: as mothers and the main upholders of morality and religious education within the family. Given these circumstances there were certain characteristics that could be applied to all female riots. They were generally spontaneous, conservative in their aims and non-violent. Moreover, the protesters were mainly older women as it was a defining characteristic of female crowd activity that those with very young children did not put themselves at risk. The average age 'for food participants in food revolts was forty, in religious and political revolts thirty-seven. But instances are found of women over seventy who frequently had a leadership rôle and may have belonged to protester dynasties' (Hufton 1997:471).

It is possible to discern three main groups of women that emerged early in the revolution: the *enragées*, the Paris market women, whose main demand was bread; the *clubistes*, formed from the political groups of women, Madame Roland being a key figure, who demanded political rights for women; and the counter-revolutionary women, whose main aim was the restoration of the Catholic faith, a faith already weakened before the outbreak of the Revolution, but almost totally destroyed during Robespierre's 'reign of terror' and, in name at least, abolished by the introduction of the 'worship of reason' in all former churches. All baptisms, marriages and any teaching of religion were forbidden. The only way forward for the counter-revolutionary women was to teach and baptise clandestinely. These women, of whom Julie and Françoise were a part, represented the largest group of women.

The first two categories of women, which included both radical and traditional women from the peasant, artisan and wealthy classes, were mainly based in Paris (Hufton 1997: 481). The counter-revolutionary women, 'the ghosts of the Revolution', as they were dubbed by the Government because they refused to bow to its will, lived mainly outside Paris, in the provinces, and were more traditional in aims. That is, they were examples of the original meaning of 'revolution'. They were restorers of the past, as far as their faith was concerned. They wished to restore their religion which had been severely weakened and abolished by the revolutionaries.

The enragées

The *enragées*, the angry crowd, were the largest group of women protesters and they followed the general pattern of women's tradition of non-violent protests, especially for food for their families. What was new, however, was the size and geographical scale of the protest. As Rosalind Miles says so cogently in *The Women's History of the World*, revolutionary France abounded in 'dangerous women' (1989:181). France was like a tinder box ready to ignite, with protest in every part of the land, but the immediate cause of the outbreak in 1789 was lack of bread. It was the artisan class of Paris, led by the only woman in the group, Théroigne de Méricourt, who stormed the Bastille on 14 July 1789. This event galvanised the market women of Paris, heirs to a great tradition of direct action in the market place, to act in the following October. These days, now known as the October Days of Women, or the March of the Market Women to Versailles, had one aim: to bring the King and his court back to Paris and make him promise to give bread to the people. Or, in the words of the crowd, to bring back 'the baker, the baker's

wife, and the baker's boy' – the King, Louis XVI, the Queen,
Marie Antoinette, and the Dauphin (Anderson and Zinner
1988:279).

The March of the Women to Versailles was a magnificent
achievement. The women of Paris had opened up the situation.
They had demonstrated how far a large and peaceful march
could go, but when their interview with the King was without
real results and guarantees, the event had to pass into another
phase involving guards and men. It was only with the help of
the latter that the transfer of the King and the Assembly to Paris
was eventually achieved.

The clubistes

The *clubiste* women were the intellectual forum of political protest of prominent individuals, generally middle-class educated
women, and they were far fewer in number than the massive
crowds of women seeking bread. It is important to give consideration to this category of women, the political women, not
because of the extent of their influence at the time but because
of the future importance of their ideas. Although the initial aims
of this group were political – to get the vote for women – their
influence extended into many areas of women's lives, educational, social and economic.

One of the leading *clubiste* women was the colourful and
eccentric Théroigne de Méricourt, who led the Storming of the
Bastille and the March of the Women to Versailles. She was a
gifted singer who had trained in London and Naples and became
a leading activist. Another was Olympe de Gouges (1748–93),
a former actress who, although largely uneducated, wrote the
first full analysis of the multiple oppressions of women in the
Declaration of the Rights of Women in September 1791:

> Woman is born free and her rights are the same as those of
> a man . . . The law must be an expression of the general will;
> all citizens, men and women alike, must participate in making
> it . . . it must be the same for all . . . All citizens be they men

or women, being equal in its eyes, must be equally eligible for all public offices, positions and jobs, according to their capacity and without any other criteria than those of virtues and talents. (quoted in Miles 1989:183)

These women understood that, especially in the cities, the low wages of women and lack of job prospects forced them into an early marriage or on to the streets. And this, coupled with their lack of education, gave men a reason for refusing women political rights and made it impossible for women to legislate for reform or to obtain the right education, wage parity or equality before the law.

To reach their ends, *the clubiste* women organised groups and institutions to represent their interest. These groups were never large until the formation in May 1793 of the Société Républicaine Révolutionnaire, which had a broader agenda, including the fight for grain, as well as political aims. It was founded by Claire Lacombe (b.1765), an actress, and Pauline Léon (b.1758), a chocolate manufacturer, and was the first to include poor, working-class women and to speak for their interests. However, a split soon emerged between the different groups of women. The *clubiste* women asked the market women to wear the sign of the revolution, the cockade, but they refused because it was contrary to their rights and duties as women and mothers, as it meant 'bearing arms and fighting' (Hufton 1997:479). Historically, non-violence has always been a key priority in all women's uprisings. The politicians eagerly seized upon the women's overt dispute and closed all women's political clubs. The women were now effectively politically silenced.

In spite of the protestations of 'liberty', women's liberty was as absent as before. The irony of the Delacroix statue of 'Marianne' (Warner 1985), who became a figurehead for the overthrow of the *ancien régime* would not have been lost on the women, whose liberty, particularly political rights, was completely taken away with the repression of the *salons* and the closing of all political groups to women. Marianne, the generic woman, was put literally on a pedestal representing the ideals of the revolution, the fruits of which she herself was totally denied. Individual liberty was only to apply to men. With the decline of the *salons* and the abolition of the right for women in 1793 either to set up or to attend political societies, women could now only participate in political life through the men in their lives.

The little that women gained politically from the Revolution is clearly illustrated by the denial of the vote to French women until 1946. Olympe de Gouges had proclaimed in her *Déclaration* that women should have the right to stand for parliament 'if they have the right to go to the scaffold' (Miles 1989:185). Throughout the Revolution, unruly women were used as a scapegoat for social evils, echoed in the words of Madame Roland, the wife of a leading Girondin and a member of the *salons*. In November 1793 she cried on the scaffold, 'O Liberty! What crimes are committed in thy name!' (ibid.:186) Many women were guillotined during the Reign of Terror, the majority being entirely innocent of any political or other action against the Government. Included among these were many of the third category of women, the counter-revolutionary women, with whom this book is mainly concerned.

The counter-revolutionary women

It fell to the counter-revolutionary women to keep the voice of women active. It is important to note that for the women involved 'it was a notable consciousness raising exercise – we did it' (Hufton 1974:18), a point not to be lost on Julie Billiart. A woman from the provincial and not the Parisian artisan class, Julie would have been aware of the situation in Paris as her great friend and provider, Madame Baudoin, a wealthy aristocratic friend from her Cuvilly days, was a frequent visitor there. Madame Baudoin fled from the revolutionaries, after her husband's arrest, to join Julie in hiding in Compiègne. Julie would therefore have known at first hand the details of the March of the Women to Versailles as well as of the other uprisings that broke out.

There was a difference between the counter-revolutionary women and the anti-revolutionary women. The former did something about it. These were the women who boycotted the Masses of the constitutional juring-priests, and who organised clandestine Masses, baptised babies themselves in the absence of priests, and taught the catechism during the difficult years of 1793–4, when almost every church in France was closed. They refused to follow the popular custom of naming their children after leaders of the Revolution, but continued to give their children Christian names. For them the revolutionary experience had been tantamount to a revival of early Christianity in the catacombs, the times of persecution.

The well-established Sisters of Charity of St Vincent de Paul were the greatest immediate success story of the counter-revolutionary women. They continued to run hospitals, help non-juring priests and perform burials for the sick who died. There was a hate campaign conducted against them in the press and in 1792 they were driven from their main house in Paris. The revolutionaries used them as an example of what would happen to other women if they would not be brought into line, and some Sisters were 'publicly struck on the buttocks' (Hufton 1974:73) by other women if they left the house and disregarded the wishes of the government.

Counter-revolutionary women were of many different types and had different ways of associating. They came mainly from the provinces and from the countryside, as did Julie and Françoise. They included both working-class and aristocratic, well-educated women. But they had one over-riding common bond, a desire to re-establish the Tridentine faith in France. Their success was mirrored in the 1801 Concordat, signed between Napoleon, from a position of strength, and the Roman Church, whereby the Catholic religion was restored to France. The Concordat, however, gave Napoleon pretty much what he wanted. He obtained the right to nominate bishops, the Pope merely conferring canonical status and the right to vet the bishops' choices of parish priests. His aim was to create a bishops' corps of 'prefects in purple' (Gibson 1989:48) in order to extend his control over Church as well as state. The clergy were to take an oath of loyalty to the government. Finally, Church property taken during the Revolution was not restored to the Church and the Pope had to recognise the rights of the new owners. The Organic Articles provided for detailed regulation of the clergy by the government. No papal or conciliar document could be published in France without the consent of the government, and no meetings of the clergy were allowed without governmental consent. This Concordat was to regulate the relationships between Church and State until their separation in 1905.

The best-known groups were those who founded or joined the new religious congregations, becoming the *bonnes soeurs* of the nineteenth century. But there was also another almost undocumented group, especially in the early part of the century, known as the *béates*. They were pious spinsters who wore a habit, were generally attached to a religious congregation, but took no vow of celibacy, lived at home and were under the authority of the local *curé*, as well as of a religious congregation. Some did later marry. Their work was primarily among the poor rural women of the parishes, in caring for the 'sick and needy (well) and teaching the catechism (badly), and lace making (rather well)' (Gibson 1989:107). They were a part of the countryside populace for most of the nineteenth century, but declined as they lacked the formalised structures of the congregations, whilst the welfare state gradually encroached into their activities.

The flowering of the women's religious congregations: the bonnes soeurs

No specific reference was made to religious congregations in the Concordat of 1801, Napoleon's attitude being 'I do not want to see any religious orders in France as they serve no useful purpose' (Gibson 1989:104). He soon, however, came to see that the orders – especially those of women – might indeed serve a useful purpose for teaching and nursing, at first leaning towards the establishment of only two congregations to serve the poor in these two ways. However, in 1808 the situation was resolved in favour of a multiplicity of congregations, possibly to avoid a concentration of power, doing similar works. By now Napoleon had recognised in them a source of cheap labour to help the poor. He not only authorised but positively encouraged them. Money was provided to promote recruitment to the female orders and in 1809 a decree conferred on them a number of favours, as well as restrictions.

The scene was set for their spectacular development, and the most phenomenal growth in women's religious congregations ever known. Of the six hundred new *congrégations*, as they were called, four hundred were female. Claude Langlois has written a formidably long and carefully researched book on this topic entitled *Le Catholicisme au Féminen: Les Congrégations Françaises à Supérieure Générale au XIXe Siècle* (1984). He points out that a phenomenon common to all these female congregations was a Superior General chosen from among their own community. And before the end of the nineteenth century over two hundred thousand women took the habit. From 1800 to 1820 foundations rose rapidly, averaging thirty-five in ten years. The period of maximum growth was 1820–60. During this time on average six new congregations were founded a year. From 1860 to 1880 a decline began to be perceptible and only 25 new congregations were founded in the 1870s.

After the fall of Napoleon in 1815, a new generation of priests were even more interested in the female congregations as a means of extending their own influence over their flock. At the level of highest recruitment in the late 1850s perhaps one girl in twelve who did not marry entered religious orders (Gibson 1989:105). In fact, more congregations were founded, especially in France between the years 1809 and 1869, than in the previous eighteen centuries, and the lack of clergy, especially between 1800 and 1820, enabled women founders to flourish. Between 1800 and 1820, 49 per cent of the congregations had a female founder. Langlois describes five categories of background of the foundresses of religious orders: 'out of a total of 174, 22.4 per cent were from the nobility; 42.5 per cent from the bourgeoisie;

16.7 per cent from the artisan or small business class (he mentions Julie Billiart as one of this class); 13.8 per cent from the peasantry; and 4.6 per cent were wage-earning domestic or urban/rural proletariat' (Langlois 1984:273).

These single female foundations tended to fare better than those with both a male and female founder. In comparison with those of the 'female clergy', as Langlois calls them, the development of male religious orders was unimpressive. Moreover, contemplative religious life, which had been gradually declining since the seventeenth century, now lost the pre-eminence it once had and the active life of service was highlighted as being the need at this time.

The Church was brought back by the populace from below, as the loss of the church for poor women had been considerable and the social conscience of the nineteenth century was largely that of women (Langlois 1984). These women protesters formed by far the largest group, and the most successful in achieving their aims: the restoration and eventually the re-education of the poor masses of France to the Catholic religion. It was also the only group that successfully united all classes of women, exemplified in the relationship between Julie, the artisan/peasant woman, and Françoise, the aristocrat. It also revealed dispositions which would have remained untapped if the extremely élitist conventual model had remained dominant. There was widespread demand for their services, and they were the only institution that offered a woman a career beyond obligatory motherhood. Langlois believes the women in these nineteenth-century congregations lived at a time when the status of women was beginning to be questioned. This coincided with a gradual shift from the Church to the state having total control over people's lives. These Sisters, therefore, were 'a long parenthesis' (ibid.:648) between the enclosed religious of earlier times, when the Church had full control over women's religious lives by the laws of enclosure, and the coming of women as an educated laity in the twentieth century, where a vowed life was no longer a necessity for the advancement of women.[6]

Protest and awakening were the bedrock for the flowering of

the four hundred female congregations of the nineteenth century. Julie and Françoise were among these women who were to found a congregation to educate the masses of the industrial poor they saw around them. These congregations are too numerous to mention but most are well-known to present day Catholics. In fact many R C women and men would have been taught or nursed by them: Society of the Sacred Heart, Society of the Holy Child Jesus, Poor Servants of the Mother of God, Sisters of the Cross and Passion, Helpers of the Holy Souls, Loreto Sisters, Holy Family of Bordeaux, the Little Sisters of the Poor, Sisters of Mercy, etc. The largest congregations at this time continued to be those founded before the Revolution: the Sisters of Charity of St Vincent de Paul and Louise de Marillac (over 9,000 members in 1878) and the Filles de la Sagesse (3,400 in 1878) (Gibson 1989:107; Langlois 1984).

The response of others was to join these women and for the first time many of the new sisters came from the ranks of the poor not the rich. These *congrégations* became an essential army of women destined to both educate and nurse the poor industrial masses in the nineteenth and twentieth centuries. They soon spread well beyond France to many parts of the world, often first to the USA, 'the land of the free'.

Reflections

The women of the French Revolution were protesters for a better way of life for all, whether they were the *énragées*, the *clubistes* or the counter-revolutionary women. They laid the foundation for the women of the later nineteenth and twentieth centuries to develop other aspects of public protest, including the anti-slavery movement of the 1840s and the suffragette movement of the late nineteenth and early twentieth centuries. St Joan's Alliance, the first Catholic reform organisation in Britain, was founded in 1911, a direct result of the influence of the suffragette movement. In the 1920s Eglantyne Jebb founded the Save The Children Fund in protest at the poverty of poor Austrian children after the First World War.

The second half of the twentieth century saw an explosion of protest movements as old ideas and institutions of society and Church no longer fitted people's experience. The mothers of the Disappeared in Argentina in the 1960s protested daily in market places for their lost loved ones, victims of the Pinochet régime. In Britain, the women of Greenham Common in the 1970s chose to set up peace camps round the periphery of the nuclear arms base. Ecological and animal rights campaigns have many female supporters, as had Jubilee 2000 – a call to eradicate the debt of the poorest countries of the world.

Given the inequalities of our time, can any spirituality be Christian if it does not have some aspect of protest? For the first time in history the twentieth century has experienced a 'massive alienation of women' from their churches, mirroring that of the male alienation of the eighteenth and nineteenth centuries (McEwan 1991).[7] This alienation of women has resulted in the foundation of modern protest groups, which I call the *salons of the twentieth century*, calling for change in all the present churches.[8] These different forms of protest cannot be separated from a growing maturation of personal and communal spirituality.

It is not surprising that protest, in its various forms, is at the root of prophetic spiritualities because it is at the core of the Biblical prophetic tradition. Its relegation to a minor, often invisible, position in the concept of holiness in spiritual literature is a strange and worrying phenomenon. Julie's and Françoise's spirituality followed this prophetic Biblical tradition of protest, born out of the personal and social context of Julie's life. It was in this furnace of suffering that her consciousness was raised and her charism, her spiritual gift, was born.

The retrieval of the importance of the protest/prophetic tradition in another time and culture is crucial, especially within religious life itself (Chittister 1996). Tissa Balasuriya OMI from Sri Lanka (1985) sees in each call a calling away from the centres of power, the establishment and the tradition-bound society. He sees certain trends, however, which develop later in religious life: the continuation of the original calling to protest against abuse and compromise is clouded by a strong tendency to be influenced by the prevalent, dominant system.

The history of the nineteenth century shows women had a revolution of their own. A new energy was unleashed by women which was to become the driving force of political, social, and eventually, in the latter part of the twentieth century, religious and ecclesial change. The responses of women were different, their immediate aims were varied, but their long-term vision was the same: the gradual eradication of poverty and the enhancement of the status of women in all areas of life. The realisation of the importance of the legacy of such women as Olympe de Gouges (1748–93) in France and Mary Wollstonecraft (1759–97) in Britain, was to lie in the future suffrage movement, brought to consciousness by the anti-slavery movement of the 1840s, of which Elizabeth Cady Stanton (1815–98) and Susan B. Anthony (1820–1906) were the catalysts.[9]

Although women played an initial and crucial role as 'the engine of the revolution' the history of all liberation movements shows that women fight first for the liberation of others, and then have to fight for their own. The women of the French Revolution were no exception, but the Revolution raised women's awareness to the extent of their own oppression. The world of women was never to be the same again. It released in many the possibility of changing their lives for the better. So it can be said that the Revolution laid the foundation of many aspects of the modern feminist movement, the movement which is striving to fulfil 'the radical notion that women are people' (Elizabeth Schüssler Fiorenza, 'Feminist Theology' (internet article, 1997), p. 1).

2

Women of Vision

'The mystic is feminist . . .' (Giles 1986:6)

The subject of mysticism and what it is has fascinated writers on spirituality throughout the centuries but the twentieth century has witnessed an upsurge of interest in this subject, beginning with such well-known writers as William James, Baron Von Hügel and his disciple Evelyn Underhill. In 1995 Grace Jantzen, in her book *Power, Gender and Christian Mysticism*, wrote the first comprehensive deconstruction of the mystical tradition from a gender perspective, and her understanding of the social construction of mysticism led her to the following conclusion:

> [I]t is obvious as soon as one stops to consider that a person who was acknowledged to have direct access to God would be in a position to challenge any form of authority, whether doctrinal or political, which she saw as incompatible with the divine will. If defining mysticism is a way of defining power then who counts as a mystic is of immediate political importance. (Jantzen 1994:187)

It is impossible, therefore, to have any clear perspective on mysticism without some reference to these changing concepts.

The 'social construction' of mysticism

The word 'mysticism' is not found in the Bible, although a direct encounter with God is recognised throughout scriptures. Etymologically, the word's roots are to be traced to Greek Hellenism. Here it referred to the disclosure of secret rites to the uninitiated in the various Greek religions, and never to any specific experience. The early Christian meaning of mysticism is to be found in the Greek Fathers of the Church. For example, Clement and Origen wrote about the mystical or hidden meaning of scripture and only those who interpreted the inner or hidden meaning of the scriptures were considered 'mystical'. As most women were excluded from education, this automatically excluded women from scriptural and theological education and interpretation. By the fourth century AD the word 'mystical' was enlarged to refer to Christ's hidden presence not only in the scriptures but also in the liturgy and the sacraments. It was only in the fifth century that a Syrian monk, known as Pseudo-Dionysius, introduced the word into the Christian vocabulary in his work the *Mystica Theologica*. This work was eventually to transmit to future generations the mystical theology of patristic times, and was destined to be very influential in the development of the mystical tradition from the twelfth century onward. (Prior to that time, the word 'contemplative' was used rather than 'mystical'.) In this work he spoke of a movement of mystical contemplation, a movement toward God beyond concepts and symbols. It was a knowledge of God by unknowing.

The twelfth-century renaissance, a renaissance which saw the beginning of the growth of towns and an embryonic centralisation of state and church government, witnessed a radical change in the general perception of mysticism when the development of scholasticism brought about an unexpected split between theology and spirituality. Mysticism now became a much more subjective and affective experience centred on the humanity of Christ. At the same time the growth of towns and universities had a great impact in accelerating the growth of clericalism and a clerical élite within the Church. These changes and the introduction of the use of the vernacular into spirituality led to significant developments in the understanding of mysticism from the women visionaries of the time. Hildegard of Bingen in the twelfth century (c.1142) marks an important transition in the social construction of mysticism. She claimed that because of men's laxity 'God has had to turn to Hildegard, a woman, and given *her* a message to be communicated by visions rather than by the "normal" method of years of prayerful study of the Scriptures' (quoted in Jantzen 1994:189). However, in order that her voice was heard she couched her strong and challenging ideas in conciliatory language. She insisted that men should be the mystical ones, because of their insight into the meaning of scripture, and that she herself was unlettered.

She was followed by an explosion of female visionaries, known as the 'golden age of mysticism', which lasted until the fifteenth century. These medieval women mystics reveal mysticism as a social phenomenon in which the mystic always reflects 'a socio-religious world and in turn affects, even transforms, that world through the creation of a new type of discourse and the formation of new religious groups'.[1] Carol Walker Bynum in her book *Jesus as Mother: Studies in the Spirituality of the High Middle Ages* wrestles with the question of this fourfold increase in women visionaries in the High Middle Ages. She concludes from the widespread evidence, especially from the nuns of Helfta, Germany, that 'the mysticism of thirteenth-century women is therefore an alternative to the authority of office' (Bynum 1994:261). Additionally, women used their visions to establish their position and to rectify the wrongdoings of the clergy. The evidence of women's widespread mystical experience led her also to the following conclusion: 'that for the first time in history we can document that a particular kind of religious experience is more common among women than among men. And women were more likely to be mystics, to gain reputations based on their mystical abilities and to have paramystical experiences' (ibid.:172). Many of these women visionaries identified themselves with Christ through suffering and they saw this as a unique form of discipleship. It was not unique to the medieval era, however: 'it has roots in the second-century struggles over meaning and identity and is therefore characteristic of most historical rendering of Western Christian self-understanding' (Miller 1999:26). What is dangerous is to over-romanticise the discourse of these visions based on eros and violent sufferings. Women used asceticism and suffering in order to be legitimised in the eyes of male clerical authority (Miller 1999).

The Church soon began to fear the growing number of women visionaries and from the thirteenth century onwards attempts were made to sideline this tradition as irrational and emotive. A gradual split developed between theology and spirituality from this time, and by the nineteenth century, this split was so complete that it led to the privatising of the tradition with an attempt to make it ineffective. Women's mystical experience was relegated even further from the public to the private sphere, in an attempt to make women's experience invisible.

After the Council of Trent in the sixteenth century, the authority of visions alone was no longer deemed sufficient for women's authority to be authenticated. The institutional Church now required an authentication of the visions of women through the discernment of a spiritual director acceptable to the institutional Church of the time. Patricia Ranft in the *Journal of Feminist Studies in Religion* (1994), points to a paradox in Counter-Reformation societies: although in this period the official Church became more restrictive and patriarchal, the Church also opened up an array of services for women religious. In Counter-Reformation society celibate women in religious communities were no longer restricted to the life of the cloistered nun but fought for an active apostolate that opened to them social roles such as those of nurse, teacher, social worker and catechist, activities that were clearly in conflict with official declarations. Ranft argues that it was the institution of the confessor–spiritual director, who not only forgave sins but also gave directions for a future virtuous life, that bestowed the stamp of approval on women's religious innovations. But while this institution authorised Catholic sisters to expand their activities, it also enabled the patriarchal hierarchy to exercise increased spiritual discipline through the penitentiary system. She traces this movement from the time of Teresa of Avila (1515–82), whose most famous confessor/director was St John of the Cross (1542–91), to Jane Frances Chantal (1572–1641) and Francis de Sales (1567–1622), Louise de Marillac (1591–1660) and St Vincent de Paul (1580–1660).

Julie learnt from her illustrious forebears and chose only a male spiritual director who could transcend at least the basic gender restrictions of the time. Julie's letters show she understood her times well; they are full of the importance of choosing the right kind of director. Julie warns her Sisters continually to discern between confessors and she herself was highly discerning in her choice of priests for spiritual direction. Julie learnt the importance of spiritual compatibility early in life, initially from the Abbé Dangincourt in Cuvilly. He was followed by a succession of good confessors–spiritual directors, including Père Thomas, who appears in the very first Letters of Julie, Père Varin, who was to urge her to begin her congregation, the younger Père Enfantin, who challenged her to make a novena and walk in 1806, and a less-known figure but a favourite in later life, Père Neujean, parish priest of St Nicholas at Liège (L387, 393, 407).

What light does this phenomenon of the mystical experience of the women of these times throw on the concept of mysticism itself? And what is the difference between mysticism and spirituality? The classic definition of mysticism is 'cognitio Dei experimentalis'. It is understood by Dorothee Sölle, in the light of the experience of the female mystics, as 'an awareness of God gained not through books, not through the authority of religious teachings . . . but through the life experiences of human beings' (Sölle 1984:86). In the same way, Teresa of Avila (created in 1970 a Doctor of the Church) declared that Christ made himself 'her living book', because of her lack of knowledge of the scriptures.

If Karl Rahner's claim is correct and the 'devout Christian of the future will either be a *mystic*, one who has experienced something or will cease to be anything at all' (Rahner 1977:51), a distinction needs to be made between the 'explicit mystics', that is the mature mystics whose inner and outer life are one and beacons for us all, and the 'implicit mystic' in all human beings. And if, as Bernard McGinn SJ writes, mysticism is a 'heightened consciousness involving both loving and knowing'

(McGinn 1992:xviii), which may or may not include explicit visionary experience, then spirituality becomes the normative, daily living out of the mystical way. Mystical and visionary experiences are therefore 'peak experiences of wholeness when the rational and intuitive are in unison (Desmond Murphy 1995:82). The mystic, like the creative artist, has the most disturbing awareness that something is not quite right, and this way of knowing is characterised by endless seeking. Although the mystics themselves generally emit great joy because of their trust in God, their heightened sense of God also leads to a heightened sense and desire to wrong the major evils of their time. Hence, the task of the mystic becomes prophetic, to reawaken the collective consciousness of society so that people can reclaim values and beliefs long submerged.[2] Mystics are therefore a corrective to all human knowledge, they break through to the next stage of consciousness, and challenge us all to move forward to greater maturity and fullness of being – the goal of all human knowledge.

The prophetic role of visions in the mystical tradition

It is not surprising that visions played a pivotal role in the lives of women mystics at a time of crisis as visions have always played a crucial role in the Christian prophetic tradition. In the words of Walter Brueggemann in his book *The Prophetic Imagination*, the prophetic tradition is where the prophet is concerned 'with the future as it impinges on the present' (Brueggemann 1978:12). The prophets are shaped by the tradition but their task is to break free from the tradition and 'to assert the new freedom of God' (ibid.:114). They are called not only to 'dismantle dominant consciousness but also energise it' (ibid.:13), and to offer signs of a genuine alternative to the present.

The Old Testament abounds with examples of visionary prophets, for example, Ezekiel, Isaiah, and Jeremiah, but it is Moses who is considered the model of all prophecy since he sought to evoke 'an alternative consciousness in Israel' (Brueggemann 1978:150), in a radical break with the social reality of

Pharaoh's Egypt' (ibid.:15). In other words, the prophets were those with their internal eyes open (Sam. 9:9; 18:9; Num. 24:3–4, 15–16), and hence they insisted on the divine origins of their visions (Amos 7:1, 4–7). Similarly, in the New Testament, Jesus declared his identity by means of a theophany at the beginning of his public life: by his baptism (Matt. 3:12–17; Mark 1:9–11; Luke 3:21–2); to Peter, James and John at the transfiguration (Matt. 17:1–8); and in his resurrection appearances to the women (Mark 16:10; John 20:18) and the disciples (Mark 16:14; John 20:24). The appearances of Christ after his resurrection are in fact foundational to Christian belief. Similarly, Paul and Peter were also gifted by visions at certain times of crisis: for example, Paul's conversion (Acts 9:1–9) and his ecstasy in the seventh heaven (2 Cor. 12:1–4), and Peter's vision that the Gentiles were not unclean and that they too were called into the kingdom of Heaven (Acts 10:9–6). Visions, therefore, are primarily for the good of others, and presuppose the gift of prophecy. It is clear, from the above examples, that at crucial times in the lives of both individuals and the church community, visions were an essential way out of an impasse. They are 'transrational epiphanies' of grace – that is, a solution to a situation not possible by the normal level of consciousness or method of reasoning.[3]

Just as Grace Jantzen has questioned who counts as a mystic from a gender perspective, (Jantzen 1995), so she has questioned the dominant understanding of how visions are experienced, by the visionaries themselves. The foundation for this understanding was asserted by William James in his book *Varieties of Religious Experience* (1902). He deduced that visions are intellectual, abstract, transient and passive, and that the visionary cannot describe, be involved in or remember what they have seen. This ineffability and privacy of visionary experience is questioned by Jantzen who is concerned both with the privatisation of visions (hence making women powerless once again) and with the way visions were experienced especially by women. She claims, although this point can be disputed,[4] that this description of their visionary experience 'would have simply baffled many of the medieval women from Hildegard of Bingen to Teresa of Avila ... who wrote about their experiences with great fluency and creativity, and at great length' (Jantzen 1994:191-2). Their visions were in no way 'negative': they saw them clearly, were frequently involved in these experiences, and could remember them graphically. The following account of Julie's founding vision at Compiègne illustrates the appropriateness of Jantzen's thought in regard to Julie. In theological terms this vision can be called Julie's great 'awakening' to the power within her.

The making of Julie's mystical identity

The first chapter has given a short account of Julie's early life and her spiritual precociousness. She seems to have been one of those people whose whole personalities learn early to attune themselves to the ways of God. Through the careful early spiritual guidance of Père Dangicourt, the parish priest of Cuvilly, Julie was allowed to receive the sacraments of the Eucharist and Confirmation earlier than generally allowed. Her paralysis gave her long hours to be in deep communion with God and it was this long preparation in contemplative prayer that enabled her to see the hand of God in all things. By the time of the outbreak of the French Revolution her self-surrender to God was complete, and her inner strength and readiness to lead others was to be clearly shown as she led the rebellion in her area in refusing to accept juring-priests in Cuvilly.

Antoon Geels in his article 'Chaos Lives Next to God' differentiates four phases in the visionary experience which are applicable to the experiences of Julie: (a) immediate preparation, (b) incubation, (c) illumination, (d) verification.[5] These phases of Julie's visionary experience all took place after the passing of the Civil Constitution of the Clergy on 12 July 1790 and its condemnation by the Pope in March 1791, but because of the necessity for secrecy the exact dates of the following developments in Julie's life are not certain. However, all occur between the years 1790 and 1793, at the height of Robespierre's 'reign of terror'.

Immediate preparation

In 1791 Julie found herself literally being hunted by the revolutionaries. The province of Picardy where Julie lived was a hotbed of revolution: in the district of Beauvais alone over 90 per cent of the clergy had taken the Oath, and in Compiègne over 83 per cent. Julie's attitude towards juring-priests was publicly known, and in spite of her physical disabilities she became a target for the anger of the local revolutionaries. She became a pursued woman when she refused to accept the juring-priest sent to her village, and she openly incited others to do the same in support of her great friend and guide l'Abbé Dangicourt, who had refused to sign the Oath. The hunted priest lived in a dark, damp hovel behind a chicken house, protected by some of his parishioners. At night he emerged to say Mass in Julie's room for her and some of her friends. Each time he left his hiding place, he risked his life. After six months of this, in early 1791, the revolutionaries were getting too close and he fled to Mt Valerian outside Paris, where the monks were hiding non-juring priests. A few months later he died there (Roseanne Murphy 1995:23–4).

Julie's influence was now perceived as so dangerous that she is mentioned in the archives at Compiègne as one of the most wanted people of her time:

> The only commune in the district where there were serious incidents concerning oaths of allegiance was at Cuvilly, situated in the north of the district on the Flanders road. This little village seems to have had a particular penchant for resistance, due to the presence of a young and very pious paralytic by the name of Julie Billiart whose 'fanatical' influence was very great in Cuvilly even before the Revolution. (Roseanne Murphy 1995:24)

The local people began to fear the great danger Julie was in and one of the rich aristocratic women whom she had befriended came to her help with the offer of a hiding place. With her niece

Félicité, her companion and nurse, who was only sixteen years of age, she left Cuvilly for the safety of the château owned by Madame Pont l'Abbé, about twenty miles away at Gournay sur Aronde. Madame Pont l'Abbé took them in her own carriage, which in itself was a considerable act of bravery. Women helping women in situations of violence, especially domestic violence, was not new in the eighteenth century, but the French Revolution introduced a new element into this custom. Madame Pont l'Abbé's own safety was now so seriously threatened that she was forced to escape to England, where, because of the traumas of her escape, she died a few months later.

But before long, Julie was again forced to flee. After searching for her all over the region, a group of revolutionaries began to suspect that she was at the château. Having torn down the Calvary shrine, so characteristic of the villages in that area, they made a bonfire of the wood and threw on it the tabernacle from the church, with statues and sacred books, to build a huge pyre in preparation for burning Julie, *la dévote*, alive. In a rage, they then turned to the château of Gournay. Hearing of their approach, the caretaker hid Julie and Félicité in the bottom of a hay cart outside the barn. Having covered both of them with hay, he rushed back to the château to meet the mob which stormed into the building demanding that he turn Julie over to them. He tried to persuade them that Julie was not in the château but they ransacked the building, swearing in drunken voices that they would drag the invalid from her bed and toss her in a blanket, and shouting that they would 'watch her dance before throwing her onto the fire' (Roseanne Murphy 1995: 25). The caretaker persuaded them that Julie was not there, but before they left they carved on the wall of the château the words 'Stuff the aristocrats with bullets'.

The caretaker insisted that Julie and her niece leave at once, so he hitched the horse to the wagon and drove right through the mob, who were still shouting blasphemies and obscenities about *la dévote* and swearing to find her. Scarcely able to breathe, Julie was jostled out on to the road to Compiègne. She and Félicité almost suffocated under the hay. They arrived in

Compiègne in the early hours of the morning and Julie was lifted out of the cart on to a bench in the courtyard of an inn. The next morning two sisters by the name of Chambon found the young girl and her paralysed aunt shivering on the bench, and offered them a room in their home.

Incubation

Little is known of the whereabouts of Julie and her niece Félicité during their time in Compiègne, except that they only remained with the Chambon sisters for two months, as Julie's presence was endangering the sisters' lives, and that they moved house at least five times. However, we do know that her favourite prayer at this time was, 'Lord, wilt thou not lodge me in Paradise, since I can no longer find shelter on earth'? (Murphy 1995:26–7).

These years were, however, to prove to be among the most fruitful of her life. It was here that her vision was born, out of her own turmoil and the turmoil of others. The Carmelites of Compiègne, who were to go to the scaffold in 1794, were among those who befriended her. While in Compiègne she also received news of her father's death at the age of seventy-five. It was while she was at her lowest personal ebb, and surrounded by the worst sufferings inflicted during the 'reign of terror', that she received a vision which was to change her life. This occurred some time during 1792 and 1793, but exactly where in Compiègne is unknown.

Illumination: the vision at Compiègne

The following is the only known account of Julie's vision, made to Monsieur de Lamarche, her priest/confessor in Compiègne in 1793, as related in the 1909 biography of Julie by James Clare SJ ed. and Mary Xavier Partridge SND. Julie herself remained reticent all her life on this major experience, only referring to it when she met certain women whom she had seen in the vision.[6] Monsieur de Lamarche related:

It was not until 1793 that I made the acquaintance of Mère Julie . . . I was then ministering to her spiritual needs . . . she was living in retirement in a small room with one of her nieces who took care of her. I went to visit her; she did not speak, or rather she only spoke in signs. When she went to confession, I had to give her an hour's notice. She then prepared herself with an intense fervour, and obtained, as she herself owned to me, the grace of articulating distinctly. It was only after absolution that she fell back into speechlessness . . . I saw her from time to time for about a year; I was more and more astonished in her progress in perfection . . . Her resignation was perfect; always calm, always united to God, her prayer was so to speak, unceasing . . . It was in one of these moments of close union with God that . . . Julie was ravished in ecstasy and saw presented before the eyes of her soul the hill of Calvary. Surrounding our crucified Lord she beheld a multitude of virgins wearing a religious habit she had never seen before. The vision was so clear, the features of some of the religious so deeply imprinted on her memory, that many years after she was able to say to some who offered themselves to be her companions, 'God wills that you enter our society; I saw you among ours at Compiègne' . . . When the time came for her to choose a Religious dress for her Sisters, without a moment's hesitation she gave orders as to the shape and material to be used; her tone was very calm and collected as she said, 'It was shown to me at Compiègne'. At the close of the heavenly vision Julie heard these words, which explained to her what she had seen: 'behold the spiritual daughters whom I give you in the Institute, which will be marked by my cross', and at that moment there was unrolled before the eyes of her soul the long series of the persecutions of her life. (Clare SJ ed. and Partridge SND 1909:35–7)

Verification

Julie's vision at Compiègne came at a time of great personal and civil crisis, and was her moment of integration of both outer conflict and inner desires. The vision was the fruit of her remarkable gift of contemplative prayer and her lifelong total reliance on '*le bon Dieu*', 'the good God'. Religious visions often occur when a person is alone and relaxed, probably in Julie's case praying before a crucifix. Antoon Geels names four main dimensions to religious visions: 'the emotional, communicative, perceptual, and cognitive dimensions' (Geels 1992:231). The dominant emotions are those of great peace, joy, security and love, and a sense of 'goodness' is communicated to the receiver. In regard to the perceptual dimension, the visual perceptions are dominant, 'sometimes in combination with auditive and/ or tactile perceptions' (ibid.:232). With regard to the cognitive dimensions Geels found that 'the more abstract, unstructured experiences are more open for interpretation than structured experiences' (ibid.). It is interesting to reflect on these four dimensions in Julie's vision.

All visions make an indelible imprint on the consciousness of the receiver, and Julie's spirituality was deeply influenced by this remarkable vision. The cross, the centre of her vision, became the focus of her spirituality, but the sense of joy and the felt 'goodness of God' never left Julie, as her letters were to show. The vision was obviously auditory as well as visual – 'behold the spiritual daughters whom I give to you in the Institute, which will be marked by my cross'. Whether it was tactile or not we will never know because there is no other known record of this vision. On the surface, it appears a very structured vision although much was left unclear, such as the details of Julie's trials with Church authorities and her opposition from some of her Sisters.

Antoon Geels remarks that 'it is striking that the contents of the visions fit so well into their situations of chaos' (Geels 1992:234). Julie's vision established order out of her chaos and it brought her the return of balance, 'homeostasis'. Julie's mystical character was to be that of a contemplative in action, marked by the cross. She called it the 'rapture of action'.[7] But the full verification only unfolded as the events of her life unfolded and she began to recognise certain women whom she had seen in her vision. As already noted, Julie's vision at Compiègne fits Jantzen's theory of female visionaries rather than that of William James. Her vision was one of great and lasting clarity. Her faculties were highly engaged and she saw her future difficulties clearly, and the faces of many of the women who were to join her gathered round the cross. This is repeatedly shown in her disconcerting words: 'I saw you in the vision at Compiègne.'

Reflections

Contemplative visions, such as Julie's, are multi-dimensional. They not only reflect the needs of the person and the times in which they live, but they also have a transrational identity. That is, they go beyond the understanding of their time and have a meaning which even the bearer of the charism is unable fully to comprehend:

> Each age brings new insights into the truth. Whatever the original founder's vision was, succeeding generations should access deeper, less concrete, more abstract and more universal dimensions. In addition, the liminal (living always at the threshold of change) future will also give expression to archetypal values, both existential and transcendental that the human race has not yet accessed, yet needs for its ongoing evolution. (Desmond Murphy 1995:210).

The acceptance of a shift in the understanding of a founding vision is crucial. Its lack was clear when change began to affect the lives of the Sisters of Notre Dame de Namur after Vatican II in 1962. There was an inability to differentiate between the socio-religious factors and the deeper transrational understanding. For example, there were many conflicts in the late 1960s between the Sisters as to whether the habit – that is, the religious dress that Julie saw in the vision – was an essential part of her charism. Time has taught the congregation that the original habit, as it was called, was not essential to being a Sister of Notre Dame – nor, indeed, was any special outward dress. It did, however, have a meaning originally, allowing 'respectable women to move freely into areas not normally open to women' (McNamara 1996:624).

The important struggle to find deeper meaning in the vision of Julie goes on. The translation of the Compiègne vision by later generations of Sisters in the nineteenth and twentieth centuries into one of the formal education – mostly of girls, including the training of teachers – though highly successful and essential for those times, narrowed down the understanding of Julie's vision. Herein lay the inherent dangers to the congregation. As the state, especially in the West, in the twentieth century began to take over the running of schools and training of teachers, the former 'shared vision' no longer answered the needs of the time. The struggles for a new 'vision', a new *raison d'être*, was born.

Any new vision arising from Julie's charism can only be born through the same process that Julie went through, an experience of chaos, struggle and almost total despair:

> Contemplation needs to be orientated initially toward the past . . . This will identify the deficiencies of the present. It will also take the original vision into a qualitatively different realm that would justify the new . . . At this point . . . [t]here is a conjunction between a particular urgent need and the nature of the vision itself. (Desmond Murphy 1995:209)

Integration and answers to Julie's dilemma were only possible through a stance of contemplative prayer. The contemplative vision which ensued was a *transrational* event, producing a vision that went far beyond the signs of the times in which Julie lived, a vision capable of many shapes and hues, of which she herself was unaware. The initial vision now has to give way to continual re-incarnations of the vision in different times and places.[8]

Her visions, along with those of many other nineteenth-century founders, although in very different times from those of the medieval women visionaries, served a similar purpose to those of Hildegard of Bingen, Julian of Norwich and the many visionaries on the humanity of Christ and the Eucharist in the Middle Ages (Petroff 1986). They were the source of their authority from which they could speak to the authorities of their time. And as the modern French writer Luce Irigaray claims, the mystical discourse is the 'only place in Western history where woman speaks and acts in such a public way' (Irigaray 1985:238). Different historical circumstances produced different needs and different solutions. I call Julie's vision at Compiègne, along with those of other women foundresses of her time and later, 'apostolic' visions, a contemplative call to action: not to run away from the world but to be centred in it. Women mystics are women who push out the boundaries for other women, beyond the norms of their society, as far as they can within the 'patriarchal' restrictions of their time. They are among the most self-actualised women of history.[9]

The time before the vision can be called Julie's 'liminal' or threshold, period, which may be described as the time that offers the most potential for enlightenment and transformation, the death and life process: the time of chaos.[10] For Julie it was her moment of spiritual maturation. 'Counter-revolutionary' woman was a 'boundary dweller' along with the other women of the Revolution, marginal to the extent that they were on the threshold of something new. The old had died, the new had not arrived. But it was by means of visions that the future was to unfold. Mysticism is God's song; or, as Edwina Gateley has said so graphically: 'The mystics are God's last resort . . . They are the dreamers not paralysed by rule and doctrine' (Gateley 1993:56).

3

Women of Friendship

'. . . friendship in God lasts for ever.' (L71:187)

The friendship between Julie and Françoise became the corner-stone of their future work. It grew out of mutual understanding and love, cemented by a shared vision of their desire to help the poor. With birth and death, friendship is the most common experience among human beings, and throughout history philosophers, theologians and, in more recent times, psychologists have discussed the question: what is friendship? There are many forms of friendship, beside the married relationship, that are well known, but documentation on friendship between women has been long neglected.[1]

In the 1840s and 1850s the women of the great quilting nation, the USA, produced friendship quilts inspired by friendships between women of different circumstances and races.[2] Yet even in 1970, Adele Fiske concentrated only on male experience in her book *Friends and Friendship in the Monastic Tradition*, and no comparable work has yet been written on the female monastic tradition. It was not until the 1980s that an awareness developed of the lack of any real thinking or scholarship on women's friendships, from a philosophical or theological view-point, even though Janet Todd, in her *Women's Friendship in Literature* (1980), has illustrated that eighteenth-century fiction was as rich in the presentation of female friendship as male friendship. Recent writers on female friendship include Janice Raymond, in *a passion for friends: towards a philosophy of female affection* (1991). Raymond has highlighted the lack of a genealogy on women's friendships. She uses this word not in the usual linear sense of tracing a family tree, but by tracing the genealogies of diverse groups of women. In this way she makes the common links between these groups to establish a counter-memory of women's lost relationships with each other (Raymond 1991:24–7). Elizabeth Stuart has reflected on the fruit of loving lesbian and gay relationships in *Just Good Friends: Towards A Lesbian And Gay Theology Of Relationships* (1995); and Mary Hunt in *Fierce Tenderness* (1991) believes that friendships between women will give us new norms, not only in personal relating, but also for societal structural change.

The friendship between Julie and Françoise is a friendship of celibate love based on a shared love of God, known to the history of Christianity as a spiritual friendship. Although this tradition has mainly come down to us through the celibate tradition, it is now no longer understood as being confined to those who have chosen celibacy but is, in varying degrees, the foundational element in all lasting friendships. Even though Mary Hunt claims that 'engaging male sources that do not take account of women's experiences seems counterproductive' (1991:78), I believe it is important to take a look at some of the key ideas from the best-known writing on Christian friendship, *On Spiritual Friendship* by the twelfth-century Cistercian monk, Aelred of Rievaulx. Therefore, I first give a short resumé of friendship in scripture and the classical tradition, then compare the friendship between Julie and Françoise, as portrayed in Julie's first thirty-three letters, with Christian texts and sayings on friendship. I illustrate that in spiritual/contemplative friendships, such as theirs, there are striking similarities, as well as differences, which cross gender boundaries. Finally, I indicate pointers that emerge from the friendship of Julie and Françoise, and anticipate some of the recent understanding on the place and importance of friendship between women.

Friendship in the Christian tradition

In the Old and New Testaments

The Bible is really a collection of stories about different forms of relationships. The key relationship is the covenant relationship between God and humanity, beginning with Abraham, Isaac and Joseph (Exod. 2:24) and culminating in the sealing of this covenant with the death of Christ on the cross – the greatest act of friendship. Two words are frequently used for friendship in the Old Testament, the Hebrew terms '*oheb*, and the most common term *rea*'. The two words have more or less the same meaning, except that '*oheb* also refers to physical love. *Rea*' is used of Job's friends (Job 2:11; 16:20; 19:21, etc.); '*oheb* of Haman's friends (Esther 5:10, 14; 6:13); and the terms sometimes appear in close conjunction or in parallel (Ps. 38:11; 88:18). Wisdom writers are on the whole cautious on the subject of friendship, but they offer detailed advice on friendships: 'a true friend is a treasure beyond price' (Sir. 6:7, 13); 'True friends stand fast and false ones fall away' (Prov. 17:17).

Re-imagining women back into the scriptures is a major task but a glance at *The Women's Bible Commentary* (ed. Newsom and Ringe, 1992) soon reveals multiple examples of women's relationships. Among them is the friendship of Shiprah and Puah, the Hebrew midwives, who by saving Moses play a crucial role in salvation history (Exod. 1:15–22). The leadership of Miriam, the prophetess, the sister of Aaron, implies friendship; she 'took a timbrel in her hand; and all the women went out after her with timbrels and dancing. And Miriam sang to them' (Exod. 15:19–21). The wonderful relationship between Ruth and Naomi, who cross the generations of young and old, of daughter-in-law and mother-in-law, is captured in the words of Ruth: 'Wherever you go I will go and wherever you lodge I will lodge: your people shall be my people, and your God my God' (Ruth 1:16), and echoed in the friendship of Mary and Elizabeth (Luke 1:39–56).

In the New Testament the word often translated as 'friend'

is *philos* and John uses the term a number of times in important contexts. Friendship was the gift of Christ to his followers at the Last Supper: 'I no longer call you servants but friends' (John 15:15). And the nature of his friendship was exemplified in his intimate friendships: 'Now Jesus loved Martha and her sister and Lazarus' (John 11:5). The friendships that Jesus experienced with the many women who followed him have been brought to light by Elisabeth Schüssler Fiorenza's concentration on the 'Jesus movement' (Fiorenza 1986), and Elizabeth Moltmann-Wendel's retrieval of the women around Jesus in her book of that title (1982). Elements of the friendship between Julie and Françoise are to be found in all aspects of this Biblical tradition and are part of our retrieval of the important metaphor of God as friend.

In Church tradition

In spite of a strong friendship tradition in the Bible, born and nourished within the relationships of the Trinity, the ideas on friendship in the early stages of the Christian tradition were deeply influenced by Greek philosophy. For Aristotle, friendship could only be based on a relationship of equality in the male political arena, the *polis*. He also developed a hierarchy of friendship: friendships of utility, friendships of pleasure and, the highest of all, friendships with people of character. He believed that the higher up the ladder of friendship the fewer the number of friends are possible. However, he did place friendship as the intersection of the contemplative and active life, using the phrase 'one soul in two bodies'. This echoes the phrase so often used to describe the friendship between Julie and Françoise, 'two heads under one bonnet'.

The Fathers of the Church also wrote about friendship. For example, St Augustine discusses friendship in *De Trinitate, Confessions* and other writings. He argues that we do not choose our own friends, God does, which is why every friend is both the gift and work of God. Friends represent the very personal and concrete way that God loves us. He also argues that every friendship should be modelled on the Trinitarian friendship of God, as friendships are a means of growing together in the love of God. True friendship converts us to God and does not lead us away. However, it was the rise in affective spirituality in the twelfth century that was to produce the best-known treatise, *De Spirituali Amicitia, On Spiritual Friendship*, by a Cistercian monk from Scotland, Aelred of Rievaulx (1110–67).

Aelred inherited from Bernard of Clairvaux the Ciceronian concept of male pagan friendship which he translated into the gospel understanding of 'friendship that does away with social barriers by establishing an equality between friends of different social conditions' (Leclerq 1979:63). He also inherited reflections on the Wisdom tradition mentioned earlier: 'a true friend is a treasure beyond price' (Sir. 6:14–16), an ally in times of struggle (37:5–6); true friends stand fast and false ones fall away (Prov. 17:17; Sir. 12:8–9; 22:23). Wisdom dictates that a friend be like oneself (Sir. 13:14–15), especially in being a person who fears God (Sir. 6:17; 9:15–16).

It was, however, on the concept of 'ecstatic dynamic' love that Aelred specifically focused, concentrating on the relationship between *amicitia*, friendship, and *caritas*, love. He regarded love as the source and origin of friendship but believed love was the more general concept and friendship the more specific. He designated spiritual friendship as *dilectio Dei*, 'to the delight of God', and said that although it 'can rise among the good . . . progress among the better . . . it can only reach its highest point among the best' (Laker 1977, Num. 38:78–9).

Aelred in his treatise reasserts the following gospel teachings which have particular application to the friendship of Julie and Françoise: (i) 'the equality given by nature, rather than the baubles [money] which greed affords to mortals' (Laker 1977, Num. 90:114–15); (ii) 'often those in lower rank, class, dignity or knowledge are received into friendship by those who outstrip them in some way. And those who do not maintain equality do not rightly cultivate true friendship, for friendship knows no pride' (ibid.); (iii) 'friendships among the poor are more certain than those among the rich, since poverty removes the hope of gain from a friendship' (ibid., Num. 70:108). He finally exclaims that friendship is 'so close to wisdom, or even filled with wisdom, that I would almost say that friendship is nothing else but wisdom', and adds that friendship bears fruit, *fructus*, in this life (ibid., Book One, p. 41 and Book Two, 'Advantages of Friendship', p. 44).

Aelred can be said to have made four original contributions to the Christian theology of friendship: (i) 'God is friendship'; (ii) spiritual friendship is necessarily Christocentric, because friends journey to God through a mutual love of Christ; (iii) friendship for him prefigures the union of all humanity with God; (iv) he admits degrees of progression in friendship: 'inferior ones may lead to more holy ones' (Recker 1997). Among other writers who throw further light on friendship are St Thomas Aquinas (1225–74), whose ideas base the nature of human friendship on 'God's goodness', Julie's favourite metaphor for God; Teresa of Avila (1515–82) for whom 'prayer was friendship with God' (Peers 1972:40); and St Francis de Sales (1567–1622) who developed Aristotle's thought of 'one soul in two bodies'. At this time Christian friendship was recognised as having another dimension, of being a means of union with God, and as such an instrument of grace and personal development with God. These understandings of the centrality of friendship in God are reflected in the letters of Julie and Françoise.

The spiritual friendship of Julie and Françoise

Their first meeting

The origin of the friendship between *La Dévote* and *L'Aristocrate* was not very promising. They first met in Amiens in October 1794, as the 'reign of terror' began to subside – although not completely, since the persecution of priests continued. The meeting took place in the house of the elder brother of Françoise, Louis-Marie-César Bourdon, Viscount Blin de Bourdon, who had offered his house, the Hôtel Blin in the Rue de St Augustin, to Madame Baudoin. She was the aristocrat whom Julie had befriended while in exile in Compiègne. She was so keen to keep the friendship of Julie that she begged her to leave Compiègne and take up residence with her in the house of Louis in the industrial city of Amiens. In her vision Julie had been given strong signs of the suffering she was to undergo in Amiens, and at first resisted the move. Madame Baudoin was so persistent that after much thought and prayer, Julie decided that she was resisting God's will and decided to go. So, in October 1794, she took her place in the roomy carriage which had been sent for her, and attended by Félicité, her niece, set out for Amiens.

It was here that Madame Baudoin invited Françoise to meet Julie. At the time of their first meeting Julie was 44 years of age and Françoise 38. It is quite clear that Françoise was not naturally attracted to Julie; indeed, she wondered if she could return again. Julie, however, immediately recognised her as the woman who was in the forefront of her vision. Françoise writes that she went to the meeting 'as a lady who had leisure in abundance, who was quite willing to come, though when she found she could not understand the invalid's laboured speech, the visits seemed less attractive' (*Memoirs* 4). In the spirit of 'Bon comme un Blin', Françoise returned to the Hôtel Blin and her initial repugnance began to subside, so that eventually 'Françoise who had come out of charity, remained out of devotion' (SND 1923:39):

> Little by little Mlle. De Gèzaincourt [Françoise] discovered the treasures of grace enshrined in the humble casket of Julie's soul, while Julie on her side recognised the rich intellectual and spiritual gifts which were characteristic of Françoise, and which were allied to such perfect distinction and charm of manner (ibid.:40).

Julie soon attracted a small group of friends around her as in her native Cuvilly: Lise, the young aristocratic daughter of Madame Baudoin, and her young friends the Doria and de Mery sisters.[3] Françoise, although considerably older, became a part of this group. At the instigation of Madame Baudoin, Père Thomas, a non-juring priest and a Doctor of the Sorbonne, who had to flee the revolutionaries, also joined the group. He and Françoise were the only two of this group destined to remain with Julie. Père Thomas became not only a close friend but Julie's trusted spiritual director.[4]

The affective friendship in Julie's early letters

Julie's first 33 letters, written in 1795–7 while she was acting as Françoise's spiritual director, are marked by an intense language of affection:

> My dear lady, what a comfort your letter has been to me. I shall never be able to tell you how much I feel in your absence ... Since your departure from our town my heart, in spite of being so poor and wretched, has never been separated from yours. I can only call you friend; my heart refuses to do otherwise, for it is too attached in the Lord; it is for him and in him that I love you so dearly. (L1:19)

The same sentiments are repeated again and again in this section of the letters:

> Fiat, fiat! Please let me have news from you, my dear lady; you know how much I love you in the Lord. (L2:23)

> I must confess that your absence is a great loss to me. At the present time, I am very much alone with the good God. (L2:22)

> You are not absent from my mind dear friend, though distance separates us. (L3:23).

> Yes, my dear and loving friend, if I listened to my heart, I'd never stop sending you loving messages. (L6:34)

> The good Lord has so to speak, linked us to you, my dear friend; it is the work of divine providence, isn't it? (L12, par. 3:51)

Yes, my dear friend ... the good God constantly speaks to me concerning you. He shows me with what holy jealousy he loves your heart. He desires it may be entirely given to him, without a rival. (L12:50)

And by Letter 29 Julie begins to speak of Françoise as '*ma fille aînée*' (L29, par. 5:58), 'my eldest daughter'.

Julie's physical sufferings in the letters

Julie manifested the sufferings of Christ in her very body and she shared with Françoise her very real understanding of the interplay between the condition of the body and spirituality: 'Above all else, never be disturbed by what you call spiritual upsets, for they are more physical than moral' (L7:36). But she only talks of her health out of consideration for Françoise when she needs to explain why she has not been able to answer letters quickly:

I have not been able to answer you before, my dear friend in the Lord ...I have had severe attacks with convulsions. (L5:30)

... my wretched health does not always leave me free to do what my heart desires. (L9:42)

I can write no more, I feel the pain coming on; it will soon attack me with full force. (L33:88)

My nausea is worse than ever, but since I have received your wine I no longer have any urgent need. (L18:62)

I have a little less inflammation, and am left with only a headache. (L25:74)

Every night I am near to death and every day the good God restores me to life. (L31:84)

Ah! Will one heart suffice me to love him as I ought, as he deserves to be loved? ... I am profoundly touched by the kindness of our good God. It seems to me I cannot do otherwise than share my gratitude with you. (L11:48)

It is not surprising that the sheer holiness of the woman deeply affected Françoise and that she responded with alacrity to her bodily needs: when Julie was struck down with the enteric fever, or malaria, from the mosquito-infected river in Amiens, she wrote:

I have such frequent and heavy perspiration that if I were to change as often as I ought, I should require a great deal of linen. What I do want to ask quite simply is whether you could send me some old towels, that I could wrap around me and change for myself as needful at night. I cannot tell you how ill I feel when all my linen, soaked in perspiration, clings to me and makes my body clammy and cold . . . You see I am making full use of the right you gave me to tell you quite frankly all my needs. (L7:34)

In her later letters, Julie always insisted that the Sisters take good care of their health without being self-indulgent. She knew the ravages of the time, and many of the young women who joined her died in their late twenties, either from fever, or the other killer of the time, tuberculosis:

Above all be careful not to drink more water than I told you. I think this poor dead sister was imprudent in this respect, and so are you. Be very prudent about your health. (L378:877)

Bettencourt

It was not till after the death of her father in February 1797 that Françoise came to live permanently with Julie, after giving Gèzaincourt to her brother and the equivalent amount in property to her sister, Marie-Louise-Aimée. By this time, Françoise had decided to join Julie rather than follow what she had once believed to be her vocation, that of a Carmelite. In 1799 they had to flee Amiens as Père Thomas was still being hunted down by the revolutionaries, and they were no longer safe at the Hôtel Blin. Four of them, including Félicité,[5] escaped by night to Bettencourt, 24 kilometres from Amiens, where one of the Dorian sisters, Josephine, made her estate available to them. They only returned to Amiens in 1803 after the 1801 Concordat of Napoleon, which restored the Catholic religion to France.

The time spent at Bettencourt was key in the evolution of this very close friendship and here Françoise experienced the happiest years of her life. They now moved into the second stage of their friendship in which they had time to get to know each other better and build up common experiences of joy and sorrow. The effect of the traumas of leaving Amiens initially weakened Julie and Françoise. Both suffered acute illnesses, but soon the quietness of the place began to heal them in body and soul. It was here that Julie began to recover her speech again, and both were able to share, with Père Thomas, in the restoration of religion (*Memoirs* 6). They were so successful that the villagers never forgot how much these good women had done for them. They transformed the atmosphere of the village from one of fear to one of love. Julie's genius as a teacher soon became evident, and her fame spread beyond the village. It was while they were here that a certain Père Varin, a 'Father of the Faith', who later became a Jesuit, came to visit them. He was to play a pivotal role in the setting up of the new congregation.[6]

Amiens and after

In 1803 they decided it was time to return to the larger city of Amiens. They were not able to return to the relatively comfortable quarters of the Hôtel Blin, as it was now occupied by Françoise's brother, but took up residence in cramped and poorer conditions on the Rue Puits-à-Brindil. Julie and Françoise, the 'two heads under one bonnet' as they were now frequently referred to, were ready to take up fresh tasks in far more difficult circumstances. As it was the custom that women taught other women, Père Varin asked Julie to help with teaching the women in the Missions that he was giving in the Cathedral of Amiens. Julie being carried in a sedan chair into the Cathedral soon became a common sight. The cry of the poor children, however, continually rang in her ear, calling her to action.

With Julie, Françoise became a founder member of the new congregation on 2 February 1804, and she witnessed Julie's miraculous cure in June of the same year, which enabled her to walk again. Françoise was Julie's main support in all the vicissitudes that she underwent in the founding of her congregation. However, Julie and Françoise throughout their lives had a wide variety of other friends. Their early friendships included not only their families but the local priests and the rich and poor of Cuvilly and Gèzaincourt. In later life their friendships extended to include bishops and even the Pope of their time, Pius VII.[7]

There is no better way to sum up the fruits of this friendship than in the words of Françoise in her later Memoirs:

[A]lthough in character, Mother Blin was quite different from Mère Julie, they were so closely united in thought and feeling, and as Mother Blin lived in complete dependence on Mère Julie, everything went on in the absence of our mother as when present. (*Memoirs* xxv)

Their friendship enabled the blossoming of their differing personalities and gifts. Women who can manifest such a degree of affection and understanding for and with each other as Julie and Françoise, could only do so because they had such a profound 'sense of respect for themselves and for others' (Raymond 1991:5).

Reflections on the friendship of Julie and Françoise

The resemblances of the friendship of Julie and Françoise to the characteristics of spiritual friendship as described by Bernard of Clairvaux and Aelred of Rievaulx are clear. This was a relationship of *dilectio Dei*, that delights in God, knowing no pride. This led to an equality between friends of different social positions, and it had the qualities of an 'ecstatic', dynamic, spiritual friendship. In the words of Graham Little, this is a 'communicating friendship, the "pure type" . . . It is about knowing and being known, about communicating singular identities' (Stuart 1995:35).

The friendship between Julie and Françoise takes us to this deeper understanding of God's love and care for us. Theirs was a way of living in relationship which prevented the ownership of goods and wealth becoming a barrier to friendship. Moreover, both knew the importance of communication for friendship and Julie was an extraordinary letter writer. Deep affection is communicated again and again in their correspondence.

> This is all the news, my good friend, and a good long letter it is. I have not yet had my breakfast. I want to have it with you. (31 August 1807)

> Good-bye my dear Mother. I'm still hoping for some gust of wind to bring you here. In the meantime, I am truly your respectful and loving daughter. (letter of 20 January 1908, in Françoise Blin de Bourdon, *Dialogue Letters* (privately published, 1996))

This tradition of intense personal love is similarly reflected in the letters of Francis de Sales to Jane Chantal, the foundress of the Visitation Order; he called the friendship between them '*the bond of perfection* which is indissoluble and never weakens'.

> All other bonds are temporal, even that of a vow of obedience which can be broken through death or other circumstances; but the bond of love grows and gets stronger with time . . . Love is strong as death and firm as hell, says Solomon (Songs 8:6) . . . this is our bond, these are the chains which, the more they are tightened and press against us, the more they bring joy and freedom . . . Think of me as closely bound to you,

and don't try to understand more than that. (Col. 3:14, letter of 24 June 1604, quoted in Wright 1985:28)

For Julie 'friendship in God lasts for ever'. It was the kind of friendship that can 'only exist among the good', a friendship made for eternity. It was the 'bond of perfection' of de Sales. She and Françoise passed on this gift of friendship to their congregation.

In her book *Fierce Tenderness* (1991), Mary Hunt discusses what she sees as the difference between male and female friendships: 'Male–male friendships have mutual enhancement as their modus operandi. Power meets power and produces more power, whereas, many women's friendships grow from the need to survive' (Hunt 1991:147). She then continues to illustrate the difficulty of ever achieving real equality in female–male relationships:

> Female–male friendships are alleged to start with mutual attraction. That model takes the energy inward, usually resulting in an enhancement of power for the male and a diminution of power for the female . . . in general this is the pattern in the west . . . In a patriarchal culture equality between female and male is chancy at the best, given the myriad of factors that structure inequality. (Ibid.)

She names the different characteristics of women's friendships as *attention, generativity* and *community*, but sees 'justice seeking' as the central focus. In fact her final summing up of women's friendships with other women is 'justice seeking friends in unlikely coalitions' (ibid.:152–7). Or, in the words of Elizabeth Stuart, they are 'a coalition of justice-seeking friends working to incarnate the passion of God between themselves and in the world' (Stuart 1995:231).

No coalition was outwardly more unlikely than that of Julie and Françoise, and no friendship was so full of justice for the poor as this one. It was certainly a very attentive friendship in every way. Françoise saw to every detail of Julie's physical needs in kind, if not by presence, while Julie was attentive to the words of Françoise, as she opened her heart to Julie on her deepest desires. To the end of her days, Julie's practical concern in every detail of the Sisters' lives is legendary. The continued growth and spread of her congregation nearly two hundred years later to over three thousand women in every continent of the world makes generativity and community clear.

Julie and Françoise, in company with many other women, found that their friendship was foundational to their lives. This relationship never became one of possessive dependency but one of interdependence and power. Without this friendship Julie would never have survived all she had to endure in the establishment of her congregation. Survival in fact depended 'on bonding and bonding facilitated survival' (Hunt 1991:49).

The spiritual friendship between Julie and Françoise has a threefold contribution to make in a renewed understanding of women's friendships with other women. First, it brings to visibility one of the missing pieces of the jigsaw in constructing the 'genealogy' of women's friendships. Secondly, it helps towards a deeper reflection on the importance of women authoring their own lives, and thirdly it shows the contribution that this friendship can bring to a new model of women's friendship.

General reflections

Is the rediscovery of lost friendships leading to a reassessment of the meaning and purpose of friendship in our lives? Stuart claims that many lesbian and gay people find themselves rejected or disapproved of by their natural family, and hence 'regard their friends as their real family' (Stuart 1995:35). I would say this claim can be found in other contexts as well. Networking has become a necessity for many. Many feminist women, and an increasing number of men, feel alienated from churches, religious communities and even former friends, because they find their outlook on life has changed so much. For the marginalised, friendship is the only means of survival, and women are more marginalised than men. This is why I can support Mary Hunt's claim that women's experience of 'justice seeking friends' has the possibility of becoming the 'prototype for a new ethical norm' for friendship (Hunt 1991:148). However, I do not think that women have the total monopoly of this model of friendship, since it is shown not only by the history of male congregations of religious men but also by very moving examples of recent male friendships, such as the captivity friendship of John McCarthy and Brian Keenan (Keenan 1992).

The spirituality and power which is ignited in these relationships is not privatised between two friends. Women bond for change, personal and communal, which is exemplified particularly in black women's writings; their struggle against race, gender and class inequalities is far deeper and harder than for most white people. One of the most important insights that 'womanist' theologians (black female theologians), especially in the USA, have given us is that women cannot afford the luxury of few friendships as many are needed for survival. This is a drastic reversal of Aristotle's male hierarchical argument for having few friends. 'One of the great paradoxes of women's lives,' says the black American theologian Patricia L. Hunter in *Women's Power – Women's Passion* (1993 ed. Townes), 'is being taught not to trust one another, yet . . . [m]y experience leads me to believe . . . [w]hen we have to walk through the valley of the shadow of death, more often than not it is our sisters who will walk with us' (194). Women have bonded throughout history in the face of insuperable difficulties, and the history of women's orders and congregations shows that women religious have played a prominent part in this process.

Women's friendship has an inherent political and religious dimension – the personal is political. An important corollary to any reflection on women and friendship is the restoration of the image of God as friend or friend(s). Sallie McFague in her book *Metaphorical Theology: Models of God in Religious Language* (1982) illustrates how God relates to us not as a parent but as a friend and, therefore, we are not alone. Moreover, the image of God as friend(s), does not exclude, but implicitly includes, women as well as many other forms of relationship – parent, lover, sister/brother. And in worship it is one of the very few images of God that is inclusive.

Friendships create a survival space in a patriarchal world, communities of resistance, working for justice, where differences have to be shared and confronted not 'hidden under the duvet of sisterhood', as Stuart says (1995:41). The origins of religious sisterhood lie in a radical bonding of women for the sake of the gospel and the new reign of God. The tragedy is that the all-pervading control of the institutional church of the twentieth century, enshrined in its 1917, and still in the improved 1983, Code of Canon Law, has stifled this tradition.[8] For example, in my early days as a religious, in the 1950s, we were only allowed out in threes, to prevent what became known as PFs, particular friendships. What is more, the 'grand silence' and 'corridor silence' of the contemplative orders were superimposed on the active religious life for many generations, and in the end were abused to curtail freedom of speech and discussion. Religious women had the equivalent of the 'institutionalisation of motherhood',[9] in the 'institutionalisation of sisterhood'. The Sisters of Notre Dame de Namur, at their Chapter of 1996, had to re-articulate the importance of friendship between and among women, personified by their two foundresses.

I believe religious women's congregations have much to learn and experience from new ways of bonding, and the worldwide networking of many women. There are insights here which have the potential to radicalise and re-vivify the justice-seeking of religious sisterhood, which McNamara claims 'in its present form will not survive the next millennium' (1996:105). Friendships are central to everyone's survival and development, but for women they are crucial for day-to-day survival at a practical level. For many women, even when married, their deepest relationships are female. If women are ever to love themselves they must also be able to love others who are like them, as well as those who are different.

Friendship

A mother with her child
Beside a foreign stream,
Afraid of ancient Egypt's might
Preserves her loving dream.

Come, weave the rushes tight
And fill the cracks with tar;
The tide will be your messenger
And bear your baby far.

Let us weave baskets now
From welcome hands of friends;
For these will bear us safely on
Towards our journey's end.

Between these linking arms
There flows a binding tar;
The Holy Spirit fills the whole
With strength'ning, joining pow'r.

These rafts of friendship make
Christ's body here on earth;
This mystic form in human shape
Can bear us to new birth.

(June Boyce-Tillman, written for Alexina Murphy, 1992)

4

Women of a Mystical Text

'It is only spiritual experience that permits us to penetrate to the heart of a sacred text.' (Waaijman 1991:34–5)

Julie's charism arose from an immediate prophetic visionary experience of God. It was the source and foundation of all she lived and wrote. The mystical text is the primary study for the understanding of the mystical process, and of the mystic themselves, and it is by submersion in the texts of the 'explicit mystic' that the 'implicit mysticism' of the reader is stirred 'by the Holy Spirit, the Ruach, and perhaps by an angel of God' (ibid.:33). Mystical texts will essentially erupt into and disrupt the reader's life. When read with the eyes of faith, they will change the way we view life, by the way they change us. The mystics show, however, that '[t]o be created after God's image does not mean that we are icons of God, but that we are following in the track of his footprints' (ibid.:32).

Mystical texts may seem easy to read, but they are not easy to understand. The same applies to all readings of scripture: the text cannot be taken only at face value. Many words and phrases have multiple meanings and complexities. The text, therefore, requires opening up and tearing apart, not only by scholarly study, but above all through being lived in by prayer for a considerable period of time to reveal at least a part of its meaning. Mystical texts are in essence eternal, and each generation will re-visit the text afresh with its own experiences, desires and needs.

For the philosopher Paul Ricoeur there are two crucial stages in the reading of any text, beginning with the 'first naiveté', the freshness and openness of discovering it for the first time. This is the uncritical stage, where we pick up the heartbeat of the text. The danger here, of course, is literalism or fundamentalism, seeing no further than the words of the text. The crucial stage is that of the 'second naiveté', the coming to a mature appreciation of the text. This is why both the scriptures and mystical texts are the most satisfying of all reading. They do not reveal their content easily, but they have untold depths, brought to life by the experiences that the reader brings to the text.

Although Julie's letters are written for another time and age, and in a language far removed from ours, they are inspirational and read aright have as much meaning in modern times as in her own. It is by praying the text that its meaning begins to spring to life. Before considering the spirituality of Julie that arises from her letters, it is necessary to have some understanding of the spiritual influences that are clearly discernible in her letters, as well as her style of writing.

The inner landscape of Julie's spirituality

The eighteenth century might be characterised as a period that borrowed much spirituality and added little of its own. This is not to suggest that the practice of the spiritual life was in decline, rather that the spirituality during this epoch was expressed more forcefully through deeds than through books. No authors of the stature of those of the seventeenth century emerged, except perhaps Père De Caussade (d.1761), famous for his devotional classic *Abandonment to Divine Providence, A Treatise On Prayer From The Heart*, often translated as the 'Sacrament of the Present Moment'. Instead the spiritual lives of Christians were nourished by the Carmelite writings of John of the Cross and Teresa of Avila, reissues of works by Francis de Sales, *Introduction to the Devout Life* and *Treatise on the Love of God*, and the late-medieval devotional book of Thomas à Kempis, *The Imitation of Christ*, which is probably the most popular book of devotion of all time.

It was from Père Dangicourt, during her formative years in

Cuvilly, that Julie learnt much of her spirituality. The Sorbonne, where he had been educated, was the centre of what has become known as the Sulpician seminary tradition, and it was the major exponent of the classical school of spirituality known as the seventeenth-century French School, a school which had a great influence on the foundation of Julie's spirituality.

It is not possible to have an understanding of the spirituality which informed Julie's mysticism in her Letters without some knowledge of this 'golden age of spirituality' to which she was heir.[1] It completely dominated the spirituality of the Roman Catholic tradition until Vatican II in the 1960s: 'the Christ-ocentric spirituality of the French school was diffused so widely that for all practical purposes Catholic spirituality in modern times could be characterised as French spirituality' (Thompson 1989:82). Much of its all-embracing influence still remains. David Tracy, in his book *The Analogical Imagination*, calls this French school of spirituality a classic and not a period piece, 'a proven source of continual human and Christian enrichment, theoretically and practically' (Tracy 1981:99). That is, it has some kind of 'normative meaning' which bring out the essentials of Christianity.

Theological characteristics of the seventeenth-century French School

In comparison with medieval spirituality, the person of Christ is so central that the French school of spirituality is often referred to as 'a Copernican revolution in spirituality' (Thompson 1989:389). The centrality of the person of Christ was closely linked to a great devotion to the Eucharist, as the sacrifice of Christ on the cross, and the sacramental system in its entirety. It was accompanied by a high Mariology which placed great emphasis on devotion to Mary, as the Mother of God, coupled with the devotion to the Sacred Hearts of Jesus and Mary as promulgated widely by Jean Eudes (1601–80). It was also there in the theology and spirituality of Bérulle, Madeleine and Olier. This school was very generative and many ecclesiastical foundations resulted from it, for example the Oratorian Fathers, and St Sulpice, where many of the clergy of France were educated, including Julie's parish priest at Cuvilly, Père Dagincourt. A surprisingly large number of women's congregations were also founded from the 'heart' spirituality of Jean Eudes, many of which still exist today.

It had a highly developed soteriology. That is, it encompassed every aspect of human salvation, but at the core of this spirituality was a spirit of *adoration*, which included abasement to the Godhead, and an understanding of the greatness and divine goodness of God. This state of adoration is the basis of our need for contemplation. The natural outcome of this was *adherence* to Jesus, which would lead to the annihilation of all traces of self-interest, and *abnegation*, submission to the redemption of Christ. Perhaps certain aspects of the harshness of the French School of spirituality, with its emphasis on sin and repentance, was inevitable after the Reformation and as an over-reaction to the excesses of the humanism of the Renaissance. However, it was tempered by the centrality of the humanity of Christ in all aspects of this school. This was also a time of a scriptural and patristic renaissance with special emphasis on the Johannine and Pauline texts. The French school built on its past inheritance, applying the teachings of the sixteenth-century Council of Trent and embodying them in the spirituality of its own times.

The many different characters involved gave it a richness, freshness and creativity which was to allow it to endure. Cardinal Bérulle was at the centre of the school, but some of the harsher aspects of its spirituality were later tempered by other people, especially St Francis de Sales (1567–1622), whose 'gentle humanism' and more optimistic view of humanity became a gift to later times. Other well-known names linked with this school include Madame Acarie, Benoît de Canfield, Jean Eudes, Madeleine of St Joseph, the first Carmelite Prioress in France, Jean Jacques Olier, Sts Francis de Sales and Jane Chantal, Sts Vincent de Paul and Louise de Marillac. It is interesting to note the crucial role women played in this school of spirituality.

Nuances of interpretation of this tradition can be found in Julie's letters. For example, although she does occasionally use the harsher language of 'annihilation' of the French school of Bérulle, her preference is clearly for the '*douceur*', the gentleness, of Francis de Sales, his 'Live Love', and foundational belief in the 'salvific will of God for all people'. In like manner her life reflects the love of the poor of Vincent de Paul, summed up in his well-known phrase 'Live the Gospel'. One thing all these founding mystics had in common was that they refused to slide into either a simplistic optimism, or a rather frightful pessimism.

Popular devotions and pastoral practices

The popular devotions and the pastoral practice of this school, which were most acceptable to the church of the eighteenth century, appear regularly throughout Julie's letters. The aim of the Counter-Reformation was to place people's spiritual and religious life directly under the control of the local parish priest. At the same time, the reform of the largely uneducated clergy was the central aim of this Counter-Reformation Church. Coupled with this was a process to centralise and control the popular devotions of the people. The Church was alarmed at the proliferation of local saints, which filled the needs of the people in times of famine and dangers. To distract the people from their local saints, the Church centralised its devotions round the events of the life of Christ; the Eucharist, which held primary position in these devotions; and the person of Mary, the Mother of God, especially devotion to the Rosary. Saints Anne and Joachim, the mother and father of Mary, became popular, as well as St Joseph. The latter became a favourite patron saint of the mystics, in particular Teresa of Avila. It is also interesting to note that Françoise Blin de Bourdon, as a religious sister, took the name Mère St Joseph.

Counter-Reformation piety encouraged 'fervour, silence and order', and many of the numerous and spontaneous local devotions were discouraged and replaced by a few which were acceptable to the Church, and controlled by the local clergy.

Much of the peasants' superstition revolved around the cult of the saints. The peasants saw religion as the only means whereby they might manipulate a largely hostile world, and their mental universe was a magical one. The Counter-Reformation and the reformed clergy of the seventeenth and eighteenth centuries were not happy about these superstitions. Hence the clergy conducted a long campaign against these local saints, either re-inventing them as clerics or replacing them with the saints of the Catholic Reformation such as Ignatius Loyola, Francis de Sales, Charles Borromeo and Teresa of Avila. The name St Eloi was often that of the local butcher re-incarnated as a bishop (Gibson 1989:14–29). The St Eloi of the church in Cuvilly where Julie was brought up could in fact have been one of these. It was in promoting Christological development, however, that the Counter-Reformation church had its greatest impact on popular spirituality, and from this arose the all-pervasive devotion to the Sacred Heart (Dupré and Saliers 1990:93–119). This first took root in France and then in Italy, and it was to reach its zenith after the apparitions of Jesus showing his Sacred Heart to Margaret Mary Alacoque, a Visitation nun, at Paray le Monial between 1648 and 1690. It was her major apparition of 16 June 1675 which ushered in the feast of the Sacred Heart, eight days after the feast of Corpus Christi. From this vision the idea of reparation was born: that is, of making satisfaction for the neglect, insults and blasphemies of many Catholics against the Blessed Sacrament.

Julie's devotion to the Cross and the Holy Child Jesus in the crib arose from her absorption into the Counter-Reformation tradition. Her devotion to the Sacred Heart of Jesus mirrored the ever-growing popularity of a tradition whose roots Karl Rahner s j has traced back to the wounds of Christ on the cross.[2] It was all part of the radical reform and control of the many medieval popular devotions that were practised by the Church after the Reformation.

The main pastoral programme of the French School was to restore and promote the faith of the Counter-Reformation, and it can be summed up under three activities, *Preaching, Missions* and the teaching of the *Catechism*. The latter was seen by the Council of Trent as one of the main ways to inculcate the truths of the faith into the minds of the people. By the late seventeenth century the production of the catechism was booming (Dupré and Saliers 1990:101–2). Julie, like all women of her time and since, at least in the R C church, was not allowed to preach, but she became involved in the education of women and children in the Missions, which were preached by the Fathers of the Faith both at Amiens Cathedral in 1795 and at nearby St Valèry. The catechism would have been at the heart of her teaching.

Other major influences on Julie

Thomas à Kempis, The Imitation of Christ

Julie's spirituality reflects the many aspects of this Counter-Reformation spirituality, especially in her devotion to the life, and passion and death of Christ. The Letters reflect this devotion, in Julie's frequent use of the most popular devotional literature of all time, *The Imitation of Christ* by Thomas à Kempis (1380–1471) (Knotts 1963), a monk who was involved in the late-medieval popular religious movement known as the *Devotio Moderna*. This pious renewal began in the Netherlands and is attributed to Gert Groote (1340–84). It was a devotion in keeping with its times, when there was a rising tide of criticism of the Papacy, and it was part of a broader development of reform within the Church, often called the 'Christian Renaissance'. This movement did not focus on institutional reform, but rather on that of the individual and the community (Rait, McGinn and Meyendorff 1996:176–93). It rejected the idea that to be a real Christian a person had to be a full-time monk, priest, or nun, maintaining that in fact it was possible to be a Christian by living an ordinary life. Education, especially free education, was also a part of this movement. The inner life of the individual was to be shaped around meditation on the life and passion of Christ. It was out of these ideas that *The Imitation of Christ* was born.

Much of the advice given in this book is not congenial to modern times, such as its emphasis on 'crushing one's natural feelings' or 'killing the old impulses'. However, Margaret Miles sheds new light on this language in her book *The Image and Practice of Holiness*. She claims that the word 'natural' needs careful interpretation: 'he seems to mean that feelings that seem to appear naturally are not to be regarded as either inevitable or normative, but can be changed' (Miles 1988:24). In other words, à Kempis, in the words of his time, is raising the consciousness of the reader to the effect of the social conditioning of many of their attitudes and habitual responses. Reading Thomas à Kempis with 'a *hermeneutic of generosity* requires that we bring to his advice the experience we have that matches the sense of intensity and urgency we get from his rhetoric' (ibid.:24). In the light of the above and the understanding of Julie's charism, it is hard to overestimate the influence of this book in Julie's spiritual guidance of Françoise.

The Carmelite influence: Teresa of Avila

Along with the gradual centralisation of the institutional aspect of the RC church in the sixteenth and seventeenth centuries, a strange and powerful phenomenon grew up beside it, a great outpouring of mystical experience, of which the major influences were the Spanish-born sixteenth-century Carmelites, Teresa of Avila and John of the Cross. No person of spiritual leanings was left uninfluenced by either of these giants of the spiritual life. Julie and Françoise were no exceptions. Madeleine of St Joseph was the first Prioress of the Paris Carmel, in the seventeenth century, when Teresa's and John's works were translated into French, and from there the Carmelite influence spread throughout France. Julie called the Carmelites 'her true mothers', and hence it was the writings of Teresa, *The Interior Castle* and the *Autobiography of Teresa: The Life*, rather than those of John of the Cross, which influenced her spirituality. Julie's natural intuition for the informality and homely descriptions of Teresa's writings is clear, and a similar simple style is found throughout her *Letters, Themes* and *Instructions* which she gave between 1812 and 1815.[3] The influence of this spirituality was equivalent to the influence and popularity of the Spiritual Exercises of St Ignatius in the latter part of the twentieth century.

Père de Caussade, Abandonment

Ignatian influence on Julie was primarily through her spiritual directors, some of whom, such as Père Varin, became Jesuits on the restoration of that order firstly in Naples in 1804, and then in France in 1814. *Abandonment,* probably the greatest and only original work of spiritual devotion of the eighteenth century, was written by a Jesuit, Père de Caussade (1675–1751). His French title *L'Abandon* has been translated into English as 'self-abandonment'. This is probably as near to the French word as our language can get, but the word can only be understood in the wholeness of his teaching. His self-abandonment is, in its primary sense, an acceptance of the will of God. It is summed up in the words of Mary, 'Be it done to me according to thy word', and of Christ on the cross, 'Father, into your hands I commend my spirit'. Abandonment of the self is therefore a very active and positive movement towards God.

This work was written for the Visitation nuns of Francis de Sales and Jane Chantal, and hence was written for those already practising 'contemplation'. 'Self-abandonment' to the love of God was a natural culmination of the seventeenth-century French School of spirituality, as developed out of the gentleness of de Sales. The words 'trust' and 'acquiescence' were preferred to the more frequently used Carmelite words of 'renunciation' and 'death to self'. De Caussade's great achievement was to make a synthesis of Carmelite and Salesian spirituality, which is the spirituality of Francis de Sales. The phrase that appears most frequently in this work is 'the value of the present moment'. In order to understand the full meaning of *Abandonment* it is necessary to read and pray the book through with Ricoeur's 'second naiveté', through the eyes of our own understanding of the 'will of God'. 'Abandonment' and 'acquiescence' wrongly understood are dangerous and can lead to infantilism. It is important to make particular mention of this work because of Julie's frequent use of the word 'abandonment', especially to her younger Sisters as they face innumerable difficulties in the founding and running of poor schools. Julie in her Letters often refers to *Abandonment* in the following words: 'God is welcome, in whatever way he comes.'

The influence of women's writings

Before leaving this general overview of the French School of spirituality, it is important to note other spiritual classics by which Julie was influenced, especially those written by women. Although she occasionally quotes from Augustine, Bonaventure and Bernard of Clairvaux, her more numerous references are to the women mystics of medieval times, for example the Rhineland mystics Gertrude and Mechtild. She also makes several references to the passionate writings of the fourteenth-century Catherine of Siena and the fifteenth-century Catherine of Genoa (Rees 1998).[4] Other outstanding female figures that Julie used as models in her teaching were St Magdalene de' Pazzi (1566–1607), a Carmelite nun and Florentine saint who worked with the poor from an early age, and the story of the widow Judith, from the Hebrew scriptures.[5] This is a story primarily about God's providence for his people, but the interesting point to note is the importance of the actions of a woman in the saving of the Jews.

The style of Julie's letters

Letters have long been a main source of communication between friends, and the letters between Julie and Françoise are no exception. There are, however, different styles and purposes of letter writers, and in the case of Julie we have letters which have all the traces of a 'mystical text'. Like all religious writings of her time, her letters are clothed in the language of the 'virtues'. It was this traditional language of spirituality that was further enhanced by the form of spirituality that arose out of the seventeenth-century French School. Many of the words of the 'virtues' that Julie uses are not words used in spirituality now. Words such as *simplicity, victim, abandonment, perfection,* even the words *humility, charity* and *union with God,* have very different meanings for us today, and have to be nuanced according to the circumstances and understanding of the time.

There are 454 extant letters written by Julie and out of these 171 were written to Françoise. The majority of the rest, with the exception of letters to bishops, priests or benefactors, were to young Sisters in their twenties who were in charge of a newly opened house and school. Although Julie's spirituality forms a whole, the letters reveal that she emphasised the aspect of her spirituality which the Sister needed at that time. The simple style of her letters was fitting for those to whom she was writing, as the majority of young women who joined Julie had minimal education, and were mainly of peasant origin.

These were not days of telephone or e-mail, but of pen and paper and delivery by horse-back – difficult times for Julie, as her personal preference was always for the spoken rather than the written word. She was forced, however, to write letters all her life, as it was the only way she could guide and keep in touch with her ever-growing religious Congregation. Although the other extant writings (*Instructions, Themes,* etc.) are all second-hand and written by Sisters, it is interesting to note a remarkable coherence between the spirituality of the letters, and these other writings. The spirituality that emerges in Julie's letters is permeated with action–reflection–action, the main structure that forms the 'architecture', the style, of her spirituality.

Julie's was an informal, conversational style of writing, without concern for grammar and quite akin to the 'rough' style of Teresa of Avila: 'writing a letter for her was like having a conversation with the person concerned . . . It was very spontaneous, not polished, but simple and full of God. Words were sometimes missing, and there were mistakes in spelling. She rarely reread what she wrote' (*Memoirs* 138–9). Her style was spiral rather than linear, full of spontaneity, simplicity, warmth and much humour. Her thoughts flowed out of her.

Julie did not leave behind any formal, coherent writings on spirituality, as did Teresa of Avila or Francis de Sales, and although letter-writing is a very living and attractive way to share one's spirituality, it also makes it much more difficult to capture the complete form of the spirituality under consideration. Like Teresa of Avila, Julie conveys the subtleties of her inner spiritual world in the language and images of her time. Teresa uses the image of a castle, reflecting the sixteenth-century landscape of Spain. Julie's vocabulary, on the other hand, arises from the everyday life of the eighteenth-century French countryside where she spent her life. Her image for 'union with God', her image of wholeness, is a sunflower, *le tournesol*, taken from her observation of the many fields of sunflowers to be found in her part of France, Picardy. She spoke simply, freely and continually of the magnetic pull of the sunflower towards the sun wherever it was: 'Simplicity is like that beautiful flower which always turns to the sun, and follows its movements.' (*Themes* 54). There is a lightness and freedom about Julie's imagery, which is firmly rooted in the reality of the earth and life.

Her whole spiritual conversation is full of these rural and familiar images, making it timeless, and hence easier to understand. These images have translated well into the rural economy of Africa, Asia, and South America, as the spread of the Congregation has shown. In many ways the Letters come to life in those continents more than in the Western economy, where agricultural images have become secondary to more sophisticated post-industrial images. Julie refers to 'cultivating the interior life', reflecting images of hard work digging both hard and soft soil, and planting good seed and bad.

It is clear from Julie's vocabulary that she had internalised the stereotypes of 'strong men and weak women'. She had little time for fearful women and her two favourite metaphors for this weakness were '*poules mouillées*', 'wet hens', and '*femelettes*', little, weak or feeble women. The former must have raised many a laugh, at the common image of damp, wet hens crouching in the corner of a very wet yard, while *'femelettes'* was a word frequently used by the revolutionaries, who wished to demean women and their practices.[6]

The alternative image she puts before women is to develop 'virile', manly, strength. The use of the word 'manly' in female mystical writing is common. For example, Teresa of Avila uses the word frequently in her writings to her Sisters. In modern terms it is called 'empowering women'. To gain this strength and independence Julie incessantly uses the word *'courage'*. Julie is so determined that all her Sisters will have this strength that she returns again and again to this theme in all her writings, not just the Letters: 'There must be nothing of the woman amongst us, we need courageous souls afraid of nothing' (*Instructions* 48).

Julie's images of God

In spite of the predominance of the 'Father' metaphor for God in the history of the Christian tradition, Julie uses a variety of metaphors for God. She refers to the scripture image of God as mother, 'as a hen gathers her chicks under her wing', and when she does use the metaphor of 'Father', it is never without reference to the best 'motherly qualities':

> When you are desirous of correcting your faults ... do not think that God will hurl thunderbolts upon you. No, he is like a kind mother. You would not expect a good mother who sees her child fall, to run and beat it. On the contrary she would pick her child up and console it. (*Conferences* 48)

But there is no doubt that her most frequently used and favourite metaphor for God was not the fatherhood or the motherhood of God, but the 'goodness of God' – '*Ah! Qu'il est bon, le Bon Dieu*', ('How good is the good God'), an exclamation she used frequently. But her life, sufferings and work transformed this common French phrase of the time, giving it depth and meaning beyond its original use. She never wavered in this belief, even in her 'darkest' times, and they were many. In fact, it is now the best-known of all Julie's words. They are engraved on the back of the cross of the Sisters of Notre Dame de Namur, and all who are, or have been, associated with Notre Dame will know those, if no other, words of Julie.

Reflections

It was out of her prayerful internalisation of the French school of spirituality, and that of à Kempis, the Carmelite Teresa of Avila, de Sales, the Jesuit influence of Ignatius in spiritual direction, and the inherited tradition from so many women saints, that Julie was able to develop an original synthesis of her own. Originality and uniqueness only grow from a lived knowledge of the tradition and every religious foundation owes its origin to a communal drive toward spiritual autonomy. With these thoughts in mind we now turn to a consideration of the heart of Julie's spirituality – 'the liberty of the children of God' – as found in her Letters to her beloved friend Françoise.

5

Women of Freedom

'Let us act in all things with the liberty of the children of God.' (L17:61)

Given that the watchwords of the French Revolution were 'liberty, equality, fraternity', it is not surprising that the heart of Julie's charism is 'the liberty of the children of God', articulated in the language of her time. What freedom is and how far it is possible to be totally free are subjects which have exercised philosophers, theologians and psychologists. But the spiritual freedom under consideration in this chapter is that of Christian liberty, the ability to be completely open to God and free from self-love, so that it is possible to discern between right and wrong choices, even against the general current of thinking or belief.

Both Julie and Françoise had experienced the inadequacy of the theory of the political freedom that the *philosophes* had brought to France. The *philosophes* had no experience to fall back on, as they had been secluded by the environment of the *salons*, and distanced from the social burden of poverty. Although they traced their ideas back to antiquity, the *philosophes* only used the word 'freedom' in a one-dimensional sense: 'Freedom could only exist in public; it was a tangible, worldly reality, something created by men ... it was the man-made public space or market place which antiquity had known as the area where freedom appears and becomes visible to all' (Arendt 1990:124). Furthermore, Arendt argues that all revolutions fall short of their ideals because the 'social question', that is the immediate and urgent demands of the poor, in the end dominates the agenda.[1]

The 'liberty of the children of God' in scripture

Christian freedom is far wider and deeper than any concepts of human freedom; although it includes the immediate 'social question', it is much more than the narrow restricted concept of the revolutionaries. Liberation and liberty are major themes in the Christian experience, but they are presented very differently in the Old and New Testaments. For example, although it is clear that God freely created the world out of God's own abundance and love, it is the human aspirations to freedom that predominate in the Old Testament (Gen. 9:25–7; Jacob and Esau, Gen. 27:27–9, 37–40). It is revealed above all in Exodus 20:2, the flight of the Israelites from slavery in Egypt – the great Exodus experience which has become the paradigm for so many freeing situations in Christian history.

The New Testament keeps the language of deliverance but Paul, John and the Synoptic Gospels introduce a new language coming from the Greek. For St Paul the free person was freed by vision granted by God. It was a fundamental experience for Paul; he was liberated by Christ at Damascus and all his life was marked by this, and freed from the exigencies of the law (Gal. 1:14; Phil. 3:6). In this way he was free to serve God: 'For me to live is Christ' (Rom. 7:25; 8:2, 9–15). Romans 6 is the great chapter on liberty: 'If we have died with Christ we believe that we shall also live with him' (6:8).

Christ, however, took it to new understandings in his own life. In the New Testament there are 800 references to the liberty of Jesus, but unlike St Paul, it is so natural to Christ that he never needs to talk about it. St John brings out Jesus' 'liberty' as his major characteristic (John 7:26–51). Unlike St Paul who made himself 'all things to all people', Jesus was always totally himself and totally in control. Following Julie's metaphor for the spiritual life, the imitation of Christ, it is interesting to note some general characteristics of Jesus' prophetic behaviour.

From the beginning Jesus proclaims himself as liberator – which the people of Nazareth could not accept – and he always spoke and acted with authority and asked counsel of no one:

'The Spirit of the Lord is upon me ... he has anointed me to bring good news to the poor ... proclaim the release of captives ... give sight to the blind ... set at liberty the oppressed, to proclaim the acceptable year of the Lord' (Luke 4:18). He always responded freely to the needs of the people, especially the most vulnerable, for example the Samaritan woman (John 4:7–39), the poor widow (Mark 12:41–4) and the centurion (Matt. 8:10). He allowed himself to be at the mercy of all he met, as in his raising of Jairus' daughter from the dead (Mark 5:21–2 and 35–43) and his curing the woman with the issue of blood (Mark 5:25–34). And throughout the Gospels, Jesus is continually surrounded by crowds who would not leave him alone but on whom he always had 'compassion' (Mark 6:34). He also rebuked those who put the law before the needs of the people and often angered those in authority. When, for example, the ruler of the synagogue was indignant because Jesus had healed in the synagogue on the Sabbath a woman who had been sick for eighteen years, Jesus replied: 'You hypocrites! ... the sabbath is made for man not man for the sabbath ... ought not this woman whom Satan bound for eighteen years, be loosed from her bond on the sabbath day?' (Luke 13:13–17) He insisted his father's house was treated with respect and his anger exploded on the money lenders. He not only turned their tables over, but he made a whip of cords to drive them out of the Temple, saying, 'You shall not make my father's house a house of trade' (John 2:13–22). Added to this, he treated those in authority as equals (Luke 13:3), exemplified in his meeting with Pilate during his passion, Jesus' supreme moment of liberty, when he told him, 'You would have no power over me unless it had been given you from above' (John 19:11).

But, above all, Jesus' law of liberty is summed up in the Sermon on the Mount in the words, 'Blessed are the pure in heart for they shall see God ... Blessed are you when men revile you and persecute you and utter all kinds of evil against you for my name's sake ...' (Matt. 5:1–11; Luke 6:20–6). To the Jews who believed in him, Christ said: 'If you continue in my word, you are truly my disciples, and you will know the truth

and the truth will set you free' (John 8:31-2); but it was to
Peter that he gave the great call to liberty in the last chapter of
John: 'Follow me' (John 21:19). The gift of Christian liberty is
a capacity to progressively participate in the life of God, through
a close following of Christ.

Julie understood freedom in this wider scriptural sense, as a
God-given gift, an inner capacity to make free decisions, to
follow Christ as closely as she could in her human life. The
similarities between Christ's understanding of liberty and Julie's
become clear as her spirituality unfolds in her letters, especially
in her first letters, and in the following chapters of this book.
To illustrate the style of Julie's spirituality, the rest of this chapter follows the methodology of the Titus Brandsma Institute and
is based on the context of these first letters (see Appendix 1). It
is the key to understanding the heart of Julie's spirituality.

Julie and Françoise

The first 33 letters to Françoise were written between their first
very important meeting in 1795 and the death of Françoise's
father when she decided to join Julie. At this time, Françoise
was living where she was brought up in her grandmother's house
in Gèzaincourt, and looking after her father who was seriously
ill, and who, to her discomfort, was still a follower of the anti-
religious Voltaire. Unfortunately, the correspondence is very
one-sided as we have no remaining letters written by Françoise
to Julie at this particular time. Françoise had asked Père Thomas,
the good non-juring priest, who resided with Julie, to be her
own guide in prayer and help discern her future calling; but
he perceived that Julie would be a more appropriate guide for
Françoise, and persuaded Julie to take on the task. The letters
clearly illustrate the degree of physical suffering Julie was experiencing at this time: besides her niece, Félicité, who cared for
her, and Père Thomas, Julie had few other direct contacts. The
only others were Madame Baudoin, who had insisted Julie come
to Amiens, her daughter Lise, and Lise's friends, the Doria
sisters.

Teresa of Avila and Julie's understanding of contemplative prayer

The influence of Teresa of Avila is clear in this correspondence, particularly in the earliest letters, numbers 1–12: 'Remember what we said about this and what we read in St. Teresa' (L4:28). An understanding of the teaching of Teresa, known as the psychological mystic because of her power to integrate her spirituality into the human development of the individual person, is a great help in clarifying Julie's teaching on contemplative prayer. However, before Julie agreed to accompany Françoise she insisted that: 'It is only according to my own experience that I can charitably sympathise with the imperfections, the problems and the miseries of others' (L32:86).

Julie knew that: 'It is by way of prayer that God makes saints' (L1:20), and Françoise had reached, in Teresian language, the transition to contemplative prayer of the 'fourth mansion'. The 'fourth mansion' is a part of Teresa's famous mandala for prayer, her image of wholeness, her rounded Crystal Castle, containing seven mansions. Each mansion represents a stage on the way to union with God, but there are many sub-divisions in the castle to denote the uniqueness of each individual's journey.[2] Teresa wrote more on the fourth and sixth mansions than any of the others because she considered these were the most difficult transitions in prayer and needed the most careful guidance. She also believed that these mansions were generally not reached until the person concerned had lived for a long time in the others.

Teresa compared the fourth and sixth transitions to undergoing an instant martyrdom. Nell Morton, a modern feminist writer, in *The Journey is Home*, sums up this process in a similar way: 'the deepest pain is dying in life not in death' (1985:60). The end result is the emergence of the 'Teresian butterfly', which I call a butterfly with 'guts' – a distinct individual whose unique colours and gifts are enhanced, a person self-actualised by their friendship with God.[3] For Teresa, like Julie, this personhood is achieved through prayer, because 'prayer is nothing more than a special relationship with God' (Peers 1972, *The Way*, p. 40).

In order to explain the contemplative prayer of the fourth mansion, Teresa uses the image of water. The entrance into the unconscious is often imagined as entrance to water. Psychologically, water symbolises the unconscious. It does not mean a regression to an inferior life, but a descent to depths. Healing and new life can be the result of entering this uncharted territory. The waters of baptism are meant to symbolise this transformation (Welch 1982:59–84):

> [T]wo troughs are filled with water in different ways; with one the water comes from far away through many aqueducts and the use of much ingenuity; with the other the source of water is right there, and the trough fills without any exterior help. If the spring is abundant, as is this one we are speaking about, the water overflows once the trough is filled, forming a large stream. There is no need of any skill, nor does the building of aqueducts have to continue; but water is always flowing from the spring. (Orilio and Kavanagh 1980, *Interior Castle* IV:2, no. 3, p. 323)

This water image is used by Julie to explain the changes that Françoise is experiencing in prayer. It is essentially a time when the person has to wait on God's time and way of doing things. The early stages of this prayer of quiet are marked by a wordless, silent, peaceful prayer. This prayer gradually develops into a prayer of a totally different order, a prayer where God takes the initiative, prayer that begins in God and ends in the person. This 'fourth mansion' or, in the more popular term of John of the Cross, the 'dark night',[4] is marked by certain characteristics which are mirrored in the experience of Françoise. In like manner, Francis de Sales says that 'prayer is called meditation until it produces the honey of devotion; and after this it is changed into contemplation ... meditation is the mother of love, but contemplation is her daughter ... Holy contemplation is the end and terminus to which all these exercises tend, and all of them are reducible to it' (Kerns 1962, Bk 6, chs 3 and 6).

Characteristics of Françoise's contemplative prayer

Loss of control

Those who can help us through this 'dark night' are the great teachers and Julie is one of these. This change in prayer comes unannounced and often at a time of crisis caused by a serious change in life circumstances – a broken marriage, doubts about a religious vocation, death of a beloved partner, family member or friend, failure at work, not being promoted in a job, forced redundancy, retirement, moving house, new job, etc. Moreover, this crisis often leads to a change in former relationships with those we have loved. Although each 'dark night' is individual there is a common experience 'that life is beyond our control' (Giles 1986:39–67). This is, however, a process, rather than an isolated happening, a time when we are tempted to cling for safety to what has been. We are in fact suspended between the old and the new: 'something new and unknown is in the making ... which surpasses the sum of the pieces at hand' (ibid.:58), but in prayer this is experienced as deprivation.

Dryness in prayer

This feeling of deprivation is experienced as dryness in prayer; all feeling seems to have gone. The person is left with emptiness. Françoise can no longer pray as she used to and the imagination is no longer helpful, to which Julie responds:

> I am not in the least surprised, my dear friend, at your state of feeling dull and lacking in sensibility in the presence of God. (L3:24)

> These times are very precious in the eyes of faith. You know that in periods of darkness we can see nothing at all, but we

can do nothing better than wait for the sun to re-appear ...
our days of darkness are perhaps our best and happiest days
for glorifying God. (L2:22–4)

However harsh his dealings may sometimes seem to you, they
are always the dealings of an infinitely wise, just and good
God, who awaits us all at the end, but after leading us by
different roads ... We must simply act like children, who on
a very dark night, keep tight on their father's or mother's
hand and allow themselves to be led. (L4:28)

But for reasons worthy of his wisdom, he allows us to be
deprived of the feeling of presence. This happens above all
that we may cling to him alone not his gifts. (L20:64)

Total trust in spiritual director

In order to help Françoise in her difficulties, Julie insists on
complete openness with her in even the smallest detail: 'You
must never think you bore me by informing me about the things
we agreed upon' (L1:20). At the same time Julie insists on perseverance in prayer no matter how difficult it is: 'I bless the
good God that you are keeping to your two meditations daily.'
Julie was well-versed in the temptations of this time and knew
with Teresa that: 'To lose one's way is – it seems to me –
nothing else but the giving up of prayer' (Peers 1972, *The Way
of Perfection*, p. 151). So Julie continually encouraged Françoise
to 'perseverance and courage' in prayer:

It is by way of prayer that God makes saints. (L1:20)

It is there we find the grace and strength to conquer every
obstacle and repugnance. I can easily believe that you find in
prayer matter for exercising your patience, but the good God
expects you to be faithful. (L11:49)

... let us often remember to reanimate our courage. (L19,
par. 6:61)

This theme of courage is re-echoed time and again in all her writings: 'Courage is absolutely indispensable to a Sister of Notre Dame. Without it, all will crumble away, like a house built on sand, which the least breath of wind overturns' (*Conferences* 51).

Emptying the mind of distractions

Françoise, like many people, found it very difficult to control her human powers of reasoning – 'her argumentative spirit'. To this Julie replies that 'the way of prayer is a way of death, especially death to our own opinion which likes to interfere in everything and arrange everything to its own liking, even in spiritual matters' (L4:27–8). To explain her teaching further, she takes her images, like Teresa, from nature. She uses images of the weather as a metaphor to explain this inner turmoil: 'Let us stand fast, however bad the weather and however strong the wind may be; the good God will grant us the grace to profit from it, if we don't waste time looking to see from where the squall is coming' (L9:44).

Teresa had explained in a similar way this phenomenon of intellectual and imaginative turmoil in images of flight – 'thoughts as a rule fly so fast' – or the sky, 'as the movements of the heavens, revolving as they do with such speed'. It is, she says, important 'not to think much, but to love much'.[5] 'For there is nothing more contrary to the spirit of God in this way of prayer than wanting to see and understand everything', as 'too much human foresight can hinder God's plan for us' (L10:45). Julie draws a further spiritual lesson against impatience: 'That is why we must not become tired of waiting for the most favourable time; the good God has waited for us so long. Oh, how good he is' (L6:33). Teresa says in her *Life* that 'although they will not find it difficult to put their learning to good use, both before and after prayer . . . in these periods of quiet . . . learning should be put on one side. The time will come when they will use it in the Lord's service' (Cohen 1957, ch. 15, pp. 107–8). She continues that one does not get very far in prayer using reason, but that reason is an excellent test for the value of insight.

'Death to self' and awakening

The effect of this change in prayer is so profound that it provokes from Julie the harsh phrases of 'death to self' and 'being a victim of God's good pleasure'. Of the first phrase, she says, 'Isn't it true that I have a peculiar method of attracting my friends?' (L69):

> Ah! Ask for me, my dear friend; above all, this death to everything, and most of all to myself, since it is in this way we find true life (L7:37)
>
> ...that he will make you advance in this precious life of death to self, though it may seem to you that a lot of work remains to be done in this respect. (L12:50)

Julie uses the phrase frequently (Letters 13, 14, 16, 17, 20 and 22). The problem is that it seems to go against the general good of women who are acknowledged as having little sense of 'self'.[6] Another way to explain this 'death to self' is 'awakening'. The concept of 'awakening' can be traced in its various meanings from the forms of Plato, where true knowledge is remembering what the soul once knew, to the Fathers of the Church, through to the present-day literature of women's spirituality (Christ 1986; Harris 1991).

The 'dark night' of women is very different from the 'dark night' for men because of the way society perceives the role of the sexes. Women by socialisation have less rigid ego-boundaries and think of their relation to the world more as sameness, not difference. This produces a sense of emptiness in their lives and as they begin to awaken to the strength of the powers within them they begin the desperate search for who they really are. It is the prelude to their awakening to their true selves. It needs to be understood that women's experience of nothingness, even when things seem to be improving, as in parts of the Western world, is more far-reaching than men's. They learn from birth that girls are inferior to boys. The most extreme though not so rare example is the forced abortion of the first child if it is a girl. But in all societies, even those that consider themselves advanced, girls and boys learn very early, in many subtle and often not so subtle ways, through the mores of family, society and religion, that girls are inferior to boys. The message is all-pervasive, especially in most religious traditions.

So 'awakening' is a more appropriate word than 'conversion' to describe women's mystical experiences in prayer. Awakening implies an ability to see what is within, once the sleeping draught is refused of compromising with the structural and cultural evil imposed on them by society. This leads to reflection on their own God-given dignity, and they are gradually healed from their former wounded nature. Julie's direction of Françoise was of this nature. She was accompanying and encouraging Françoise in this finding of her self, affirming the emerging person and assisting in the death of the previous conforming personality.

In the realisation of this vacuum, this emptiness of who they really are, women come to an awakening of their true selves: 'For women awakening is not so much a giving up, as a taking on' (Christ 1986:19). Or in the words of Julie: 'Nothing is better able to draw God's gaze upon us than the conviction of our nothingness and our poverty before him ... he is so rich in good, what ought we not to expect from his liberality?' (L20:64) In Julie's eyes, this is what true sainthood is: 'death to self'. She concludes, 'let us ask to be saints' – i.e., whole human beings.[7] It is often said that the 'pattern of female development suggests one reason why mystical experiences are easier for women to achieve than men' (Christ 1986:19).

'Victims of God's good pleasure': becoming our true selves

Julie's second phrase, 'victim of God's good pleasure' (L4:27), refers not to the kind of victimisation of women that is now so well researched and documented,[8] but to the fact that by allowing God to take control of our lives we become our authentic selves. Spirituality is full of paradoxes. We 'lose our lives to save them'. So the use of the word 'victim', which Julie is using here, must be very carefully understood: it is 'the character, the one that God gives, not the character we fashion ourselves' (L182:485).

Virtues: strengths gained in contemplative prayer

Inner freedom is both marked and supported by what the language of the spirituality of Julie's time calls 'virtues', predominantly simplicity, self-abandonment and humility. Recent women's spirituality uses words such as *awakening, discovering, creating, dwelling, nourishing, traditioning* and *transforming* for women to recover their authentic, inalienable selves (Harris 1991). Harris's gentle but provocative book demonstrates that when women give themselves permission to be contemplative – to attend to their own needs and to be the women they were created to be, rather than what others expect them to be – they are nourished in a way that satisfies their spiritual hunger as well as their physical needs. The words of Harris denote a clearer understanding of the needs and shape of women's spirituality for modern times, but in Julie's time there was only one spiritual discourse for men and women and it was from this form that she chiselled the structure of her spirituality.

Simplicity

Simplicity is a key word in the charism of many women's religious congregations (Huls and Bloomestijn 1995). Simplicity means keeping an inner eye on 'God alone', 'being as wise as serpents and gentle as doves' (Matt. 10:16), for '[i]f your eye is healthy your whole body will be healthy' (Matt. 6:22–3). Or, in the words of Julie, 'As the spirit of God is a simple spirit, it is much safer for us to remain in dispositions that bring us nearer to simplicity of faith' (L4:27–8). This virtue is the one that corrects a predominant weakness among women of being 'too diffuse', concerned about the 'too many things'. The sin of 'pride' is, in fact, a predominantly male sin, except where women assume patriarchal power, because women on the whole have not enough sense of themselves to begin to understand it. The temptations of women are different, because of their 'feminine' socialisation. Valerie Saiving in her groundbreaking article 'The Human Situation', first published in 1960, explains the situation in the following way:

> They are better suggested by such terms as triviality, distractibility, and diffuseness; lack of organising centre or focus; dependence on others for one's self-definition; tolerance at the expense of standards of excellence; inability to respect the boundaries of privacy; sentimentality, gossipy sociability, and mistrust of reason – in short, underdevelopment or negation of the self. (Christ and Plaskow 1979:37)

However, women can also be guilty of the sin of pride when they allow themselves knowingly to be co-opted into the hierarchical, dominating system. Co-option and compromise are always tempting, as in the garden of Eden.

Simplicity is the virtue which overcomes this weakness. Julie uses her favourite image of the sunflower to explain simplicity as total focusing on and listening to the voice of God:

> [T]he sunflower . . . follows all movement of the sun and ever turns towards it . . . the mind and heart . . . who possesses the virtue of simplicity is always turned towards God alone . . . the light which beatifies and guides her, and the warmth which vivifies her. (*Instructions* 74)

> The simple soul is always happy, my dear sisters, always at peace, no matter what emotions arise in the inferior part of her nature. (ibid.:75)

The connection between simplicity and quietness in prayer becomes clear. The term used for this is 'perfection', a word frequently used by Julie in her letters to explain a process on the way to union with God.[9]

Self-abandonment

'Self-abandonment' follows 'death to self', the concept which originated in the eighteenth-century spirituality of the Jesuit, Père de Caussade, and which means personal, total trust in God, no matter what happens – Mary's '*fiat*'. Julie explains it in the following way: 'Let us turn to him in the beginning of all our actions. Then try as far as we can to preserve his holy presence, and abandon everything else to his providence' (L7:43). The ultimate self-abandonment, to which all other smaller steps lead, is that of Christ on the cross. Julie continually urges Françoise to remember that '[y]ou and I, my dear friend, must live in blind abandonment' (L11:48) . . . 'Ask for me total abandonment to the good pleasure of our Divine Master' (ibid.:34). It is not a once-and-for-all but a continuous life-long growth in human and spiritual maturity. It is the fruit of the growth of spiritual freedom and is dependent on it.

Humility

Last but not least of these virtues is humility, whose origin is in *humus*, the soil, the foundation of all growth. Humility holds a fundamental place in Christian spirituality, and is essential for a contemplative life. The 'lowly handmaid' of Mary's Magnificat (Luke 1:48) is a prelude to the Beatitudes. 'Lowly' is the translation of the Hebrew word meaning 'poor', and it is the poor whom Jesus blesses first in the Beatitudes (Matt. 5:4). Jesus is also a model of humility (Matt. 20:27–8; 25:40; Mark 1:43–5; Luke 22:26–7; John 8:50; 13:2–17).

This is the key which opens up the secrets of Julie and the full flowering of her spirituality. Julie was clear that humility did not mean making oneself into a doormat for others. She likened humility to the wings of a bird 'which cannot rise in the air without them; for the soul cannot rise to God without humility' (*Themes* 139). But it was one of Julie's great predecessors, Julian of Norwich, who reversed the traditional understanding of humility to accepting and receiving the overwhelming love and delight of God in us, not of being ashamed of who and what we are.

In early Christian spirituality, St Benedict noted twelve stages or degrees of humility, but from medieval times they were generally reduced to three. These concepts now are understood as a metaphor; the use of the word degrees or stages is better explained as deep changes in our levels of consciousness of how reality has been formed, which are reflected in changed attitudes and behaviour. These changing forms of consciousness are well known to those who are familiar with the 'three degrees of humility' in the Spiritual Exercises of St Ignatius. Taking these exercises as a guideline, it becomes clear in Letter 4 that Julie's personal response was the third level of consciousness – the testing 'third degree' of humility of Ignatius. *The Spiritual Exercises of St. Ignatius* sums up these three kinds of humility in the following way:

> The First Kind: is necessary for salvation ... I would not consent to violate a commandment ... that binds me under pain of mortal sin. The Second Kind: is more perfect than the first ... I neither desire nor am inclined to have riches rather than poverty, to seek honour rather than dishonour, to desire a long life rather than a short life, provided ... I would promote equally the service of God our Lord. The Third Kind: This is the most perfect kind of humility ... I desire and choose poverty with Christ poor, rather than riches; insults with Christ loaded with them, rather than honours; I desire to be accounted as worthless and follow Christ, rather than to be esteemed as wise and prudent in this world. So Christ was treated before me. (Puhl 1951:69)

Julie sums up this third kind as follows:

> So you do not yet want to be good for nothing, to allow God

to be glorified by others? You do not see yourself fit for that, my good friend? (L4:28)

And again,

It is from prayer that you must draw the grace to be very humble, since the good God causes you to feel the need of it ... Yes, I shall ask the good God with all my heart, for you as well as for myself, that we may become very humble, that we may have a vast contempt and that we may not be amazed if others feel the same contempt for us; the good God will help us in this. (L10:46)

In her *Instructions* Julie uses the imagery of Judith as a model for humility, an Old Testament model used often by the Carmelites at that time, perhaps learnt by Julie from her association with the Carmelites at Compiègne: 'Humble ourselves before God', Judith kept repeating it to the inhabitants of Bethulia. 'Let us humble ourselves before Him, and continuing in a humble spirit in His service let us go and ask the Lord with tears that according to His will, so He would show His mercy to us (Judith 9:16–17).

This third degree of humility is the closest following of Christ and the deepest transformation and change in consciousness of all – the making in psychological terms of the *transrational identity*, the authentic marginal, liminal person, the characteristics of the prophetic person.[10] Julie considered this degree of humility, of transformation of consciousness, to be essential in the mystical process of self-actualisation. Yet the words are hard and strange – being despised by others, even friends, poor for the sake of the kingdom, and 'to be accounted as worthless and a fool for Christ's sake' (Puhl 1951:69):

Yes, I shall ask the good God with all my heart, for you as for myself, that we may become very humble, that we may have a vast, a perfect self-contempt for us; the good God will help us in this. (7:46)

You tell me you have made silly mistakes. As you know well, my dear good friend, our blunders must not be an obstacle to the work of God's grace in us. I can tell you God often makes use of us after these awkward mistakes, because he then finds us in our proper place, convinced that we are good for nothing. (L6:32)

This level of consciousness or humility gives birth to a mystic, prophetic spirituality, that of a person who often unknowingly is called to awaken a deeper consciousness in others. Or as Desmond Murphy writes in his book *The Death and Rebirth of Religious Life*: 'The call of the prophet to transformation inherently arouses anxiety in the listener for it involves the prospect of being required to leave the security of the present mode of adaptation. The core construct is threatened' (Murphy 1995:205). Hence, the effect of transformation in prayer is revealed in transformation in life. Prophets energise even though their stance is very challenging.

Julie's teaching on contemplative prophetic action in the perspective of Enneagram spirituality

Although, initially, Julie concentrates mainly on Françoise's experience of prayer, this teaching was going on during the ordinary daily life of Françoise. In the following letters (numbers 13–27) she concentrates as much on the daily choices of Françoise as on reinforcing her teaching on the prayer of the 'dark night' – the 'fourth mansion' of prayer.

Richard Rohr, in the book *Discovering the Enneagram* (Rohr and Ebert 1996), claims that the Enneagram is a very powerful tool for this transformation of consciousness. The Enneagram comes from the Sufi tradition, but its origin is not known. It is reputed to have originated almost 2000 years ago in Afghanistan, and to have infiltrated into Moslem circles in Asia and India. It was an oral tradition until the twentieth century. The term 'Enneagram' is derived from the Greek word *enneas*, meaning nine. According to this system there are nine, and only nine, personality types. Each personality type is identified in a negative way, arising from the specific compulsion of each type. The compulsion is a kind of 'hidden sin', which pervades all behaviour, where sin is understood as a kind of paralysis or hindrance in becoming one's true authentic self. St Paul (Rom. 7:14–23) often presents sin as a power which enslaves a person. If the Enneagram is to be useful we must discover the negativity of our own personality. The Enneagram enables us to discern which of the nine basic predominant passions or compulsions control us. The sixth-century Pope, Gregory the Great, enumerated seven major ways of being trapped in one capital sin, and the Enneagram added two more major sins, deceit and anxiety, to these traditional seven, making them nine. These predominant faults are divided in the following way: (1) over-perfectionism; (2) over-helpfulness; (3) avoidance of failure; (4) avoidance of ordinariness, a desire to be special; (5) storing knowledge for oneself; (6) over-anxiety and fear; (7) avoidance of pain; (8) avoidance of revealing personal weakness; (9) avoidance of conflict. God uses our style, our predominant fault, for our transformation, and all nine personality types are characterised by one of the following being our predominant mode of responding: from the heart, the head or the gut.

Françoise's 'predominant fault': timidity and fear

Reflecting on the Enneagram as a tool for unearthing the predominant fault of Françoise, I think she was probably a number six, because in these first letters she seems initially to reflect both the loyalty and the fear and timidity of the sixes. In fact Françoise reflects some of the main faults so often associated with women, summed up in the words of Joanna Wolski: 'Women have rarely been alerted to those vices to which their socialization prompts them, for example, weak submissiveness, fear, self-hatred, jealousy, timidity, self-absorption, small-mindedness, submersion of personal identity and manipulation' (Wolski 1986:39).

Julie shows her skills as a director by following the experience of Françoise and gently pointing out the cause of her reactions to different situations:

> You have a very timid nature and that has a great effect on you. Therefore our father [Père Thomas] is right in saying: Such people need much practice. He gave himself as an example; when he was young he was extraordinarily timid, but by dint of exercise he has changed to what he is now. (L7:36)

> You need liberty of spirit to rid yourself of all these miseries! (L15:57)

Françoise often showed this fear and timidity by responding too quickly to her 'first impulse', and like others both before and after her, it led her into many troubles:

> The first impulse is always too quick in you. If you allow yourself to be caught by it, it will rob you at times of the peace of the children of God that is to be much desired ... You need a very gentle humility, my dear daughter, to get back to a calm state of mind. (L24:73)

> There must be nothing of the woman among us, we need courageous souls, afraid of nothing. (*Conf.* 18)

This is why Julie, in common with Teresa, calls her women to be 'manly souls', to overcome this learnt fear and timidity. In other words, to resist the way women are supposed to be, seen and not heard; to be prepared to speak out, hold their own position and be focused on the matter in hand.

Françoise also had a propensity to day-dream: 'You know my dear daughter, that I have always recommended you not to daydream; that can only cause your soul to be disturbed' (L32:84). The other weakness was to lose her temper very quickly on occasions, which made her worry even more about her ability to help others. To this Julie replied:

You should not worry, even though you should happen to have one of your outbursts of temper. There is nothing astonishing in this. You must even take it as permitted by God ... When you perceive your blunder look at it quite calmly. (L31:84)

Little practice in the 'works of mercy'

Françoise learnt the hard way. Julie continued to raise the issue again and again because of her 'little practice in the works of mercy': 'You have a very timid nature and that has a great effect on you' (L7:36). She continually returns to this weakness and by Letter 8 warns Françoise that 'the devil ... will not fail to fill timid souls with alarm in order to prevent their contributing to the greater glory of God' (L8:36).

[T]hese reactions come from a certain self seeking in the things of God ... we resemble worldly women who often go back to their mirrors to see whether anything's lacking in their attire. Oh, how much more refined is grace! Let us behave as much as possible with simplicity ... let us avoid self complacency because we do not like to see any defects in ourselves. (ibid.)

If you allow yourself to be caught by it, it will rob you at times of the peace of the children of God, that is so desired. (L24:73)

Do less yourself and you will see that the good God will do his work in you in peace and quiet. It is in this way that grace is communicated to a soul ... Always wait until your first impulse is spent, without worrying about its turbulence, as if refusing to notice it. Then put yourself into the holy presence of God as if nothing had happened. (L22:69)

Rome was not made in a day and neither is the elimination of a predominant fault, as Françoise discovered. However, Julie saw this as a good thing:

You are still reproaching yourself for making blunders . . .
you are only too lucky that the good God grants you the grace
of noticing them . . . show them to God with all the tranquillity
of a child showing his mother a small hurt . . . Well, my daughter, would the mother take it into her head to increase her
child's sufferings because he hurt himself by being disobedient?
No, she would apply any useful remedies . . . for his injuries.
In the same way the good God asks of us, when we have hurt
ourselves by our too great haste, our over activity, to repair
our injuries by acts of humility and by accepting the humiliations that may be the result. How good the good God is . . .
he gives us an easy means of drawing profit from everything,
even from our imperfections and weaknesses. (L27:78)

Julie was probably influenced by the writing of Francis de Sales
on this question of the predominant fault, which he referred to
as 'loving our abjections'. In Latin 'abjection' means 'humility':
to love our 'abjections' is to love ourselves, as we are loved, in
our wholeness. It is also to have compassion for ourselves. It is
to see that our true transformation is not in our gifts but in our
weaknesses. To love our abjections is to shatter our images of
self-perfection (Wright 1993:85).

The liberty of the children of God

Julie led Françoise to a gradual understanding of the 'liberty of
the children of God' in guiding her in the perennial difficulty
for counter-revolutionary women in their refusal to support
juring-priests. For a juring-priest, Julie's response was unequivo-
cal: 'without hesitation for a single moment, you will tell the
mothers of families, and other persons who ask you . . . they
cannot in conscience go to the sermons or the Mass of intruders'
(L8:39). A non-juring priest evoked a very different reply:

The little stirring of human respect you may experience at
the place where you go to assist at Mass: you have to expect
it. First of all it will be a new thing for these people, who are

not accustomed to seeing anyone receiving [Holy Communion]. The idea of attracting notice and disapproval may trouble you. But you know with a single glance of faith all this soon disappears . . . What are a small handful of people in the presence of God? He alone is great and all these people are nothing but a breath of wind which he can still by a single act of his will . . . Thanks be to God you know the devil's tricks . . . For nothing is better able to lift our hearts to God than the contempt shown us on these occasions; you know that already. (L11:49)

Julie uses these occasions to say to Françoise, 'I want to lead you into pastures much vaster' (*Conf.* 29). That is a better, fuller way, to live and to respond, and as the correspondence progresses Julie begins to name these vaster pastures in her growing call for 'liberty of spirit': 'you need liberty of spirit to rid yourself of all these miseries' (L15:57); 'in all things act with the liberty of the children of God' (L17:61). This theme of 'liberty' culminates in Letter 27:

What I would like to give you is the liberty of the children of God . . . You cannot believe how useful this holy presence is in everything . . . familiarising yourself with it is not to be preoccupied about knowing what to do or say on some occasion or other that you foresee, perhaps in the distant future. From the moment you notice this untimely working of your spirit, drop it all by leaving it quietly in God's hands. Preserve your peace of heart in entire abandonment to Divine Providence. There lies the secret of the interior life, which very few people know, because we always want to see which way we will go and what we ought to do. That is the wisdom of the worldly wise. (L27:78)

The 'devil and his tricks'

Before leaving this section, mention needs to be made of the way that Julie dealt, in Letters 28–33, with temptation, which she called the 'devil and his tricks' or 'the scurvy'.[11] This is now called the testing of good and bad spirits. Françoise was undergoing the spirit of resistance that often develops towards the spiritual director, at a certain stage of discernment. Julie is well-versed in the ways of the testing of the spirits and soon recognises the signs in Françoise. Françoise seems to lose trust in Julie, and becomes highly critical of her actions. This is manifested in Françoise by her cutting accusations that Julie was not paying 'enough attention' when reading her letters. Julie is not fooled by this attitude; she recognises it for what it is, as her prompt reply shows:

> You would be very unjust to my heart in thinking that . . . I do not doubt the devil makes every effort at this moment to disgust you with me. Moreover, he knows only too well what he is going to lose not to present to you as ridiculous one so opposed to the spirit of the world. And no doubt, my daughter you will see very great imperfections in me; yes, they exist . . . Do not spare me . . . tell me all the faults you see in me and ask the good God that I may become a saint, whatever the price may be. There is still much work to be done, I warn you. (L32:85–6)

The conflict only served to deepen the understanding between the two women, forging the 'bond of perfection' of de Sales. Julie makes Françoise aware of the root of the problem: 'The enemy of salvation will stir up all sorts. But a woman of faith, who puts all her confidence in God and leaves all to him, will enjoy great tranquillity even in the midst of storms and squalls' (L31:84). Julie's words are echoed in the book that was so important to her, *The Imitation of Christ*: 'The Devil sleepeth not, neither is the flesh yet dead; therefore, thou must never cease to prepare thyself for the battle; for on the right hand and the left are enemies that never rest' (Knotts 1963, chs 9 and 12).

The relationship is quickly restored to its former trust:

As soon as you notice these little horns, you'd better not let them grow very long, as we are naturally all inclined to do ... We shall make a saint of you, my daughter, a saint without horns, of course. Our father (Père Thomas) and I will do it together, if I cannot do it all by myself. So don't worry we shall fulfil your plans in this respect. (L33:87)

Françoise's immediate growth in 'liberty'

One of the first-fruits as Françoise grew in this spirit of inner and outer liberty of action was her desire to be 'poor in spirit' by taking a vow of voluntary poverty. She wished to be free of personal possessions and follow the call of Christ more closely. The Letters show that Julie in no way influenced Françoise in her choice; in fact, the evidence is quite the reverse: 'the good God does not ask everyone to practise it with the same perfection' (L15:57). Françoise promptly informed Julie of her desire but Julie waited till she saw clearly that it was the way for Françoise, and only then came the response:

I must not forget to say a word about evangelical perfection. You write that the poor are the beloved members of Christ. I have realised that limiting you to giving alms was not what you needed to reach the object of your desires. May what I say satisfy you, my dear friend, since you want to serve the poor by being poor. (L17:59)

The next clear evidence of Françoise's growth in liberty came with her ability to make a decision on her future. On her father's death, she realised that her future life was to share Julie's vision:

As soon as I heard of your father's death, I saw you throwing yourself into my arms. This sight struck my heart with great feeling. It seemed to me that this was the great moment when the good God would give me to you, in such a strong tie that death alone would separate us. (L29:82)

Julie has guided Françoise successfully through this most difficult time of transition in prayer and life choices – the Fourth
Mansion of Teresa. Julie had built up such trust between Françoise and herself that Françoise was able to abandon herself
completely to God's guidance through Julie. And Julie was able
to lead Françoise to an understanding of freedom as 'a liberation
from fear but not from pain' (Fiand 1987:38). Françoise and
Julie were now able to witness to the truth that 'there is no
freedom of God without the politics of justice and compassion
and there is no politics and compassion without a religion of
the freedom of God' (Brueggemann 1978:18). They could live
out contemplation in action to the full: the 'rapture of action' so
dear to the heart of Julie rather than the 'rapture of the cloister'
forced on so many religious women from medieval times.

Julie's 'liberty of spirit'

Julie had been thoroughly versed, since her childhood, in the
spirit of the scriptures on freedom and the spirit of the *Imitation
of Christ* by Thomas à Kempis, thanks to her parish priest, Père
Dangicourt. Moreover, she was no stranger to making decisions
that were not acceptable to her times, as is shown in her early
first communion and her vow of celibacy at the age of fourteen.
Her public opposition to the powers of the Revolution over the
Civil Constitution of the Clergy show a fearlessness similar to
that of Christ in the face of authority she could not accept as
God-given.

Julie learnt, in the school of suffering, the cost of God's grace,
and from an early age she never hesitated to follow God's will,
once it became clear. Any slight knowledge of Julie's life shows
she was completely imbued with the 'spirit of her good God' –
the spirit of freedom. This was the great Christian gift, her
charism, which she could not but help pass on to the Congregation of women she was to establish. Julie, moreover, in her
letters to Françoise shows that this gift can only be received
fully from God, and lived in life, with the help of skilful guidance
from one who has gone before and who knows the way. This

movement towards and living in the spirit of contemplative prayer evokes the spirit of abandonment to the goodness of God – God's will. It is a gift only acquired through a depth of contemplative prayer that led John of the Cross to call it the *nada*, the 'nakedness', the 'complete nudity of spirit'. The philosopher Kierkegaard used an even more startling term to express his experience: 'to jump about stark naked' before God. Julie, however, preferred the more scriptural term of 'liberty' to the graphic terms of John or Kierkegaard.

Reflections

The experience of the 'dark night', skilfully navigated, led Françoise not to death but life and a reshaping of her interior and exterior landscape, echoed again and again in the developing understanding of women's spirituality. It is a continuous process that returns at deeper and deeper levels. A precondition for these changes is allowing God to free up an inner space, to remove the clutter of our thoughts, to die to our false selves and come alive to our true identity in God. This understanding continually grows, in accordance with the depth of the action of God within us. Fullness is only achieved in those gifted to live at the greatest depth of consciousness of all, 'the third degree of humility'. This is a person who, through God's grace, has achieved a unique Christian self-identity. It is never completely attained, as human factors and experiences always clog the way. The predominant fault never dies; it is only tamed by experience. Julie, with the other great teachers on contemplative prayer, is claiming the possibility of a degree of freedom once the way is well understood, but it is only after secure self-boundaries are developed that spiritual liberty is effective. Self-abandonment is only possible after knowing oneself. Liberty of spirit allows a person to live out the mysticism of everyday life, finding God in all things. It makes a person truly human by opening up an immense longing for more than this life can give. The following chapter on the Cross clearly illustrates how 'liberty' consumed the whole of Julie's being in all her actions and decisions. She was never rushed into decisions but always waited for the prompting of her 'good God' who never failed her.

Following in the footsteps of Christ, the gift of the 'liberty of the children of God' enables people to become fearless catalysts for change in the times in which they live. For example, women are praying and thinking their way out of 'patriarchy', and as women grow in inner freedom, there is a developing realisation that 'patriarchy' is not built on a superiority of thought or the Word of God, but on silencing all other voices. From the many and varied experiences of the 'dark night', properly traversed, the butterfly of Teresa and the transrational person of psychology emerge, exemplified in the song and dance of the Asian woman theologian Chung Hung Kyung at the End of the Decade on Women at Harare, Zimbabwe in November 1998:

> We are changers
> we are movers
> everything we touch changes
> touchers, movers,
> everything we touch changes

Julie and Françoise, consumed by the power and 'liberty of the children of God', were part of the vibrant changers and movers of their generation. They followed the law of liberty lived by Christ. Their legacy demands the same of all who follow their way to God.

6

Women of the Poor

'We exist only for the poor, only for the poor, absolutely only for the poor.' (letter of 1808, L86:225)

The rise and fall of the Napoleonic Empire, 1804–16, was the historical background against which Julie founded her Congregation. Although in this chapter it might seem that Julie went from place to place founding houses very smoothly, nothing could be further from the truth. The next chapter will show the struggles Julie underwent: not only those with bishops and priests, over the governing of her Congregation, but also a bitter dispute with some of her most trusted Sisters. To this can be added Julie's continual health problems, her long journeys on foot, donkey or stage coach, and the problems of her Sisters when French soldiers flooded through northern France in the last two years of her life.

Julie's answer to the profound poverty of her time was to found a Congregation for the education of the 'poor of the most abandoned places' – initially the poor, young, orphaned girls she saw all around her. All forms of education had been severely disrupted by the French Revolution and this period marks a watershed in the history of education and set the whole idea of education in a new direction. It marks the general acceptance of the principle that popular education should be controlled by the State, not by the Church, and that the State is responsible, at least for primary education. This was accompanied by the abandonment of the classical curriculum of the grammar schools, and the start of secular and modern subjects. However, the Church did not give up its hegemony over education without a struggle.

The dominant views of education were those of Rousseau, who wrote in his educational treatise *Émile* that women were to be 'educated for ... domestic life. Their purpose is to perpetuate the race, to watch over the development of their children and to rule men by *la puissance irrésistible de la faiblesse* (the irresistible power of their weakness) ... And they should not leave home except in special circumstances.'[1] A few lone voices, such as that of Condorcet, were beginning to articulate a more egalitarian approach for girls' education. Although the question of girls' education was dealt with in many reports of the Revolutionary Assemblies, it was not until the Guizot Law of 1833 that a detailed system of primary instruction was provided for girls. Secondary education in France had to wait until 1880. In 1789, the standard of literacy was still only based on whether a person could read or write their name. It is little wonder, then, that the question of education was uppermost in the minds of the thinkers of the day.

Napoleon's educational reforms as Consul and later as Emperor reflected his social attitudes and contempt of women. Like those before him, he saw the purpose of education as to equip young people for service to the state – the boys as doctors, civil servants and officers, or simply as craftsmen, labourers and common soldiers; and the girls as dutiful and obedient housewives and mothers. What is more, the poor should only benefit from a modicum of instruction, and therefore the primary schools could be left to the local municipalities to support and be supplemented by the numerous Church schools to which the Concordat of 1801 had opened the door.

In May 1802 Napoleon reorganised the public secondary schools, created for boys during the Revolution, under a Director of Public Instruction; thereafter the Church was allowed to invade the field. Napoleon's distinctive creation was the *lycée* for the training of leaders and administrators, with a strictly secular curriculum directed by the State. Places at these schools were reserved for the sons of officers and civil servants and for the most able pupils of the ordinary secondary schools. As for the education of girls, it was of relatively minor importance and for the greater part could be left to the religious orders and thus save public expense. Writing from his headquarters at Finkenstein in Germany during the campaign of 1807, the Emperor urged his Minister of the Interior to see that the girls in the new high school at Ecouen should receive a solid grounding in religion. 'What we ask of education', he wrote, 'is not that girls should think, but they should believe'; and he added that 'care must be taken not to let them see any Latin, or other foreign languages'.[2]

Poverty in the eighteenth century

The main source of support for families in France in 1789 was the land. With an average family of four to five children, nine tenths of French families had insufficient land to support them. *Les Pauvres*, the poor, covered a wide spectrum of vulnerable citizens: 'The best estimation of the poor can be made from the number of *passive* poor citizens, that is, adult males whose tax rating was the proceeds of two days labour ... In 1790 around 39% adult males were in this position' (Hufton 1974:23).

The term used for those suffering absolute poverty was *les indigents*, but the difference between *les pauvres* and *les indigents* was only one of degree, as it was so easy to fall into absolute poverty. This happened in Amiens in 1795, when the entire town was hit by famine and food riots resulted. Urban historians have suggested that up to 20 per cent of the total town populations were *nécessiteux* (Roseanne Murphy 1995:40). The survival of the poor was a triumph of human ingenuity, as they had come to expect very little from anyone.

Poor relief in France was still based on the predominant ideas of 'Catholic Poor Relief' of the sixteenth and seventeenth centuries, with the Church still preaching unflinchingly 'the God given nature of the social order' (Gibson 1989:13). God had ordained that some should be born rich, and others poor, and the latter were there to help the rich do good works and so get to heaven. The spiritual efforts of clergy, in the second half of the seventeenth century, were directed towards arousing in the rich an awareness of their obligations towards their weaker brethren. To thinkers such as Montesquieu and Robespierre, it was this Catholic Poor Relief which encouraged the growth of the idle poor, and they wished to replace it with a soundly based, objective, state assistance. To this end a *Comité de Mendicité* was set up to look into the numbers and reasons for the begging poor of France. 'Eighteenth century France was the uncomfortable arena in which the Catholic philosophy of poor relief came into open conflict with the anti-clericalism and social idealism of the Enlightenment.'[3] This old structure of voluntary charity was destroyed in July 1793 when all hospital property was nationalised and in 1794 with the passing of the Poor Law. To understand the causes of poverty fully, an analysis of the gender element is necessary.

The specific poverty of women in the eighteenth century

Les enfants trouvés

Women's poverty pivoted on their child-bearing role. The rapid dislocation of eighteenth-century society had led to a great growth in illegitimacy. 'Up to 17 per cent of all births in certain French cities by the end of the old regime were outside marriage' (Hufton 1997:131). The Church considered men the unwilling victims of this increase of illegitimacy, and not only blamed women for the immorality of the time, but also branded illegitimacy a sin. It is significant that even St Vincent de Paul regarded the children unquestioningly as a product of sin, though he believed them worthy of compassion. He is, moreover, said to have worked long hours to persuade Louise de Marillac that foundlings were the children of God and, as such, worthy of human pity. That the foundress of the Sisters of Charity should herself have recoiled from these children is indicative of the general distaste felt for them.

However, as poverty grew worse during the century, not only those with children born out of marriage but married women also were increasingly forced to abandon or even murder their own children. The penalty for child-murder was death, though fortunately this was not rigorously enforced. The Church and police often worked together to uncover the place of burial of these children; they would descend on an unsuspecting girl and often find the corpse of the baby. Others, to escape the authorities, resorted to putting their dead children down drains. In Rennes, for example, in 1721, in the course of rebuilding the city, a drain was opened to reveal 80 skeletons of very young children. Although this crime was punishable by death, few were brought before the courts, except in Brittany where it was rigorously enforced. Execution for these young girls consisted in being broken on the wheel before being hanged.

Most villages and towns were familiar with 'the sight of such little corpses, usually with the umbilical cord untied, still blood-streaked from the birth process, and dead from suffocation, found in ditches, cellars, and most frequently drains' (Hufton 1974:351). Abandoned children who were found alive were called by the state *enfants trouvés*. These were to be Julie's initial 'poor of the most abandoned places'.

Prior to the Revolution, three quarters of these children were barely a month old when they were abandoned, and racketeers began to trade them for money. The practice was highly developed and lucrative, and many parishes, either for reasons of conscience or money, worked with the racketeers in this profitable but dreadful enterprise.[4] We learn from the Sisters of Charity, who ran a large hospital for these foundlings in Paris:

> The infants were bundled upright in groups of four or five in pannier baskets strapped to the backs of donkeys. Those who died on the journey were discarded en route, however, the more children that reached Paris alive, the more the carters received. Hence the nuns claimed the carters gave children wine to drink not milk, for convenience, to stop the crying, to make them sleep, or keep them alive till the end of the journey. (Hufton 1974:345)

The children generally arrived in a terrible condition and syphilis was rampant.

Prostitution

Prostitution was then, as always, another sign of poverty among women. Although the courtesan or the royal mistress was a well-known figure, these women are not to be compared with the young girls who were forced by economic circumstances into prostitution. Most went into prostitution either full or part-time in order to feed their families. A large majority of full-time prostitutes became camp followers, similar to the young Philippine women in Japan in the Second World War – the 'comforters'. Approximately one adult woman in thirteen in Paris took to prostitution for a whole or part of her income. Perhaps with London as a contender, 'Paris contained the widest range of prostitutes in Europe, as Rome had done 200 years earlier' (Hufton 1997:322). In certain parts of France, especially in ports such as Toulouse, 'the commonest street walker was the girl from the *Comminges*, an ex-servant camp follower, trailing from garrison town to garrison town' (Hufton 1974:313).

Unfortunately, we know little of the stories of the girls themselves as most could neither read nor write. But we do know that 99 per cent of the evidence on prostitution reflects the attitudes of men as legislators, magistrates, ecclesiastics and philanthropists (Hufton 1997:308). Julie must have had a profound knowledge of women's sufferings and we can now look back, with some historical perspective, on the vital spirit of the early days of her Congregation.

The founding of the Congregation

It was against this background of poverty and the relative political stability of the Napoleonic reforms that Julie was to found her Congregation. Its foundations were underpinned by the deep friendship between Julie and Françoise, and by a shared and developing understanding of the meaning behind Julie's vision in Compiègne in 1792. Its origins, which were poor and simple, began where they had first met, in the house of Françoise's brother in the Rue Neuve, Amiens, at Mass on 2 February 1804. Julie's earlier work in helping with the Missions given by the Fathers of the Faith soon attracted attention, and by 1804 they had eight poor little abandoned orphans to teach. Julie and Françoise had already attracted a third young woman to join them in making their first vows, in the presence of Père Varin: Cathérine Dûchatel, a young woman from Rheims. They promised 'to devote themselves to the education of orphans and especially to the formation of teachers, who were to go wherever they were needed – never fewer than two – to instruct the poor, free of charge' (*Memoirs* 8). Père Varin gave them the Rule of The Institute of Mary, written for another group, as a preliminary guide to follow until they could draw up a Rule more suitable to their needs. Unfortunately, Cathérine was not in good health and she died eighteen months after her consecration.

On 20 February two other women in their early twenties, both with some education, asked to join: Victoire Leleu, later to be known as Sister Anastasie and *le petit conseil* of Julie, and her good friend Justine Garson. A few days later they were joined by a young woman from Bettencourt, where Julie and Françoise had laid the foundation of their friendship, Geneviève Gosselin, and the work of educating the orphans began seriously. In the early days in Amiens, the Sisters would go out into the streets with a bell to 'let you know that the Sisters of Notre Dame have just opened free schools for little girls. Go tell your parents the news' (Roseanne Murphy 1995:69).

Julie's cure

Julie's foundation of an apostolic congregation was a great act of faith, as she herself was still severely crippled and unable to walk.[5] However, under the influence of a young and enthusiastic priest, Père Enfantin,[6] Julie's new spiritual director, she agreed to join him in a Novena to the Sacred Heart, for a special intention – not knowing it was for her. Françoise writes:

On June 8th, the Feast of the Sacred Heart, when Julie was in the garden Father Enfantin stepped up to her and said: 'If you have faith, Mother, take a step in honour of the Heart of Jesus'. Julie rose and took a step, something she had not done for twenty-two years. 'Take another, another, that will do: you may sit down' . . . The next day she went upstairs as she usually did, sitting on the stairs and using her hands to raise herself from one step to another. At the landing was a low chair, which she generally used to get to chapel; but now she picked it up and carried it to her place, and at Communion, instead of dragging herself on her knees . . . she walked to the altar . . . Finally, on Tuesday when thanksgiving after Communion was over, we went downstairs to breakfast as usual. We were in silence when two of the children who were near the door cried out: 'Mother is walking downstairs!' We were so amazed that we made no move to meet her. Our mother came in with a firm step while we fell on our knees to praise the Lord. Then we went to the Chapel and sang the Te Deum. (*Memoirs* 10)

Julie's journeys

After 22 years of being unable to walk, Julie was to spend the rest of her life 'on the road', in establishing and visiting houses for poor children. Françoise calculated that she did at least 119 journeys, yet an argument can be made that Julie actually made 378.[7] Although she frequently walked, especially between Fleurus and Gembloux, or at other times went on a donkey, most of the time she either went by coach, or hired a driver. Her letters are filled with references to her difficulty in booking seats on a coach or hiring a suitable driver. She was never deterred by the weather – cold, heat, snow, ice or rain – and her journeys can scarcely be imagined, except by those who have lived and worked in developing countries. The times that she walked are emphasised because they are so amazing for a woman who was once paralysed. At her beatification in 1888, when a malformed bone was discovered in her foot, it was perceived as a mystery that she could ever have walked at all, let alone covered the miles she did. Françoise notes in her *Memoirs* her fears for Julie while she was on the road:

> To go alone on such journeys at her age and in her frail state of health, in public conveyance where she had to hear so much cursing, swearing, raillery, and familiarities, she needed courage and the maturity and religious bearing that were hers. She was over fifty when she began these journeys; her face, though bright and animated, was that of a much older person, and this often protected her from insult. Ordinarily while travelling she met neither raillery nor disrespect because she knew when to say nothing, how to speak to the point, and how to use her gift of repartee without wounding anyone's feelings. In the company of cultured travellers, she usually inspired a certain reverence. (*Memoirs* 110)

The stories of her travels are legendary, including travelling with drunken men in a carriage in which she was left alone when the horse bolted off on its own. She often said, 'I would rather go on foot than travel in a coach' (L291:722). On another occasion, she travelled with a very poor driver, who stopped to rest at an 'inn of disrepute'. Many a time she had trouble on horseback and she would relate her adventures with much humour:

> Do you know, my dear daughters, I owe it to your good prayers that I did not fall into a pond as I was returning? I told you I had come back with a horse. My little guide wanted it to go and drink in the pond, with me sitting on it. Then suddenly a whim got hold of it and it took me right out to the middle of the pond and did not want to come out. But my good angel helped me just in the nick of time. May the holy name of my God be blessed for ever. (L128:346)

No wonder she would say 'It is impossible for me to visit you before the thaws. The horses cannot keep their feet' (L377:873).

Even after such a day's journey, she would still find time and
energy to write to her 'dear young sisters', who needed help: 'I
have done plenty of walking ... I have asked the good God to
grant our little girls all the graces they need. Our dear Sisters
must ask the good God for me: I need them so much, and I
count very much on their good prayers' (L148:401).

The foundation of poor schools: 'the rapture of action'

It was in the foundation of schools and houses for the Sisters,
twelve in all (of which only eight schools in Flanders remained
by her death), that Julie's struggles and sufferings for her Congregation were unremitting. Yet Julie always referred to these
struggles as 'the rapture of action'. At each step, she met difficulties and opposition, and it became a firm principle with her
that she would never establish a school and house where the
local bishop or clergy were not supportive. Julie had learnt her
lesson well from the opposition of Père Sambucy in Amiens (see
chapter 7, pp. 141–152ff.).

The four early houses and schools that Julie established before
1807 were doomed for closure: three were in France and one
in Flanders. On 2 February 1804 the first house of the Congregation was founded in Amiens, in the Rue Neuve. In August
1806, it was closed and the Sisters and their pupils moved to
larger premises at the Faubourg-Noyon, a move made possible
only with the help of the wealth of Françoise and one of their
great friends, Madame Jeanne de Franssu. By this time the
number of Sisters had grown to eighteen. They were accompanied by only four orphans, so as soon as they moved Julie
sent a Sister out into the street with a bell calling any poor child
to school. It was while she was here that Père Sambucy was
made the spiritual director of the Sisters. Nevertheless, in spite
of this background of personal suffering Julie continued to
establish houses.

On 17 December 1806 St Nicholas in Flanders was founded,
the first house established outside Amiens. Here Julie was
warmly received by Bishop Beaumont of Ghent who had the

same vision for the Congregation as Julie. It was in his episcopal house that the Sisters were able to wear their habit in public for the first time, of which occasion Julie said how charming they looked in their little outfits (L45:114). Their dress was that of the Flemish women of the time. Unfortunately, this foundation was not to survive. The conditions were so poor with dampness and 'bugs' that it was closed in favour of a house in Ghent in 1810. Julie later also closed this second house as she found the premises too damp for the Sisters; in fact, the young Superior of the house, Sister Jeanne Garson, contracted tuberculosis while she was here and later died. Moreover, Julie found little co-operation from the people – even the very poor. Nationalism raised its head – the Flemish did not like the idea of their children being taught by the French. The house was closed and the Sisters moved to another house in Ghent. On 21 February 1807 Montdidier, the only other house Julie founded in France, was established twenty miles south of Amiens. This was also closed after Julie's dismissal from Amiens. The very young Superior of the house, Marie-Gaudine Caroline of Montdidier, was later renamed Sister St Jean, and became the Superior of St Hubert in Flanders.

On 7 July 1807, the house at Namur in Flanders was opened. Françoise, now Mère St Joseph, became the first Superior of the house, which, after the dramatic dismissal of Julie and her Sisters from Amiens by Bishop Demandolx, was destined to become the Mother House of the new Congregation. With the arrival of Julie and the other Sisters from Amiens in 1809, a new chapter opened in the history of the Congregation. Other smaller but no less important foundations followed that of Namur: Jumet, Flanders (23 March 1808); St Hubert, in the Ardennes, Flanders (13 August 1809); Ghent, Nouveau Bois, Flanders (15 February 1810). It was here that some of the Sisters closest to Julie, led by Sister Cathérine Daullée, severely challenged Julie's flexibility in the application of the Rule outside the Mother House at Namur – the suffering which caused Julie the greatest pain (see chapter 7, pp. 152–159ff.).

It was while the Napoleonic wars were reaching their climax

that the last four houses and schools were founded: Zele, Flanders (11 November 1811); Andenne, Flanders (6 October 1813); Gembloux, Flanders (11 October 1813); and Fleurus, Flanders (21 June 1814). Julie's journeys were made even more dangerous, as the war was encroaching on French soil and the Sisters' lives were seriously endangered.[8]

Julie quickly showed her skill as a businesswoman and negotiator. Françoise, meanwhile, proved to be a very able administrator with a rare gift of getting things done thoroughly and quickly without any fuss. Although it was always essential to gain the permission of the bishops and priests with whom she worked, Julie was also shrewd in harnessing local dignitaries as benefactors to her new foundation, and made sure they kept to their word. For example in the parish of St Hubert, Flanders, she was asked by the local Mayor, a Monsieur Zoude, a baker by profession, to send two Sisters to run some of the schools. He agreed to provide a building and pay an annual income of 25 francs, a considerable sum of money for that time. However, when he failed 'to send a load of faggots', Julie wrote to the young Superior, Sister Jeanne, 'Do not let him forget it; write him a very courteous letter to remind him' (L128:345). She added that we must, on the other hand, always 'pray to God for our benefactors' (L131:351).

Julie's educational principles

The poor

Julie did not have the benefit of the sophisticated theories of education and assessment we have today, but she was a natural educator with an intuitive instinct for the needs of her time. She was a creative, flexible and courageous educator who, from personal experience, understood above all the needs of the very poor. She clearly articulated this central place of the poor in all her works at Montdidier, a town twenty miles south of Amiens, in her words *'We exist only for the poor, only for the poor, absolutely only for the poor'* (L86:225). It was in the foundation of this house that Julie was forced to begin to lay down clear principles for all the schools. It arose over the question of fee-paying pupils. A young Sister, Marie-Caroline, 24 years of age, was sent to be Superior of this new foundation only one year after making her vows. She was accompanied by two other young women. Julie wrote:

> They said they were no longer able to earn a living with the decrease in the number of children still coming to their school. Monsieur Cottu,[9] who informed me of everything, gave me a message from his Lordship that you should receive definitely only the poor. I answered that I had already written you . . . and you told me about having sent away some of those who were paying. I ask you again to receive only poor little girls who cannot pay at all. Collect as many of them as you can. If any money was taken from anyone it was, so to speak, against my will. If you have a few who pay send them away immediately. Thus people will say you are not giving instruction out of a spirit of self-interest. Let us not worry, my dear daughter, who is going to feed us. Our good father in heaven will. If what you have in the future is only sufficient for two, the good God will feed the third . . . Goodbye, my three good daughters. Do what I command for the poor little girls. May they be your treasure. (L86:225)

However, these little fee-paying pupils did not go quietly:

> I am not surprised your children caused such a stir over leaving your school. We must bless the good God for it with all our hearts. You must show the mothers it is not self interest keeping you three in Montdidier . . . You have not done it, but Providence has done it for the advantage of the town . . . You remember what I told you at instructions: a manly courage, my children. Oh yes, how much it is needed in the holy service of the good God! . . . let there be nothing low, which smacks of the spirit of the world. I speak of those mean little tricks that are considered fitting to attach people

to ourselves . . . It is for the poor children the good God has sent us to Montdidier. (L87:227–9)

Julie urged the sisters to '[l]ove the unpleasant ones . . . the unattractive ones most; be especially kind to them, and ask Our Lord to show you when you need to be firm . . . you don't catch flies with vinegar, but with honey' (Linscott 1969:52). As for numbers, she would say: 'I absolutely forbid you to think whether children will come to you after making their first Communion . . . If there were only two in your class, you ought to kiss his hand if the good God grants you the grace of being useful to them . . . Let us not listen to the illusions of the demon under the pretext of zeal' (letter of 1811, L259:667).

Her letters continually illustrate this priority throughout her life:

> The demon is very jealous because we deprive him of many victims in these unfortunate little girls who would otherwise be on our streets. (to Françoise: L147:486)

> We have nearly three hundred children in our house: one hundred day [fee-paying] pupils, little ones as well as big ones; and then, the poor, the poor, three classes of them. (from Namur to Sr Anastasie at Jumet, L330:797)

On another occasion, when jealousy was aroused against the work among some of the parishioners, she said: 'Tell them that it is the poor that we want to teach. No one will be jealous of our privilege in that direction' (Linscott 1969:53). Her innate respect for the poor was shown in her deep concern for their 'temporal as well as the spiritual needs' (*Memoirs*, 109): 'My dear good daughter here are two small parcels for our poor women . . . They contain some chemises for them' (from Namur to Sr Julienne at Fleurus, L348:820). Moreover, at Fleurus the Sisters had some of the poorest children of all – the lace-makers: 'The one thing I wish is for our poor children to have a fire in their classroom. You do not tell me how many poor children you have. You know my desire is that you always have fifty at the beginning' (L360:839).

In like manner, at Ghent the children had no decent toilets:

> I have had conveniences made for our poor little girls. I searched every corner of the house so that it would cost less. On Friday I went to the market to buy all kinds of things for locking the doors, which I had made from bits and pieces as well as new wood. For if we had not put on any doors we might as well not have made them. I had a good workman who does anything I want. We understand each other very well. I am very pleased that it is finished. The children were delighted ... Ghent is unrecognisable, everybody is so busy. I hope when all is finished the pupils will come. As the good God wishes – may his most holy will be done! They are getting on with the chapel: one part is erected and very majestic. All the children will assist at mass in the big corridor ... The altar is like those in church. I was told to do it all this way. Here I am again with orders, just as in our house in Namur. (letter of 1811, L148:400)

'Teach them what they need to know for life'

Julie's second major educational principle was, 'Teach them what they need to know for life.' For Julie's 'instruction in Christian doctrine' (L427:965) was by far the 'greatest work on earth' (Linscott 1969:61–77). Secular subjects for her were but 'hooks for catching souls' (L138:372). Moreover, she insisted that these subjects must be trimmed to the needs of the unlettered poor – the three basics of reading, writing and arithmetic. The poor, she said, needed 'bread and butter' subjects and skills for life, not the affected education of the schools for the rich. Hence, she banned the 'dancing' master, and other frivolities, such as embroidery: 'We have destroyed a good big mania; that of embroidering. It is absolutely forbidden under any pretext whatsoever. Our holy Institute is not made for teaching all the wordly things milliners have in their shops today' (L270:689).

Julie's common-sense approach to education was also reflected in the 'good order' and high standards she demanded from her Sisters: 'You must insist on your Sisters not scribbling, for nothing spoils a person's handwriting more than that. There is time for everything' (to Sr Julienne at Fleurus, L370:858). She was a stickler for good order, especially in classrooms, and had no time for laziness. But, above all, she demanded innate respect for the poor: 'after all,' she would often say, 'the souls of the poor are the same as everyone else's.' She showed this consideration on many occasions: 'the little girls whom I forgot by mistake in my last letters: I kiss them so heartily that they must hear it a hundred miles away' (L43:112–13).

The preparation of the teacher

Julie's third great educational principle, without which none of the others would be attainable, was her insistence on the education of her Sisters. 'Study', she said, was 'one of their chief duties'. While Julie taught catechism and spirituality, Françoise taught them grammar, spelling and arithmetic, but 'even these simple requirements were at times remarkable rather for their originality than for conformity to recognised standards, and whenever the Sisters were free from their class studies, they became pupils in their turn' (*Memoirs* 90). Julie also put riders on her concept of academic work, because she feared it could be done for its own sake alone.

The personal qualities of the Sisters were her first concern and, as with Françoise, she quickly became aware of the predominant fault in the Sisters who joined her. The Letters echo with her dealings with peevish, lazy and downright disobedient young women. In all her dealings she was gentle but firm, and on many occasions very forthright. For example, she reprimanded Sister St Jean at St Hubert, the former Marie-Caroline of Montdidier, for being a giggler with another Sister, for she knew it could harm their work: 'Not that I am annoyed about your good humour. I bless the good God for it. But you might find that if your two characters are not restrained, they might soon degenerate into contempt for each other' (L128:344). Julie's correspondence with Sister Anastasie (the former Victoire Leleu, whom Julie called her *petit conseil*) at Jumet showed that she had many troublesome Sisters. Julie found Anastasie needed to be 'a little firmer' (L70:456) with the young Sisters, because they were beginning to lose respect for her. There were others like Luce, who loved penances, which she received 'like children receive sweets' (L170:455), but without giving much time or thought to her real work, the teaching of religion. So Julie suggested that instead of her self-made penances, she be put to making beds; then, she said, 'We shall see how far her virtue goes and what she will complain of in you' (L173:461).

Sister Elizabeth, on the other hand, was peevish, 'the height of womanish behaviour' for Julie (L173:461). Moreover, her character was inflexible, a warning sign that she lacked the spirit of the Institute: 'when the character remains inflexible ... then we must be on our guard' (ibid.). Then there was Sister Angelique who 'would be a little devotee, remaining still as a statue' (L233:607). Julie frequently remarked that 'it is hard work forming young persons in the spirit of our holy Institute ... [but] I bless the good God a thousand times that your little house is going as well as human weakness can make it go' (L234:609).

Julie's model of poverty

Julie's poverty was the model put before Françoise. They were both recognisable in town and country in their cheap dyed cloaks. Françoise's relatives were frequently ashamed to meet her dressed so poorly, and urged her to take more care with her appearance. The Sisters were so poor that they first adapted the clothes they had and 'put their motley garments into a big dyeing tub where they were subjected to a transformation to a colour chosen by Julie, a shade of maroon. Into the process came the rich trousseau of Françoise ... the garments were distributed to all irrespective of person' (SND 1964:60). Julie's and Françoise's personal poverty was apparent to all. Françoise so admired the poverty of Julie she sometimes fell into exaggerations. For example, she insisted on cobbling her own shoes, and once refused to wash for a week to overcome her fastidiousness. She never demanded any special concessions and was adamant that any money or possessions that she had been bequeathed by her father should go to the new Congregation.

There is a further story about Julie's dress in Ghent, when on one occasion a young Sister, called Marie Steenhaut, refused to sit with her in the Cathedral because young boys were laughing at Julie, saying she looked like a witch. Julie did not hear the remarks, but asked the Sister what they were saying. When she heard the words, she laughed heartily. Julie, through her action, taught the young woman a lesson in humility, not to worry about what others thought.

Julie wrote her daily letters with a goose-feathered quill pen that had to be cut every evening. Her own room was never grand, often lacking personal conveniences – for example, the room in which she was living at her death had no fireplace. We have seen how in her illness and the early days of her friendship with Françoise, she never asked the best for herself. Knowing the value of money, she was always careful not to waste anything. Julie also demanded poverty in death: 'we must be poor in death as in life so the burial must be poor' (L318:771).

However, the model of poverty Julie set before her Congregation was not one of destitution. The sisters were to work and earn their own bread, and to share what they had with each other, as well as others:

> Try to plant many potatoes in every place where you are not going to have other vegetables ... Ask your good ladies for a mattress, so that two won't have to sleep on one ... A bed of good straw is very good ... As for your shoes, tell me the right size so that I can have some made that fit. Otherwise there is a risk I will send some that do not fit. That would be against the spirit of poverty. (L394:910)
>
> ... a bottle of wine for four days is very little, especially as you will be in class from morning to night. (L131:351)

Julie knew that work needed good food and health. She always demanded that the sisters looked after themselves, with a prudent care for their health: 'Take good care of your health, without softness, as you well know' she says to Marie-Caroline of Montdidier, in the midst of all her school problems with fee-paying pupils (L86:226). And again to Sr Anastasie as she grappled with the number of young Sisters in her community, she wrote: 'Let us practise what the holy book of *The Imitation of Christ* tells us . . . Whatever may happen to others, let us not neglect ourselves. Above all, well ordered charity begins with oneself' (L440:996). And the question of health was paramount when in the early days many of the houses bordered on destitution, which was never Julie's preference: 'But my good daughter, I ask you for the love of God not to go short of anything necessary. The good God would be very displeased with you' (to Sr Jeanne at Zele, 1813, L245:632).

Julie's happy spirit and air of gaiety pervaded all the work of the Sisters. Her happiness depended on her ensuring that the young women who joined her Congregation, 'the Sisters of Notre Dame de Namur, were given the opportunity to grow in simplicity and trust and to find the same freedom that she enjoyed' (Hughes 1994:400). The effects of Julie's spirit and living this form of poverty were evident: in fact she regarded true gaiety as a proof of the spirit of the Institute. She was free, joyous, utterly dedicated and sincere. To sum up, it was her *liberty of spirit* which enveloped all that she did. She always waited on God for foundations and decisions, even though a temperament like hers would have found waiting naturally irksome. She would often remark that time was a great master but her decisions were made irrespective of human respect and public opinion. She accepted, on one hand, as possible Sisters, poor girls who had been in service and, on the other hand, would refuse candidates whose relatives or clergy put great pressure on her to take them. She held out for day scholars at Namur and always insisted that poor children predominated over fee-paying. In everything she knew when to be adaptable and when to be firm (Linscott 1969:57).

Julie's principles of life and education emerged clearly during these early years. All were to be called Sisters; there was to be no distinction between lay and choir Sisters, as in previous congregations. All goods were to be held in common and those houses with more goods had to share with those who had less. The Sisters were not to live off alms but to work for their living. Education of the poor dominated Julie's horizon, hence all the schools were only to teach what the pupils 'needed for life', but above all Christian doctrine was to be uppermost. Flexibility, courage and hard work were keys to her success. Nothing daunted Julie if it was for her beloved poor. This was the foundation laid by Julie which was later consolidated in the first Rule of 1818 drawn up by Françoise.

Reflections

Julie's understanding of poverty was born out of the needs and understanding of her time. She inherited the concept of Catholic charity where the helping of the poor by the rich was the latter's way to heaven. The French Revolution, on the other hand, was primarily about change of attitude, resulting from an understanding of the structural injustice of the *ancien régime*. But as chapter 1 has pointed out, the ideas of *liberty*, *equality* and *fraternity* never applied to women. It has taken until the latter part of the twentieth century for women to begin to have any real and effective revolution of their own. Gaining the vote was just the beginning.

Julie saw the poor around her and she could identify with their needs. She responded in the only way a woman could, at that time, by teaching or nursing the poor. It was not until the second half of the twentieth century that reflection from the poorer nations on the injustice of the effects of colonisation inflicted on them and control of their economic systems by the richer nations became evident. A great debt is owed to the liberation theologians of the developing countries for giving us all a wake-up call. However, the first generation of liberation theologians, even people such as Gustavo Gutiérrez, failed to analyse the sexist structure of so much poverty. It took organisations such as the Ecumenical Association of Third World Theologians (EATWOT), of women theologians from all continents, to open the eyes of even the most conscientiatised male theologians towards the plight of women.

In the latter part of the twentieth century the women's movement, which had almost gone underground after the initial burst of energy at the beginning of the century to obtain the vote, burst forth, and this time on the theological scene as well. It was influenced by books and films such as *Roots*, which told the story, through the eyes of a black man, of what it was like to be black and to live in a society where the black population were segregated and treated as inferior. The popularity of doing history from the point of view of the victims, the 'underside of history', coupled with the Civil Rights movement of the 1960s in the USA, led to a period of rapid conscientisation in that continent. Women such as Rosemary Radford Ruether were greatly influenced by this movement and their feminist consciences were formed. From the 1960s women began to reflect on their lives and research developed in earnest on the conditions of women's lives. Perhaps the greatest shock of all was the uncovering of the complexity of the multi-faceted causes of female cultural and economic poverty and the theological underpinnings with which it was upheld. So much that was accepted about women was now looked at with a 'hermeneutic of suspicion'. The cosiness of the academic world was shattered: a new breed of women were preparing to challenge some of the dearest long-held assumptions, and these were now found wanting. This second and most crucial phase of the women's movement spread rapidly to all parts of the world.

The philosophical and theological flaws in the formation of Christian theology were gradually revealed. The origins of what is known as 'dualism' were traced back to Aristotle. He took the dualistic opposition between male and female as his starting point, and he used it 'as the model for the relation of form and matter . . . Form is rational and active; matter is irrational and passive' (Garry and Pearsall 1989:56). Thus, far from being an aberration in Aristotle's thought, it became the central way of understanding the difference between men and women. According to Aristotle only the free adult male qualified as a full person, because only he had rational capacity. To him, to be born female was the most common kind of deformity.

This thought was taken into the young Christian tradition and embedded in the theology of the Fathers of the Church. It was articulated clearly and almost unashamedly in the theology of Thomas Aquinas. He wrote that women were 'misbegotten males', whose only function in life for men was as an aid to reproduction, 'since for other activity – work or play – man would better be served by a male helpmate' (Radford Ruether 1974:217). Dualism now became imbedded in all philosophy and theology, and later can even be found in the psychology of Freud and Jung. In brief, women were considered to be the bodily function and men represented the higher intellectual part of life. Women were prone to their emotions and their role was to be passive to the wishes of the man in all spheres of life. The effect of this fault line in inherited philosophy and theology has been enormous. It gets to the root of the unease many women feel with the way the Christian tradition has been interpreted in their lives, and has led to the ambivalent attitude women feel towards the Christian tradition which has both nurtured and wounded them.

This new understanding of theology gave a renewed impetus to the understanding of why theology was so important in any change in women's lives. In the name of God women have been, and still are, starved, battered, raped and denied authority in most Christian denominations and other major religions. Coupled with this, women of all races and creeds have begun to raise the close connection between sexism and the racism that they have experienced in their lives. The women at the 'bottom of the pile' – coloured women – now challenged white women as racist within their analysis of sexism.

This understanding of multiple forms of female deprivation, Julie's 'poor of the most abandoned places', culminated at the end of the twentieth century with the United Nations Conference on Women at Beijing in September 1996 and the World Council of Churches' 'End of the Decade on Women' in Harare, Zimbabwe in November 1998. The people who attended these conferences gave many proofs from their own continents and countries that women still do 'two thirds of the world's work, earn one tenth of the world's income, and own less than one hundredth of the world's property' (United Nations Report 1980). As Elisabeth Schüssler Fiorenza so often has said, 'Until all women are free, no woman is free.' In the next chapter the question of the philosophical and theological underpinnings of women's poverty is developed under the theme of 'scapegoat' theology.

This general shift in perception was codified in general terms in the 1984 Constitutions of the Sisters of Notre Dame de Namur, but a full and informed understanding of the *patriarchal/kyriarchal*, multiple structures and attitudes that keep *structural* poverty in place have still to be lived and worked through:

We work with others
To transform unjust structures and systems
As we participate in creating new ways of relating
Which enable all to experience more fully
The goodness of God. (1984: Cons. 23)

Julie realised the demands of each generation would be different:

This is not only an ordinary Christian life but a supernatural life, spiritual and ecstatic, so that we can love poverty, humiliations and sufferings, living in a world contrary to its maxims . . . no one can live this life unless called by God . . . Moreover, as no ecstasy can be considered true without this transport of action and operation, let us throw ourselves into it, my good Sisters, with all our heart. (*Themes* 59–60)

7

Women of the Cross

'If you live by crosses you will die of love.'
(S.J. Clare ed. and Partridge SND 1909:34)

Julie's life was no life of ease. All the time as she moved around founding new schools for the poor, in all weathers and often in great personal pain, she underwent great misunderstandings from bishops and priests as well as from her own Sisters. It was during this time that Julie came to a full realisation of the meaning of the words she had heard so clearly in her vision at Compiègne: ' "Behold the daughters whom I will give to you in the Institute, which will be marked by my cross", and at that moment there was unrolled before the eyes of her soul the long series of the persecutions of her life' (Clare ed. and Partridge 1909:35–7). As she travelled from place to place opening and closing schools and houses for her Sisters, persecutions dogged Julie every step of the way; to which her only reply was: 'If you live by crosses you will die of love.' Julie's cross took two particular forms. The first was her bitter power struggle with some Church authorities over the governance of her Congregation; the second, which she considered worse, was the criticism of her judgment from some of her Sisters.

The problem is that the cross, as the central Christian symbol, is no longer acceptable to many people, often women, because of the way it has been used to make women the scapegoats for suffering in the world.[1] The mystical tradition has played a major part in overcoming this 'scapegoat syndrome' and has kept alive the understanding of the cross as a life-giving, not death-dealing, symbol, summed up in St Paul's intuitions of equality (Gal. 3:27–8): 'For as many of you as were baptized into Christ have put on Christ. There is neither Jew nor Greek, there is neither slave nor free, there is neither male nor female; for you are all one in Christ'.[2]

Julie's understanding of the cross is part of this crucial retrieval. Moreover, her 'trials' bear a striking resemblance to those of Christ's betrayals – conflict with the religious authorities of her time and opposition from some of her closest friends and disciples, the Sisters. To these troubles Julie's most frequent response was, 'The work of God needs to be tested, so that its foundations may be more solid' (L74:199). Julie's close following of Christ was never clearer than during these times.

The complexity of cross theology

The dominance of the doctrine of atonement, in its various historical interpretations, initially attributed to the twelfth-century St Anselm of Canterbury, has led many women and men to become greatly disillusioned by the cross as the central symbol of Christianity. Anselm's theory of atonement arose from the penal laws of feudalism, summed up in the well-known words *victim*, *sacrifice*, *satisfaction* and *expiation*. This was the means by which the 'wounded honour of God' was to be restored for the sins of the world. Mary Grey, in her book *Redeeming the Dream*, illustrates the many historical variations that this theory underwent in the further radicalisation of this moment of freedom. But she, with many other theologians, starkly concludes that the 'power of the cross has presented the greatest paradox for religious women. Identifying with the sufferings of Jesus on the cross . . . has contributed to women remaining transfixed as a victim and scapegoat of society' (Grey 1989:118). The importance of Grey's theology is her desire to transform the image of the cross from Anselm's negative interpretation of satisfaction for sins and expiation, to a theology of right relations with people and the earth, all of which are fuelled by a 'passion for justice'.

The 'scapegoat' interpretation of the cross has become the

theological/ideological means of keeping women in both subservient and violent situations, often within their homes, making even 'abuse' to be seen as redemptive. Aruna Gnanadason in her two books written for the end of the Decade on Women, 1988–98, of the World Council of Churches, *No Longer A Secret: The church and violence against women* (1997), and *Living Letters to the Churches* (1997), clearly illustrates the worldwide problem of violence against women, whether physical or psychological, and its theological underpinning in all religions. Gnanadason states that one of the most poetic of the Declarations she heard came from the women of the Pacific who met in Apia, Western Samoa, in March 1996. They spoke of what they called the violence 'beneath paradise':

> Strengthened and encouraged by each other and the unconditional love of God, we reached out to each other and shared our painful experiences and stories of the violence against women throughout our Pacific islands.
>
> We heard of the lack of support by governments, churches and the society as a whole for women in violent situations whether at home, in the church or at work or in society . . . We wept for the thousands of women who, because of cultural and religious pressures, have suffered violence silently and alone . . .
>
> We acknowledge that the kind of theology taught by the church not only perpetuates violence against women but often condones it. We listened to the stories of the betrayal of women and children's trust by the clergy through acts of sexual harassment and abuse . . .
>
> We affirmed that we are the survivors of violence and committed ourselves to struggle until justice is done. We listened, we heard, we shared, we struggled, we wept and we prayed . . . (Gnanadason, *No Longer A Secret*, 1997:67)

To this example could be added myriads of others, especially from poor women. The imperative necessity of re-visioning the heart of the Christian message from another perspective is very clear, if women are ever to be lifted out of their acute poverty and achieve a sense of themselves, especially when the idea that 'Christianity is an abusive theology that glorifies suffering' is rapidly gaining ground:

> Christianity has been a primary – in many women's lives *the* primary – force in shaping our acceptance of abuse. The central image of Christ on the cross as the saviour of the world communicates the message that suffering is redemptive . . . Our suffering for others will save the world. The message is complicated further by the theology that says Christ suffered in obedience to the Father's will. Divine child abuse is paraded as salvific and the child who suffers without even raising a voice is lauded as the hope of the world. Those whose lives have been deeply shaped by the Christian tradition feel that self-sacrifice and obedience are not only virtues but the definition of a faithful identity. The promise of resurrection persuades us to endure pain, humiliation and violation of our sacred rights to self-determination, wholeness and freedom. (Carlson Brown and Bohn 1989:26)

The Irruption of the Third World *women*[3]

Although there is no doubt that the interpretation of this theological formula has promoted the dehumanisation of at least half the human race, there is, on the other hand, another story to tell of the cross that the women of the *Living Letters* and other women of colour are telling. It is from these women that I find a richness and a different interpretation of the cross, much more akin to Julie's understanding. The book *Irruption of the Third World* (1983) has given expression to the depth of consciousness of these women to the triple oppressions of sexism, racism and extreme poverty. They are the people at 'the bottom of the pile' who have suffered the worst effects of the world that has become our reality. They understand structural oppression in a way that few white women and men do. From them arises a sense of sin, as alienation from God, neighbour, and/or self, a different way of knowing.[4] The articulations of these women are essential for the development of women's theology.

Their theology is not the analytical theology of the West where the 'European-American experience is taken as the norm' (Townes 1993:8), but it vibrates with the struggles of personal stories, the sermons of famous foremothers, such as Zora Neale Hurston's *The Wounds of Jesus*,[5] and songs such as the negro spirituals. Their theology is *inductive*, from their experience, not *deductive*, from any preconceived theory, and it is not monolithic in voice or tone. These experiences and sources have taken on new meanings. Great sufferings have led them to a spirit of 'outrage' at their condition (ibid.:4). The story of Julie's sufferings needs to be seen in the same light. She did not set out to write anything as grand as a cross theology. Like theirs, Julie's story is deeply inspired by the historical life of Christ and the scriptures. Julie, in like manner, was 'outraged' by the condition of the poor in the France of her time. Her visions were the source of her channelling her 'outrage', her anger in a positive fashion. It was 'the power of anger in the work of love' (Harrison 1985:3–21).

This shared sense of 'outrage' led to a theology of 'resistance to evil' and the cross not as *a* factor but *the* source of their liberation, to another way of living and being. Shawn Copeland in her article 'Wading through Many Sorrows' illustrates through the evidence of the negro spirituals that the slaves understood God 'as the author of freedom, of emancipation' (Townes 1993:120). So a theology of suffering from this perspective is a theology of *resistance*, a theology that remembers and retells the lives and sufferings of those who 'came through' and those who have 'gone on to glory land' (ibid.:123).

In a similar way, Cynthia Crysdale, a white American theologian, in her book *Embracing Travail: Retrieving the Cross Today* (1999), places her experience of the cross as liberative into a similar perspective from the viewpoint of a white woman who has undergone the suffering and joy of childbirth. Birthing, one of the strongest metaphors for the development of any liberative cross theology, is at the basis of so many women's experience. The world is the life-giving, pulsating, 'womb of God'. The cross is the sign of the ever-returning daily struggle of birth and new life – the sign of a compassionate, all-loving, all-forgiving God. This is the God with whom Julie was permeated, exemplified again and again in her continual cry of 'How good is the good God'. A cross of resistance against evil is not easy and in no way takes away the pain or all the fear, but persistency in action comes from a deeply held certainty of the rightness of personal stances and action. I am reminded so much of the impact of the horrors of the Holocaust. In the face of such violence the sheer heroism of so many involved reduces me to the silence of awe.

Julie's cross theology of compassion, resistance and liberation

The retelling of Julie's birthing of her Congregation, against a background of opposition and intrigue, is her story of resistance to the evil of an all-consuming, addictive need, by certain people within the Church, to control her every thought and move. Julie's 'glory land', her place of freedom, was to be Namur, Belgium, where her Congregation at last found a home.

Julie was among the earliest of all the nineteenth-century foundresses who found themselves in deep conflict with Church authorities. Julie is so significant in this area that Jo Ann Kay McNamara in her book *Sisters in Arms* gives her special mention (McNamara 1996:602). The struggle to have a Superior General from their own Congregation was the outstanding characteristic of all the women founders of the nineteenth century (Langlois 1984). This is not surprising as the 1830s were to witness the growing clericalisation of the Church, as we know it today, which was still in its early stages in Julie's time. Two forms of authority began to emerge in the women's congregations in the nineteenth century. The first, most generally accepted and best known up to this time, was a congregation under the direct authority of the local bishop, known as a Diocesan Congregation. Bishops often preferred these congregations, founded for the specific needs of their diocese, over which they had more personal control. However, for many nineteenth-century foundresses, this model of government did not suit the *raison d'être* of their new apostolic congregations, which was to go all over the world – in the words of Julie, to have a heart *'vaste comme le monde'*. They needed to choose a Superior General from among their own Sisters, and keep the ultimate authority over their congregation in their own hands, subject only to the authority of the Pope, thus becoming a Papal Congregation. This desire for a Superior General, to enable the new congregations to spread all over the world, is a striking religious outcome of revolutionary thought. Just as the revolutionaries desired to spread the ideas of the Revolution beyond the borders of France, so too did the many religious congregations that were formed as a direct result of this Revolution, albeit by different means.

A clear founding vision is essential in any new venture and Julie had this in abundance. Her 'good God' had sown the deep conviction in her mind, at Compiègne, that she was called to go 'all over the world'. This was confirmed in a second vision on 2 February 1806, the feast of the Purification, at Amiens:

> . . . while she was singing the words 'lumen ad revelationem gentium', 'a light to the revelation of the Gentiles' (Luke 2:32), her gaze was lifted to the crucifix, she stopped singing and her eyes became fixed on the image of our Lord, who seemed to draw her to himself from the depths of her soul. Light radiated from her countenance and for some time she remained motionless. She would have remained so longer, but just then Madame de Franssu [their great friend] came in. Someone blew out the candle and made a good deal of noise, and an impulsive young Sister threw her arms around her mother, who quietly came to herself and went to her room. (*Memoirs* 211)

Her conviction was later confirmed through the words of the new Bishop de Buoglie of Ghent in April 1809, 'Mère Julie, it is your vocation to go anywhere in the world: you are not made to stay in one diocese' (L114:304). This vision, with that of Compiègne, was clear but the path to its birthing was covered with thorns. She never foresaw her actions but always waited on her 'good God'. Julie's voluntary participation in these sufferings was part of the wider picture of redemption, of 'making right relations here and now' (Grey 1989:89), of turning the world 'rightside up again'.[6] By Julie's death she had founded twelve houses either in France or in present-day Belgium. Three houses, however, were of particular significance in her struggle for the government of her Congregation: Amiens, Namur and Ghent.

Père de Sambucy and Julie's cross of resistance

The major defamation of Julie's character centred on the person of Père Sambucy, but the conflict in the end transcended this two-way conflict. As the story unfolds, it is clear that other clerics, including some bishops, were equally involved. There was, however, a real difference between their actions and that of Sambucy. While others eventually repented of their former judgments, he never sincerely retracted. He was a caricature of the worst form of cleric that a patriarchal church can produce, a young man of great pride and conceit and little discernment. Louis-Etienne Sambucy de Saint Estève was spoken of as a young cleric who was 'enterprising, and absolute in his notions, a man of letters, gifted with a brilliant imagination, but whose character was restless and changeable . . . a lover of the acrobatic, an unquiet genius in constant motion' (*Memoirs* 278). He was trained at the leading seminary in France, St Sulpice, and after his ordination affiliated himself with the Fathers of the Faith where his intellectual gifts gained him quick promotion as a professor at the seminary in Amiens. At this time Père Varin, who was Julie's great friend and adviser from Bettencourt days, was Superior of the Fathers of the Faith, and he appointed Sambucy to the influential role of confessor to the new Congregation. He became a professor at the college of the Faubourg-Noyon in Amiens. Father Varin, the head of the College, named Father Leblanc rector of the College, and ecclesiastical superior

of the Sisters of Notre Dame.[7] At the same time he appointed
Père Sambucy as confessor not only to Julie and her Sisters but
also to the foundress of the Sacred Heart Sisters, Sophie Barat,
later known as Mother Barat. Both foundresses were to suffer
grievously through the power wielded against them by Sambucy.

The 'hardness of heart' of Sambucy (Matt. 13:13–17) was
pitted against the 'purity of heart' of Julie (Matt. 6:22–3). From
the beginning, Sambucy not only considered that he should guide
the drawing up of the Rule of the new Congregation, but took on
the role of the founder, determined that the new Congregation
should bear the marks of his ideas and character, not Julie's. He
had little respect for Julie because of what he considered her
humble origins and lack of education. He did, however, have a
little, but not much more, respect for Françoise, as she was obviously of aristocratic birth and educated in the classical sense.

From their first meeting, he insisted that Julie consult him
over everything, accused her continually of meddling with the
Sisters' consciences, and reprimanded her for presuming to give
the young Sisters spiritual talks. But he was determined above
all that Julie's Congregation should remain only in the diocese
of Amiens and be under the control of the local bishop.
Unknown to Julie, Bishop Demandolx of Amiens was in very
poor health, from a growing brain tumour, and Sambucy used
this weakened state of the Bishop to his full advantage. Hence,
he easily persuaded the Bishop to support him against Julie's
desire to establish her Congregation beyond the diocese of
Amiens. This conflict is so full of details and sudden twists and
turns that it is easier to understand if it is divided according to
its main stages.

Conflict over the Rule and the founding of Namur, 1807–9

'There is something about Namur very dear to my heart.'
(L72:197)

After the founding of her first house for poor children in Amiens,
Julie's fame spread rapidly and she was soon asked to establish

poor schools, not only in Amiens and Montdidier in France, but in the northern part of France, Flanders (modern Belgium). Two bishops in Flanders viewed favourably her desire to establish schools in more than one diocese. Foremost among these was the Bishop of Namur, Bishop Pisani de la Gaude, and the other was the Bishop of Ghent, Bishop de Beaumont.

It was when the Bishop of Namur asked Julie to establish a house in Namur that the conflict initiated by Père Sambucy, and acquiesced in by Bishop Demandolx of Amiens, became clear. Sambucy used the Bishop of Namur's request to gain complete control over the Amiens house. He insisted that Françoise and not Julie should be the Superior of the new house in Namur, in an attempt to weaken their friendship, and that the inheritance of Françoise should not only remain in the diocese but also that he should become its chief executor. Then, in the absence of both women (as Julie accompanied Françoise to Namur), he replaced Julie's appointment as Superior, Sister Anastasie, with his own, a Sister Victoire, who was far too inexperienced for such a position. At the same time he insisted all the Sisters change their names from those Julie had given them. This was accompanied by systematically poisoning the opinion, not only of Bishop Demandolx of Amiens against Julie, but even that of her great friend, Père Varin (who had been so influential in the founding of the Congregation). He did this either in writing or by conversation – by calling Julie a 'gadabout' and a proud, ambitious woman, who was trying to supplant the power of the priests to whom she owed obedience.

After escorting Françoise to Namur, Julie returned to Amiens via Bordeaux and Paris, mostly on foot. In spite of her obvious exhaustion, when Julie stopped in Paris, after a five-day walk and three nights in the stagecoach, she was greeted with coldness and harshness by her mentor, Père Varin, and even by her great friend, Sophie Barat, the foundress of the Sisters of the Sacred Heart.

Although Julie was shocked by these receptions, and became very ill, she never faltered in the belief in her God-given vision for her Congregation. Additionally, the defamation of her character by Sambucy made it very difficult for her to re-enter the Diocese of Amiens. Julie learnt that the situation in the Amiens house had become so impossible under Sister Victoire that Sambucy had been forced to replace her with a Sister from another Order. There was no way he was going to admit he had made a mistake and restore Julie's choice, Sister Anastasie. After staying with a friend for two days, she obtained an interview with the Bishop who, seeing how ill she was, finally allowed her to return to her own house. Julie returned in secret and hid in the top of the house for several days, until the word began to spread that 'Julie had returned'. Françoise said that even now 'Julie blamed everything on her own sins, but I think the devil's anger against our new foundation was really the explanation. I believe at the time there were many evil spirits roaming the house' (*Memoirs* 67). She knew that God's dew fell on the unjust as well as the just, and she waited.

As soon as the Sisters realised Julie had returned they began to visit her secretly, and told her all that had happened in her absence. Pressure began to mount from both the Sisters and the parents of the children in the school for Julie to be reinstated to her former position as Superior of the house. Demandolx's attitude towards Julie was now more favourable and he restored Julie to that position. Père Sambucy thought it prudent to concede to the Bishop's request and he was replaced by Père Cottu as the ecclesiastical superior of the house.

But neither Sister Victoire nor Père Sambucy acquiesced in the situation. Sambucy did not accept that he was not the founder of the Congregation or that he had been removed from the position of ecclesiastical superior of the house. Bishop Demandolx was getting increasingly anxious at the non-resolution of a Rule for the Congregation and forbade Julie to leave the diocese. Julie became a virtual prisoner in her own house, but saw the irony of the situation: 'I do not know whether the good God asks me to remain inactive, when in his great mercy he has been kind enough to give me the use of my feet' (L72:193). Previously she could not return to the diocese; now she was forbidden by the Bishop to leave it.

Françoise had no inkling of what Julie was going through until she received a letter from Julie dated 20 March 1808 (Letter 72). Julie refused to act either as a 'victim' or as the 'victimised'. She blamed no one and kept her own counsel. Julie refers to this time as 'the fogs of the Somme', concluding: 'The good God must have some hidden design in all this, for everything to be so disturbed without reason' (L72:197). 'I am completely submissive to God . . . God alone is necessary for his work, since he has permitted things to be as they are' (L74:203). It was in the darkness of not knowing that she was continually transformed. But Julie had learnt the importance of working through pain with patience, if change was to be effected: 'The good God's time will come; let us adore his divine delays' (L71:189).

Sambucy was now determined to force both women out of the diocese and he pressurised the sick Bishop of Amiens to insist that Julie accept Sambucy's version of the Rule and government of her Congregation – to remain a Diocesan Congregation in Amiens, under the full control of the Bishop (*Memoirs* 62). In desperation, Julie again turned to Père Varin for advice, but he had his own concerns. He was in some turmoil himself, as Napoleon had ordered the suppression of his own Congregation, the Fathers of the Faith, and he insisted that Julie accept the Rule proposed by Sambucy. Françoise spoke of this as

> the peak of the persecution against our mother when bishops and priests, everywhere esteemed for their rank and virtue, held her in contempt and overwhelmed her with abuse – or should we not rather say, offered her to drink of the chalice which God had prepared from all eternity? These persons persisted in their mistaken judgment until very late in the affair; then they had a change of heart. Their dignity and worth oblige us to respect their judgment. (*Memoirs* 30)

For Julie and the 'counter-revolutionary' women of her time the Church was their all-consuming relationship and they believed that '[t]o oppose the Bishop was to revolt against God' (McNamara 1996:607). So when the Bishop summoned Julie to meet him, Françoise, who had returned to Amiens to oversee her inheritance, accompanied her, knowing full well how painful this meeting would be. Françoise said of this interview:

> [I]t was worse than any of the others; the prelate's tones and gestures were so harsh that, though her soul was unshaken, the effects of the shock to her nerves were with her for days afterwards; the bishop's voice kept echoing in her ears. The complaints had centred on Mother Victoire, Julie was making her miserable; Victoire was an angel and Julie was jealous as a tiger; and so on . . . These rebukes lasted a long time, the bishop stamping his foot for emphasis. Mère Julie was too deeply religious not to find a bishop's anger overwhelming. (*Memoirs* 51)

This interview so unnerved Julie that she immediately sought and obtained confirmation from the two bishops who believed in her mission, the Bishops of Namur and Ghent. Julie and Françoise now waited for the final sign from God whether they and the Sisters should leave the diocese. Julie asserted her power from her marginalised position for the sake of her Congregation. She did not acquiesce in the will of the Bishop.

Julie is among those women who have helped redefine the caricature of the Christian virtues of women from those of the passive, silent, subservient, suffering woman. Her actions translate the gifts of the Spirit – forbearance, long-suffering, patience, love, hope and faith – to a new meaning. Women redeem their identity by their active resistance to the sufferings inflicted by the unjust abuse of others. Julie continues to praise her good God throughout all these adversities – 'let us love him with all our hearts' (L80:213). This same spirit is to be found in the sermons of Sojourner Truth, the nineteenth-century black-American freedom fighter.[8] For both women their encounter with Jesus brought such joy and sense of self, that no pain could take it away. They became overwhelmed with praise for the God who had freed them. Their active resistance was their liberation. To live a life guided by the Spirit is to live on the boundaries of change, to live an 'ethic of risk'. Any life such as this 'whether nascent or mature will be counter-culture' (Crysdale 1999:147). The cross is liminal living, living on the threshold of the new.

Dismissal from Amiens and Julie's liberation, 1809

'There is something about Namur which is very dear to my heart, and about a good bishop who is not taken in by anybody, on whose word one can count and who is so zealous for the glory of the good God. Let us be patient, let us be patient, my good friend!' (L72:197)

To the relief of Julie and Françoise, the letter of dismissal finally arrived on the morning of 12 January 1809.

> Bishop Demandolx sent a letter to Julie through Père Cottu, who had signed it as Vicar General. The Bishop informed Julie that since he had rented the house at the Faubourg-Noyon to the Sisters of Notre Dame, and since the foundress was guiding the Sisters in a very different spirit than the one he had expected, that she might leave and go to any Diocese she chose. He, on the other hand would take back the house and form true Sisters of Notre Dame. Julie's heart filled with a sense of gratitude; it was clear to her that God was speaking through this letter and was now pointing the way for her. Père Cottu said she could take any Sisters she chose with her, Julie immediately sent for Françoise, and asked him to repeat what he had said, so that she too heard the permission given for the sisters to leave. (Roseanne Murphy 1995:103)

They were now convinced it was God's will and Julie acted with decisiveness. Namur was to become the centre of the Congregation – the new 'Mother House'. Julie told the Sisters that 'those who love us come with us. But I wish to make it clear that no one is under any obligation. I will accept anyone who wishes to come and I will feel no ill will toward anyone who prefers to remain' (*Memoirs* 72). However, she followed this with the warning 'that anyone who remained in Amiens would no longer be a Sister of Notre Dame' (ibid.:73). Victoire was the only Sister who decided to stay and even she was feeling remorse.

Julie acted with firmness over every detail, and never more so than in the case of Françoise's inheritance, which she had bequeathed to the new Congregation. She wished to take it all with her, and only later conceded to leaving the tabernacle, as well as the ciborium, because it had been the gift of their great friend, Madame de Franssu. Julie did not only have the Sisters to care for, but also her own nephew, Norbert, who was eleven years old. She had promised her brother, Louis, to look after him after her brother's death, as there was no one else to care for him.

Sambucy's response to Julie's action was to intensify his mischief and deceit. First, he persuaded the sick Bishop Demandolx, to renege on his promise that no Sister would be prevented from following Julie to Namur. The test case was that of the high-spirited Sister Ciska who, because she was not under vows, refused to acquiesce in the Bishop's wishes.[9] Secondly, he determined to make the removal of Françoise's inheritance to Namur as difficult as possible. Françoise says of this time:

> No judgement is intended, but the truth is that he often accomplished his ends by roundabout ways and secret means. Even his words were ambiguous, and his remarks were full of implications. In short, his manner of speaking and acting was diametrically opposed to Mère Julie's openness and frankness. Her way was so different that it is very true she found him had to deal with, and although she tried to see things from his point of view, she had never found in him the understanding God gives those who are working together for his glory. Father Sambucy felt the same way. I can only explain this lack of sympathy as part of God's mysterious plan. (*Memoirs* 38)

Julie's last action was to visit all the poor children in the school, although they had no idea she was leaving. On 15 January 1809 she finally left with six Sisters, leaving Françoise behind for the final closure. Julie and Françoise left their native land to establish their Congregation in Namur, a place at last where 'all felt at home, in a new world' (L85:247).

Julie's ability to keep up others' spirits as well as her own, in very difficult times, was almost super-human. The journey to Namur was long and dangerous, and on arriving at her destination Julie soon realised that her troubles were far from over. In fact, they had followed her there. On arriving at Namur she was greeted with coldness by Bishop Pisani and even by Père Minsart, a great supporter and spiritual guide of the Sisters in Namur. The Bishop had received a missive from both Bishop Demandolx and Père Sambucy, restating the case against Julie. Julie sat in silence for two hours and listened to all the allegations against her in these letters, which she said were 'enough to throw me into prison on the spot' (L96:248). But she kept her composure, and then quietly asked the Bishop if he had received Françoise's letter explaining the reasons why they were all leaving Amiens. His disposition visibly changed when he read the letter. He had grown to trust Françoise in a very short time, and as he read the content of the letter he began to understand the amount of damage Sambucy was trying to inflict on Julie and the fledgling congregation, a congregation which, through his recent encounters with Françoise, he had learnt to regard most highly.

The final paragraph on Amiens was not written until September 1812 when Julie received letters from a repentant Bishop Demandolx, asking her to return to his diocese (*Memoirs* 156). In 1811, Père Sambucy had been imprisoned by the Imperial police because of his political activities. He had become an embarrassment to the Bishop, who now saw the error of his ways:

> . . . I wish to see you back in Amiens, to resume the office of superior of the Sisters of Notre Dame in my diocese, from

which you were dismissed through an error of judgment on my part because I relied on a person I thought I could trust. I am wiser now and I do not hesitate to admit that I was deceived in your regard . . . (*Memoirs* 179)

Julie had effected deep changes in the attitude of this bishop and was touched by his letter asking her to return to his diocese. She had no desire for retribution, only the desire of her 'good God' who led her. However, she feared she was only being asked to return because of a rumour that the house was in debt. So it was only after discussion with the Sisters that she decided to return, saying: 'I do not know at all what I am going to do. The good God will show me moment by moment what I have to do' (September 1812, L225:585). Julie returned to the former convent, but, as she entered the courtyard of the Faubourg-Noyon, she heard the words of Christ: '*Look at me and follow me*' (L228:593; *Memoirs* 181). In a letter that was later destroyed at her request, Julie confided to Françoise that she saw Christ carrying his cross *away* from Amiens. It was a vision, she said, that she could not easily forget.

The message of this vision soon became clear. At first, Julie thought all was well in the house at Amiens, but she began to be slightly disturbed when she experienced a stiffness of manner among the Sisters, coupled with irregularity in attending community prayers. Her fear of debt was soon realised. The house at Faubourg-Noyon had become too large for the needs of the fourteen Sisters and their ten boarders. The people were so desperate for the Sisters to stay that offers of gifts of money and even houses were made to Julie. Finally, part of a factory was offered rent free to the Sisters, provided they taught the young women who worked there. When the Count de Rainville offered to buy the house in the Fauborg-Noyon, Julie believed this would pay off the Sisters' debts, and she felt able to leave for Namur. Then all began to go wrong. The factory-owner decided that he could no longer offer the factory rent free and the Count de Rainville withdrew his promise to buy the Faubourg-Noyon. Added to this, the young Superior, Sister Marie, who had been loaned from another Congregation, decided to return to her own Sisters.

Julie took all these reverses as signs from God that the house in Amiens should be closed. Bishop Demandolx agreed as he could not afford to finance the Sisters. The house was finally closed by mutual agreement in January 1813. The same fate awaited the other small houses near Amiens, and by 1816, the year of Julie's death, all connections with France were severed.[10] All these changes were no shock to Julie:

> When Julie was faced with a difficult decision, she did not say, as many do, 'I will think it over, I will see about it.' She used to say 'God will show me what to do when the time comes. She was quick and decisive by nature, yet she had a wonderful patience; she could await God's moment (Memoirs 208)

The struggle for institutional power

Julie was one of those exceptional women who did not allow her creativity to be thwarted by all the devious ways that 'patriarchy' could conjure up. In the struggle for institutional control of her new Congregation she left a legacy for her Sisters to ponder, that 'women cannot feel redeemed, if their only bodily experience is of being *object* within power-dependent relationships, which preclude the possibility of genuine mutual relationships' (Grey 1989:159). Julie left an example of trying to work for relationships of mutuality even with those who opposed her. 'Poor Monsieur de Sambucy to work so hard for the designs of the good God without knowing it . . . My very dear friend, the good God is very good and men are not always good!' (L104:274) Françoise shows similar insight into the behaviour of Père Sambucy:

> All that was said or done against Mère Julie at this time resulted from a long series of mistakes and misunderstandings on the part of persons who were zealous and good, but who

seemed, as it were, *blindfolded*. In cases like this, one can only adore the permissive will of God, without attempting to pass judgment. Besides, God can make use of these errors, inconsistencies, and misjudgments, imprudent words or hasty actions, to carry out his designs. And he readily pardons such things when they do not proceed from malice – as we know these do not. (*Memoirs* 100)

It has already been noted that this continual struggle by women for autonomy, in the governance of their congregations, was reflected over and over again in many of the female congregations of the nineteenth century. In medieval times women were cloistered by the Church, as a means of control. Canon Law to the present day, and the Sacred Congregation for Religious in Rome, continue this long tradition of curtailing the autonomy of religious women, the 'loose' women of the church (Raymond 1991:71–114). These conflicts are a part of the inherited struggle of women to be women against the very dark and subtle psychological forces of what Fiorenza names 'kyriarchy', to signify the multiple oppressions which burden women. Often a generation of women make strides forward, only to become invisible again. Herein lies the importance of our 'foremothers who have broken new paths for women in a hostile and forbidden world' (McNamara 1996:6). They have left 'footprints' for us to follow in. Julie was a part of the widening freedom sought by women of which we are the heirs. Julie's struggle is not ours, but her struggle is now most clearly expressed in the struggle for women priests. Subordinates do not create the conflict; all they do is expose the conflict which is already there.

Women and broken relationships; conflict with the Sisters

Chapter 3 on the friendship between Julie and Françoise revealed women's relationships at their best, echoing the words of Aelred, 'relationships reach their highest among the good'. Conflict between women is one of the most difficult to unravel, as the talk of 'sisterhood' has been so rampant. For me, this tension between Julie and some of her most trusted Sisters is a reminder that just as 'patriarchy exalts motherhood for its own purposes, sisterhood too – despite its egalitarian basis – can be exalted out of all proportions' (Grey 1989:163). The following story of Julie can be multiplied in so many other congregations, male as well as female. Mary Ward is probably one of the best-known examples (Peters 1991). The whole question of the persecution of the 'good' by the 'good' is a continual mystery throughout known history.

No sooner had Julie extricated herself from the débâcle in Amiens and settled in Namur than she was faced with another serious threat to the future of her Congregation. At the centre of the rebellion against Julie were the Sisters at Ghent, led by their Superior, Sister Cathérine Daullée. Those who followed her lead were some of the Sisters who had given Julie the greatest support during her troubles in Amiens, among them Sister Ciska who had spoken so strongly against the desires of the Bishop of Amiens to keep her in his diocese. The roots of their criticism lay in the early days of the foundation of the Congregation. The first was a political controversy, external to the Congregation – the implementation of a *Universal Catechism* by Napoleon in May 1806, when he was at the height of his power. The second arose from a serious misunderstanding of how the tentative Rule of the Congregation should be lived in circumstances which were totally different from that of the Mother House at Namur, where Sisters were first introduced to the Rule.

The *Universal Catechism* of 1806 was a part of Napoleon's grand desire to control the mind and heart of the Church in his bid to establish an Empire which stretched from the Rhône to the Volga. It was a natural corollary of the 1801 Concordat, by which all appointments of bishops and the establishment of any religious community had to be approved by the government. By 1806, he had already conquered Italy and set about re-organising the Italian Church, as he had the French. Napoleon seized the Papal States and declared himself Bishop of Rome. He was immediately excommunicated by the Pope, Pius VII, and in 1809 Rome was annexed to France and the Pope was arrested in the Vatican. He was held in captivity for five years, first in Savona, Italy, and then in Fontainebleau, in France, where Julie visited him in 1813. Napoleon had learnt from the mistakes of the revolutionaries, that without the re-establishment of the Church in France (though under his terms), he would never fulfil his dreams. By 1806 he was strong enough to implement further this control over the hearts and minds of the French. The *Universal Catechism*, which was to be studied in all the classrooms of the Empire, included such questions as: What are the duties toward Napoleon I, our Emperor?

Needless to say this catechism was condemned by the Papacy and Napoleon retaliated by arresting any bishop who opposed it. Among those arrested was Bishop de Buoglie of Ghent. On the other hand, the Bishop of Namur, Bishop Pisani, seemed immune from persecution, partially due to the influence of one of Napoleon's ministers, who was a loyal friend of the Bishop.[11] We learn the final truth of the situation from Françoise, 'that not only did the Bishop of Namur not introduce the Universal Catechism into his Diocese, but it was through his efforts that the government finally gave up the idea of imposing the catechism on his country' (*Memoirs* 212). Julie felt this condemnation of the Sisters so much that she wrote the following to Père Le Surre, Vicar General of the Diocese of Ghent:

> You are aware, Monsieur, of the difficulties which have arisen concerning religious opinion regarding the *Universal Catechism*. M ... has put into the minds of the young Sisters of Ghent some fears that I might be following the views of my Bishop, to whom he attributes suspect opinions. For several years I have been attacked in the most extreme manner about him. I have nothing against my bishop, whom I regard as my superior, and I am not concerned with all these matters. But that is what has turned the gentlemen of Flanders against me. They have managed to prejudice the Sisters in my regard, saying that sooner or later I would be likely to draw them into error. In fact, I have suffered the most violent attacks without giving any occasion for them.

I have turned for counsel to Father Van Schouwenberghe, secretary to the Bishop of Ghent ... And by the grace of God I have done nothing without his advice ... Each time I went to see him, I took Sister Catherine Daullée with me ... On each occasion she was witness to the counsel I received, but being entirely out of sympathy with the Bishop of Namur, she misrepresented, or misquoted ... (*Memoirs* 356)

In spite of the external scandal inflicted on Julie by the Sisters over her support of the Bishop of Namur, it was her final struggle with these same Sisters that challenged the heart and mind of the Congregation for which she had given her life, and threatened to split it. The Sisters were following the Rule of the 'Institute of Mary' and although it was not intended as the final Rule, some of the Sisters, especially in Ghent, did not fully understand its main purpose of introducing the Sisters to the values of religious life, and accused Julie of laxity. Even when Julie reminded them that 'nothing is finally settled as yet' (*Memoirs* 213), they still insisted that every 'jot and tittle' of the Rule should be lived in all the houses, as it was lived in Namur, the Mother House. Julie's liberty of spirit could only insist that the present Rule must be adapted to suit local needs: 'I do not adhere slavishly to a regulation when I see a greater good to be done, because for us nothing is really settled' (*Memoirs* 213).

For Julie, the questioning of her loyalty to the Church by the Sisters was deeply painful, but the questioning of her judgment over her own Congregation, by some of the Sisters who were closest to her, proved devastating. What is more, although Sister Catherine Daullée saw the error of her ways before she died in 1814, others, including Sister Ciska, did not acknowledge their mistake until after the death of Julie. What was even more alarming was that some of the clergy of Ghent wanted to divide the Congregation diocese by diocese, threatening the very government Julie had struggled for so long and hard. It needed the intervention of her great friend and supporter, Bishop Pisani of Namur, to save the Congregation from splitting.

It was these last trials that Julie referred to as 'the bitterest ... of all' (*Memoirs* 215), of which she had been forewarned in her vision at Compiègne:

> Daughter there is still one more trial I must endure ... It was predicted that I [Julie] should be persecuted by bishops, priests and the Sisters. All is not over yet.' Françoise replied, 'No Mother, that can never be. You went through so much at Amiens'. (*Memoirs* 211)

Julie's friendship with Françoise was even more crucial at this time, yet Julie was so disturbed by the betrayal of the Sisters that she even occasionally doubted Françoise's loyalty: 'You are the only one left – you will fail me too, one day – it will come.' But her faithful friend hastily added, 'That day will not come.'[12]

In the last chapter of her *Memoirs*, after Julie's death, Françoise testifies to the greatness of Julie in the following words:

> As I say, her qualities were those of great souls: her heart was filled with zeal, energy, and courage. She was always even tempered, never moody, sad, or constrained ... During the twenty-two years I knew Mère Julie I never saw her lose her peace of soul, never noticed the slightest impatience. She found means of drawing profit from everything; she never acted out of human respect nor did she indulge in resentment or bitterness of heart. She did not permit herself to remember injuries; she put them out of her mind. And yet none of these could be ascribed to weakness ... She was not constrained or ill at ease in the presence of the great; she maintained a liberty of spirit which appeared in her whole manner of speaking and acting. (*Memoirs* 205–9)

Julie died on 8 April 1816 with this conflict between the Sisters and herself unresolved. What is more, these last years of her life were also marked by the tragedies of war fought on French soil. Namur narrowly escaped attack but three houses, Fleurus, Jumet and Gembloux, did not escape the horrors and dangers of being broken into by marauding soldiers. The Sisters' lives were often in danger – Gembloux was entirely ransacked.

Julie died as she had lived for most of her life, an invalid. At her death there were 58 Sisters and 25 young women in formation to become Sisters. It was left to Françoise to guide the growth of the new congregation, in the spirit of Julie, through the next difficult 28 years until her own death at Namur on 8 February 1838. Françoise is now buried next to her beloved friend in the chapel in the garden of Namur, where their tombs can be seen today. Julie was eventually canonised on 22 June 1969, and the street where the house is situated in Namur was later named Rue Julie Billiart.

Reflection on the conflict with the Sisters of Ghent

Women's lives are constructed from a different starting point from men's lives in society. Women have been made the 'carriers' of morality and relationships and their identity has been built on a sense of connection with others. This means they often find dealing with conflict in relationships very difficult and have a tendency to blame themselves for their failure. For some women, even their very self-identity can be damaged. Moreover, society transmits, to a greater or lesser extent, the concept that women's culture and very being is inferior to that of men. And men and women deeply internalise this lesson early in life.[13]

In order for a woman to reach any kind of maturity, she will have to spend much of her life unlearning and unravelling the reasons behind her deep sense of inferiority. In some cases there may result a complete lack of any sense of self. On the other hand, men, who understand themselves as the dominant ones, have to learn to view the world from other perspectives and give up their illusion of a sense of power over others.

Women, therefore, start from a position of being subordinate; Jean Baker Miller, in *Toward a New Psychology of Women*, traces the root cause of conflict between women from this position imposed on them by society. She writes:

> Subordinates (in this case women) absorb á large part of the untruths created by the dominants; there are a great many blacks who feel inferior to whites, and women who still believe they are less important than men. This internalization of dominant beliefs is more likely to occur if there are few alternative concepts to hand ... Within each subordinate group there are tendencies for some members to imitate the dominants. (Baker Miller 1988: 11–12)

In other words, those who feel inferior take it out on their own kind rather than uniting against the structures which are the cause of much of their sense of inferiority. This is just the situation dominants want, whether it is women against women or blacks against blacks, etc.

For me, the suffering of Julie is an example of this more recent understanding of women's sin and why women turn on women. Julie called it 'the devil and his tricks' – in our language, women's 'socialised sin'. Julie had known rejection many a time, but this was the most critical: 'I have suffered the most violent attacks without giving occasion for them' (L340:811). And she wondered how far she was to blame: 'Is it possible to be at fault without realising it?' (*Memoirs* 213). Of this time, Françoise said: 'God willed to draw her closer ... by allowing her to pass through a trial that would wound her heart and bring to perfection all her virtues; it was the last brush stroke of the Divine Artist on a soul that would soon receive the sweet reward of her bitterest trial' (ibid.:215). To say this last trial killed her might be too strong, but it weakened her even further, and '[i]t was impossible to discover whether she wished to live or die' (ibid.:202).

Because women have been made the main bearers of making and maintaining relationships in human society, their sense of failure when these relationships appear to break down is all the greater. Elisabeth Moltmann-Wendel, in *His God and Hers*, sees many parallels to women's experience of the difficulty in accepting and dealing with broken human relationships in the Easter morning flight of the women.[14] The despair of Mary

Magdalene and the other women at the sight of the 'empty tomb' was almost too much to bear – 'they have taken away my Lord and I do not know where they have laid him' (John 20:13). It takes the words of Christ, '*Noli me tangere*', 'Do not touch me' (John 20:17), to awaken Mary Magdalene to the stark reality that not only her relationship with Christ must change but also her relationships with others. Mary Magdalene is now called to, 'Go tell my brethren', and St Augustine was to name her as the 'apostle to the apostles'. Resurrection is a call to change: it is a call to action: it is a call to 'right relation'.

General reflections

The early part of this chapter reflected on the dangers in the historical atonement theories of the cross, and the need to redis-cover and re-frame theologies of the cross which are life-giving for all, especially those which reflect women's positive experi-ences of the cross. However, Linda Hogan in her book *From Women's Experience to Feminist Theology* stresses that women's experience is not the most important just because it is women's experience *per se*, but because

> the experience of oppressed groups may be in a position to have a more complete vision than their oppressors . . . Not because they have 'a priori' access to truth, but because of women's particular location in history . . . the feminist vision is valid, because women (and feminist men) attentive to the voices of marginalized groups, have collected, analysed and critiqued 'in communities of resistance and solidarity'. Because of the values it inspires feminist theology (throughout the world) may claim an ethical priority. Feminists may not claim a universal enduring significance for their vision: how-ever, we do maintain that the commitments central to the feminist vision are foundational to our age.[15]

The cross has no meaning without the resurrection, and the resurrection no meaning without the cross: 'If Christ is not risen then ... your faith is vain' (1 Cor. 15:14). So no reclamation of cross theology by women is complete without the re-proclamation of the Mary Magdalene tradition of the resurrection and the 'empty tomb'. In the latter part of the twentieth century this tradition assumed much greater importance. As Fiorenza writes, the road to Galilee is open:

> In sum, the imaginative space of the empty tomb leads to the proclamation of Jesus as the Resurrected One who has been vindicated. The Living One can only be found when we experience that he 'is ahead of us' and that he opens up the future for us. Christian Testament sources ascribe the proclamation of this 'revelatory' experience and the future-orientated empty tomb message primarily to women. (Fiorenza 1994:123)

She names two early traditions of the resurrection, one based on the experience of the women at 'the empty tomb', the other on the male 'visionary experience' in 1 Corinthians 15:3–8:

> For I handed on to you as of first importance what I had received: that Christ had died for our sins in accordance with the scriptures, and that he was buried, and that he rose again on the third day in accordance with the scriptures, and that he appeared to Cephas, then to the twelve. Then he appeared to more than five hundred brothers at one time, most of whom are still alive, though some have died. Then he appeared to James, then to all the apostles. Last of all, as to one untimely born, he appeared also to me.

This second tradition, where not one woman is named, became the dominant tradition and was used to legitimate male authority (Fiorenza 1994:123–8). Moreover, Fiorenza disagrees with a large number of feminist theologians and maintains it is futile to try to reclaim the atonement theories of the past, as they are all patriarchally/kyriarchally based (ibid.:50–7). That is why she believes we have to go right back to the earliest pre-Biblical sources.

Julie's understanding of the cross, as one of birthing freedom, means she hangs in the tension of living in 'liminal', threshold, space, between the death of the old and the coming of the new. In this way she has left a very rich cross heritage to the Sisters who have followed her. Women theologians, black and white, taking women's experience as their primary tool of interpretation, now understand the cross as Christ in solidarity with the suffering of all humanity, rather than the image of Christ suffering alone for individual sins. This is beautifully illustrated in *Struggle to be the Sun Again* by the Korean theologian Chung Hyun Kyung. She writes from the 'broken bodies' of Asian women, from the spirit of the *han*, the spirit of those who have suffered so much: 'Asian women are discovering with much passion and compassion that Jesus takes sides with the silenced Asian women in his solidarity with all oppressed people. This Jesus is Asian women's new lover, comrade and suffering servant' (Chung 1990:56).

The cross, therefore, is now beginning to be understood not as a ransom, to give satisfaction to an angry God who demands expiation for the sins of the world, like a demanding child, but as the inevitable result of working to eradicate the multiple oppressions imposed by unjust patriarchal attitudes. These are given structural form in state and church, and made to appear as right and inevitable. In the twentieth century the name given this form of sin was 'structural sin', or *kyriarchy*, as Fiorenza prefers to call it: 'Social-political causes . . . the *kyriarchal* paradigm that underlines all scripture' (Fiorenza 1994:106). Sally Purvis in *The Power of the Cross* sums up the developing understanding of the life-giving reality of the cross as 'not primarily a cry of pain, though that is not silenced, but the exuberance of life as it breaks free from control and violence it has confronted and moved through' (Purvis 1993:92).

Womanist and feminist theologians have searched for terms to illustrate their understanding of the joy of this freedom. They have come up with words which initially shock, when used to evoke God's actions. Audre Lorde was the first to speak of the 'erotic' power of the cross, not to be understood in any pornographic way, but as a term rich in meaning for our need to touch and be touched by one another.[16] The French writer Julia Kristeva uses the gender-exclusive metaphor *jouissance* for the joy of the cross.[17] Both concepts evoke the spontaneity of God, the power of the touch of God, the unpredictability of God, which leaves us with the responsibility to live 'into the power of God . . . the power to enhance one another' (Purvis 1993:43).

For Julie, her Christ was her co-sufferer for justice. She overcame the 'power of control' of the worst forms of patriarchy. She refused the stifling of the Spirit attempted by Sambucy and colluded in, for a time, by others. Instead, she substituted the exuberance, the eroticism, of the 'power of life'. Julie's theology of grace was grounded in 'an ethic of risk lest grace be robbed of its very nature of gift' (Crysdale 1999:135). She was one of those women who could discern and act against inauthentic authority, whether it was with Church leaders or her Sisters. Julie knew, instinctively, both in her dealings with the Church and her Sisters, that 'an ethic of control necessarily ends in coercion . . . and the resolution of evil leaves human freedom intact' (ibid.). Her struggle for the form of government suitable for her new Congregation demanded all the courage she could muster. But it was the misunderstanding of her charism and the breakdown in relationships with some of her most trusted Sisters which nearly destroyed her.

Julie's message of compassion, resistance and liberation was only possible because of her refusal to be made a victim, rooted in her profound friendship with her God. For her the 'power of life' is always dominant even in the midst of the greatest sufferings. It is the transformation of the '*Christus Victor*' symbol of Jesus as innocent lamb, delivered up to slaughter for a ransom payment, to a metaphor based on the image of 'new birth' (Grey 1989:75). Mary Grey relates this new life to a 'theology of right relations', of 'claiming power-in-relation' and a 'theology of connection', with people and the earth, all of which are fuelled by a 'passion for justice'. The resurrection is not simply the survival of the soul but the 'transformation of the world as we know it' (Fiorenza 1994:121). Liberation means not just self-liberation but an ethic of protest. Julie's charism was born out of protest and it reached its zenith in her anger at the poverty that raged around her. But her anger was channelled into the life-giving powers of the resurrection, the *viriditas*, the 'greening', of Hildegard of Bingen.

> God of all our growing,
> take our roots down deep
> in the long, dark winter season
> of our grief.
> Nurture the resurrection life in us,
> in the secret places of the soil
> in the barren, frozen earth, underground,
> where no eye can see.
> Send your Spirit where the cold season rages
> And speak to us of the promise of spring.[18]

8

Women on the Threshold of Change

'A small group can change the world, in fact that is all that ever did.'[1]

This book has tried, through placing Julie Billiart's spirituality in the historical context of the French Revolution and Napoleonic times, to present a rounded picture of the structure and depth of her spirituality: a spirituality born out of her vision of protest and awakening, rooted in friendship, the cross, and the poor, and permeated by her spirit of contemplative prayer, her charism, 'the liberty of the children of God'. Julie's spirituality was greatly influenced by the classical tradition of the seventeenth-century French School of spirituality, which was transformed into a new synthesis from her own experience. And her letters, her mystical text, have relevance for all times. Her charism and understanding of the cross have the power to weave deftly, not the devastation of the 'power of control', but the life-giving possibilities of the 'power of life'. In order to understand the importance for religious to live on the threshold of change, a brief critical historical survey helps to put the present-day problems of religious life into perspective.

Reflections on the historical development of the Congregation

In July 1994, Dr Susan O'Brien gave a paper to a meeting of the British Sisters of Notre Dame de Namur entitled 'Women Religious; Historical Past – Future Perspective'. In the light of her analysis of women's congregations in general, I want to reflect on the growth of the work of Julie's Congregation from a four-phase historical perspective. This reflection includes highlighting both the strengths and weaknesses of each phase, from the founding of the Congregation to the dawn of the twenty-first century.

1800–1914

This the longest phase of all and there is a very close similarity between the findings of Dr O'Brien for this period in general and the experience of the growing Congregation that Julie left behind. O'Brien highlights four specific characteristics: innovation, risk-taking, optimism and confidence. It was a time of establishing large-scale institutions and building from scratch. And the Victorians, 'far from being solid bastions of security and stability . . . were risk-takers' (O'Brien 1994:9). In fact: 'The speed with which such institutions were created is a source of some astonishment to us in the late twentieth century' (O'Brien 1994:10).

O'Brien goes on to say the religious sisters were on the cutting edge of change till about the middle 1850s. That is, 'They were ahead of their society, or at least among the movers and the shakers in a number of key ways' (O'Brien 1994:11). However, she argues that by the end of the nineteenth century it is far harder to see 'that religious congregations were keeping pace with the changes in society, or that they were at the cutting edge in serving the poor or meeting the needs of women' (ibid.). They were not part of the foci of the action for change, especially in women's lives, such as the fight for the vote; or alongside Josephine Butler in her successful struggle for the repeal of the Contagious Diseases Act, in the second half of the nineteenth century. There was 'a distinct shift taking place towards collective action by the marginalised themselves in which women religious were not taking part, either overtly or even covertly'.[2]

It was with one of the foremost members of the British Province of the Sisters of Notre Dame de Namur that the first public signs of the Sisters' lack of involvement in the political affairs of women surface. Sister Mary St Philip, a distinguished educationalist and first principal of the Training College, at Mount

Pleasant, Liverpool, gave the following advice to students before leaving Mount Pleasant College: 'Never distinguish yourself as a woman who is perpetually standing up for her rights. Be womanly not womanish' (ibid.:11). And these were words from a formidable educationalist, an outstanding instance of the pioneering individual Victorian woman, described by the Chief Secretary of the Education Department as 'a woman who might fearlessly put her hand on the helm of State'.

The attitude of Sister Mary St Philip illustrates Dr O'Brien's crucial insight, that 'women religious operated in what the Victorians called the "public sphere", which was normally seen as a male prerogative, but they did so without political consciousness and without taking a public or political position in matters of church or state' (ibid.:7). The inability to develop a more critical public stance on women's concerns was to have serious repercussions on the development of understanding of the 'signs of the time' in the Congregation in the latter part of the twentieth century. O'Brien also concludes that: 'Perhaps it is the absence of any clear positive lead from the congregations on the questions raised by the "woman question" that has led to the neglect of their contribution to female education in the histories of education in Britain' (ibid.:11). It took until the second half of the twentieth century for secular historians, such as Olwen Hufton, to begin to retrieve the crucial role these women played in the education of a large percentage of women and some men of the nineteenth and twentieth centuries.

However, the seriousness of this inherited weakness did not impede the growth of the Congregation. Notre Dame, like so many of the Superior General Congregations, spread rapidly to other parts of the world. The tales of the daring and courage of the early Sisters of Notre Dame are legendary, and their hardships equalled Julie's. They were certainly women of courage. This adventurous spirit took them first to the USA (1840), then to Britain (1852), and by the end of the century to Africa. The first openings were in 'the Congo in 1894, then came Rhodesia 1899, and an invitation to South Africa not long afterwards' (Linscott 1966:65). They were the willing cheap labour of the state in a growing industrialised world. Geographical spread into primary and secondary schools was not the only aim; the education of teachers was always to the fore, since the days of their early foundations. This enterprise was soon followed by the establishment of a further college in Scotland, as well as the establishment of child guidance clinics in Scotland and London. A similar, equally successful pattern of a three-fold system of education was established in the USA. Nuns founded 30 per cent of women's colleges in the USA (McNamara 1996:620).

1914–1965

For the Roman Catholic Church, this period was one of a profound rejection of modernism and an attempt to shield Catholics from anything that was new. The new Code of Canon Law (1917) left little room for individual charisms or creativity. The totalising and stifling hold of the Ultramontane Church took hold. Catholicism during this time had a sense of timelessness about it; it was solid, sure and self-contained. Catholics had created their own spiritual state equivalent to the secular state to meet what they perceived to be their spiritual needs. After a period of pioneering, perhaps a period of institutionalisation was inevitable. This was the time that these congregations became 'respectable', but much good work was accomplished and the foundations were laid for the growth of an educated Catholic female laity, for the second half of the century. During this period of consolidation the Sisters numbered well over 5,000, while missionary activity continued; the Sisters expanded into Japan in 1924, Nigeria in 1963 and Kenya in 1965. However, 'religious congregations (male and female) ceased to see themselves as missionaries when they were in the West and saw mission as something specialised that happened overseas' (O'Brien 1994:12).

Vocations were ample until the 1960s, but then the rapid growth and success of state education, at least in the West, began to take its toll on the religious orders. The success of the congregations can be measured in the degree of self-confidence they gave to many women through their education and the important positions many of these women gained in their professional lives. It was during the latter part of this period that I joined the Congregation: a time when all the schools and colleges were flourishing and the inherited vision of formal education at all levels, as the main work of the Congregation, was in the ascendant.

1965–1990

This third period is the shortest and the most difficult to analyse. The post-war generations seemed to question everything, in contrast to the acceptance of the previous two generations. The rejection of formal orthodoxies began and there was a new emphasis on personal fulfilment. In the RC Church also, change was happening. John XXIII threw open the doors and windows of the Church in calling the Second Vatican Council, and proclaimed in *Pacem in Terris* (1963) that 'those who have rights must claim them' (par. 36:17). The concepts of Liberation Theology and structural economic injustice now entered the vocabulary of the Christian. These insights began to release the theological ability and energy of women and it was in the 1960s that a theological education at university became possible for more women. The insights of Liberation Theology also affected the thinking of the Sisters of Notre Dame and the 1970s witnessed their expansion into South Africa – Peru, Brazil, Nicaragua and Mexico.

For religious congregations O'Brien cites 'de-institutionalisation' as the characteristic of this period, at least in the affluent Western world. If the decline in numbers of those who joined was dramatic, equally dramatic was the number of those who left. The withdrawal from, or handing over into secular hands of, the well-established schools was a matter rather of pragmatism, than the desire of the sisters. O'Brien names this as a time of 'slimming down'. The closure of large convents where community life was obvious gave way to sisters living in smaller houses, or even alone, for reasons of ministry. The concept of community also had to be rethought, accompanied by new forms of leadership more relevant for small group living and a growing mixture of ministries. Most congregations will recognise this period as a time of 'position papers' and meetings, which took a long time with seemingly little effect. In spite of this gradual change in mentality and the more obvious signs of change, such as the removal of the veil and religious 'habit' for most female congregations – and, I would add, male congregations – many of these changes proved difficult to assimilate.

1990–2000: a call to prophetic/critical ministry

O'Brien believes that the future lies in the realm of

> ideas (not production), of information and service (not production) and in the application of intelligence (not materials). The realms might therefore now be theological and spiritual education and leadership, political action and all that goes with giving informed and intelligent voice to the marginalised and powerless. Above all, giving the prophetic voice. (O'Brien 1994:14)

The women's movement, both secular and religious, has led the way in this area, a movement that gathered tremendous momentum after the 1960s. Theologically, there was a great outpouring of first-generation feminist theology and later the theology of women of colour. The driving force of this change of thought came initially from Roman Catholic women, a direct corollary of the vision of Vatican II. Mary Daly, in her book *The Church and the Second Sex* first published in 1968, gave the first full critique of the patriarchal tradition of the Church. The growing realisation of the dominance of male experience and structures in the Roman Catholic Church was strongest among some women in the USA and Canada in the 1970s. It was not until the early 1980s that much of this thought began to influence the wider world, including Britain, in any profound way.[3]

In spite of great efforts being made, the re-education into a renewed understanding of both theology and church from a feminist and womanist perspective has proved difficult. Sisters were attracted and trained in these congregations for another age and time. The inability to grasp the depth of change in theological thought that is required is, in my opinion, holding back the present life and future growth of religious congregations. In striking contrast, the latter part of the twentieth century experienced a great growth of women's critical organisations throughout the world. In the Christian world, organisations based on the growth of women's theological insights began to reclaim the prophetic/critical ministry of Christ for a new age. They moved to the cutting edge of change and often in the most difficult place of all, their churches. The members of these organisations relearnt the meaning of being boundary, marginalised or liminal people (see below).[4] It is almost as though the Spirit, from the 1970s onwards, had to move outside these congregations in order to break through in a different way. Langlois was not wrong when he said the nineteenth-century congregations were 'in parenthesis' (1984:648) between the cloistered woman religious and the coming of the lay woman.

Women on the threshold of change

As stated in the introduction, my experiences in the women's movement, far from drawing me away from Julie's spirituality, have led me into the heart of the transforming power that lies within it. It was an intuitive living out of Julie's spirituality which enabled me to make the transition from patriarchal Christianity to Christian feminism. The past has not had to be jettisoned for the present or for the future. It has enabled me to stay with the chaos and make some sense of it. Protest takes on many forms at different times, giving rise to visions of a better future. My experience has taught me that it is out of protest and awakening that a deeper consciousness is reached, and a new, shared vision is arising out of renewed theological reflection on the collective experience of the poor, especially the experience of poor women. Time has not changed my commitment, it has only shaped it differently.

During the writing of this book the reasons why I have stayed in religious life have become clearer to me. Others have given me the words and ideas around which to express my experienced new reality, especially the writers Diarmuid O'Murchu, in his *Reframing Religious Life* (1995), and Desmond Murphy, in his *Death and Rebirth of Religious Life* (1995). Now I would like to explore further two of their concepts: *liminality* and *value radiation*.

Towards a renewed spirituality of 'prophetic liminality' and 'value radiation'

'Liminal' comes from the Latin word *limen* meaning 'threshold' and refers to experiences of marginality, or being at the frontier. Reference has been made, in chapter 1, 'Women of Protest', to the fact that the 'counter-revolutionary' women were boundary or marginal people. Those who take a stance of public protest become marginalised or liminal persons. Diarmuid O'Murchu explains and then reflects on this concept of liminality. However, the deeper meaning of liminality is a 'subconscious drive for wholeness, for completeness, for tangible connection with the Originating Mystery ... whether we consciously acknowledge it or not. It is an inner orientation of the human spirit, that defies logical or rational explanation' (O'Murchu 1995:48). The cross is, therefore, a liminal symbol: the tension between the death of the old and the coming of the new.

He explains that the call to *liminality*, being at the cutting edge of change, is a way of life older than Christianity itself. Through the vowed life (in all religions) people in general seek to explore and articulate 'those deeper universal values to which we all aspire' (O'Murchu 1995:49). These groupings then become the official 'value radiation' centres of liminality. They should radiate the values which society is in danger of losing, or is unaware that it needs, or is frightened to embrace for fear of losing human respect. In each generation the needs will be different. God works through human means and liminars are called out by the people, rather than from within the liminar herself/himself, to live intensely the higher values of life.

Liminality and value radiation are always at work in every age and in all religions and cultures. In fact, the origin of this call to liminality and the values which it radiates is much older than Christianity itself.

People with the gift of liminality become centres of 'value radiation', both personally and communally. Julie and Françoise and their new Congregation were amongst the liminal people of their time, who radiated the values the society of their time needed but neglected – to work for the education of the very poor, especially women, and teach them to be articulate about their beliefs. But what does it mean to be a liminal, boundary person? What does it mean to be a person who radiates the lost values of one's period?

Who and where is the liminality for the twenty-first century?

'What happens when the official liminars, the orders and congregations, fail in their task?' asks O'Murchu. He concludes that most religious, because of their domestication by the institutional church, are no longer fulfilling their liminal and value radiation role in an appropriate way. Over the years their very successes have made them lose sight of their liminal origins, and unable to acquire the knowledge and experience of being on the cutting edge of change. Others, therefore, have been called out by the community to fulfil this task. O'Murchu cites alternative movements with liminal qualities which have arisen in the twentieth century, such as Greenpeace, holistic health movements, alternative technologies, workers' co-operatives, base communities, attempts at ethical investment, attempts at discerning alternative socio-economic and political strategies as an alternative conscience for the planet, anti-racist groups, lesbian and gay groups, but above all, ecological and feminist groups (O'Murchu 1995:53–4).

My experience has taught me that the accelerated rise of the women's movement has been the most radical and all-round source for change in the twentieth century and will be in the twenty-first. It is because it demands such a fundamental and radical shift in the way reality has been constructed, that ideas arising out of women's experience receive so much opposition. This shift in reality encompasses all the above new liminal movements. It is called a paradigm shift of ideas. Theology uses the phase *paradigm shift* for this seismic shift in ways of thinking, believing, and acting. The word *paradigm* is taken from the scientific definition of Thomas S. Kuhn, which is 'an entire constellation of beliefs, values, techniques and so forth shared by the members of a given community' (Küng 1995:60). A 'macro-paradigm', i.e. a major paradigm shift, is the replacement of a previous one in every area of life (ibid.:111). These shifts take a long time to mature and they are made up of previous minor shifts. The new paradigm always carries certain elements of the previous paradigm with it.[5] This non-violent revolution will take far longer than other revolutions, as it is not tangible as were the agrarian and industrial revolutions, but there is not a single aspect of our lives that is not being or will not be touched by it. It is a crucial part of the development of the fullness of Christianity. A Christian identity, framed from a feminist and womanist perspective, will be very different from the present Christian identity framed from a patriarchal/kyriarchal mindset. And so too will any future form of religious life.

This is why I am moving to the belief that the first and perhaps most relevant vow a person who has a religious vocation should take is a vow to live a life of liminality and all that implies. I would rename this form of life *a call to liminality*. The signs are that this new way of being may not be for life and may not necessarily entail being celibate. The taking of the three vows of chastity, poverty and obedience would depend on the individual calling of each person. In this way, the Holy Spirit is opening out the former understanding of religious life to a much larger and more diverse group of people, and membership will probably be ecumenical.[6]

My experience of the marked differences between many religious congregations and women's groups worldwide very much resonates with that of O'Murchu. Through a study of the spirituality of Julie, I can now begin to articulate the reason for my eventual unease and dissatisfaction with the life to which I was strongly called. In other words, through close working with other unexpected liminars, I have found my true vocation as a religious, not in the place where I had formerly looked, but unexpectedly, at Greenham Common, through feminist theology and spirituality and in the women's movement in general.

Spirituality for active threshold/liminal living: Women-Church

Rosemary Radford Ruether's book *Women-Church, Theology and Practice* (1985), is about liminal church among Christian people – women and men.[7] Women-Church is not easy to define because it is not a new church, but represents a transitional stage between the old forms of institutional church and the coming of the new. Many people who participate in these groups are members of different churches, while others have left their churches altogether. These groups are essentially networks for those who are no longer nourished either sufficiently or at all by their churches. The aim is not to set up a new church, but to point the way to change in the Christian tradition, particularly to the full inclusion of women in a changed form of ministry. They are always ecumenical in composition and a great emphasis is placed on reclaiming theology and experimenting with new liturgies. Community, both local and international, especially the poor, is at the centre of their *raison d'être* (Radford Ruether 1985).[8] One of the major functions of Women-Church is to create communities to resist present gender roles and to create new ones. It is perhaps significant to note that Victoria Erikson's vision for further studies in the area of gender, in her book, *Where Silence Speaks: Feminism, Social Theory and Religion,* recommends

> small-scale detailed studies of women's religious groups, such as *Women-Church* communities, in order to discern how they are resisting and recreating gender roles. Erikson focuses on

new women-centred rituals which seek to break out of the inherited repression of women's experiences, a tradition which denies them the right to be considered *holy*, and which represent liberative practices that re-sacralize women's lives. (Erikson 1993:230)

A Final Reflection: the feminist/womanist paradigm shift

Hans Küng, in his book, *Christianity: The Religious Situation of Our Time* (1995), divides the history of Christianity into six major shifts, finishing with the 'Contemporary Ecumenical' paradigm. I believe all these previous paradigms were paradigmatic variations of a patriarchal/kyriarchal culture, and that the present age is in transition to a totally new non-patriarchal culture. This is why people are losing their familiar footholds and there often seems to be no ground under their feet; all previous value systems seem to be shifting. The value systems of a small percentage of predominantly white men are no longer considered the dominant norm. Others, men and women of all races and cultures, are claiming their place in the world on an equal basis, and the values of the old system no longer feel comfortable nor fit.

I do not leave religious life because my understanding now of my vocation as a call to liminality through the charism of Julie enables me to attempt to be a bridge-builder between the former liminal group and the new. This is a difficult time of transition, and blame should not be laid at anyone's door. Many of the former official liminars are trying to adapt to the new. The call in many of these congregations for a new shared vision, as the former vision dwindles, is a sign they have lost sight of the original call to liminality. Liminality can no longer be contained in one way of life, as before. As the new liminars, in their diverse hues, begin to realise the importance of their calling, they too need the help and the wisdom of those who have gone before them. I see the process as two-way. There is much in the 'official liminars'' spirituality, when it is eased out of its narrow casing of religious life and the language of a former time, which can and should be transmitted to the developing and experimental spirituality of the new liminal groups of the present day. The former liminars need the energy, the dynamism, the daring, the thirst for justice, which newer groups have. They can relearn the power of vision from them.

The challenge for all liminal groups is to be willing to learn from and listen to each other without fear. The former official liminars have a long if unrealised history of liminality in their founders, while the latter, those called to challenge in a different and more provocative way, need to learn to integrate the best of the past with the best of the new. This age above all is an era of discernment. There are few old paths to follow. It is clear that the task of the prophetic liminal group is to concentrate not on social structure but on social change – that is, a deep radical change of attitudes. These groups pose a threat to the order and stability of the status quo, and are generally disturbing to mainstream culture. Attitudinal change, as Julie learnt in her struggle with the Church, was by far the hardest to implement.

A full living out of the charism and structure of Julie's spirituality leads inevitably to a return to the value system of liminality. Julie and Françoise were liminal people and in the nineteenth century, as today, the majority of these groups were female. The spirituality of Julie and Françoise arose out of circumstances of protest. Their liminality was deeply embedded in finding an answer to the 'social question' – i.e. the direct needs of the poor. Julie and Françoise chose education as their main tool and they exercised their liminality in a very real and effective manner. This response lasted until the middle of the twentieth century. Today the 'social question' without deeper analysis is no longer enough. Embedded within all poverty are capitalism, racism, sexism, classism and homophobia. These 'isms' in fact pervade all societies and regularly reinvent themselves not only in the state but in all religions.

Liminality for Julie and Françoise was a liminality dictated by the possibilities of their time and gender. Any form of deep change for justice evokes response, and the negative response generally predominates in the initial stages. For the dominant group it is a response of fear – fear of losing control, fear of power slipping away. Liminal groups of counter-culture are feared because the power of the shadow sides of our nature is feared. In Christianity, the conflict of the Cross will remain central to any new attitudinal change. The raising of awareness or 'conscientisation' is difficult and it is generally done by the few for the sake of the many. This was always the role of liminal groups.

No one can live this life of liminality who has not responded to a variation of Julie's request to Françoise: 'So you do not yet want to be good for nothing, to allow God to be glorified by others? You do not yet see yourself fit for that, my good friend? Well then let us await God's own good time' (L4:28). None of us can avoid this 'dark night', this sense of loss of control, personally and communally. In spite of continual backlash from those who fear or resist change, the Spirit will always call some people to be the 'salt of the earth' – to the vocation of liminality. But it is the power of the Resurrected One who will ensure shifts to new ways of being and acting. The lives of Julie and Françoise serve to illustrate this. The history of the Congregation shows that other forms of liminality will be necessary, and the call for any major shift will always be heralded by individual and communal descent into the chaos of the 'dark night':

> I have only time enough to tell you that the good God is very good ... Ah! Work, work at fitting yourselves for the great labour to which the good God calls you. We do not know the value of it until the good God puts us to the task, but we must prepare ourselves well beforehand. (L50:133)

> What expressions I use to wish you a happy New Year ... death to ourselves, utter renunciation ... we may advance on the royal road of the cross. (L13:52)

'Ah, qu'il est bon le Bon Dieu'

Appendix 1

The 'structural dynamic' approach to mystical texts

Introduction

Over thirty years ago the Titus Brandsma Carmelite Institute of Spirituality (TBI) in the University of Nijmegen, Holland began to research a very particular methodology for reading and understanding spiritual texts, called the 'structural dynamic' approach. The TBI claims that this methodology is particularly beneficial to many religious congregations, who are often not clear what their charism (special gift) is because

> the second generation of their people tried to work the original charism into a system or routine – a simplified form – to make it more applicable. These interpretations led to distortion and falsification of the texts; the dynamic structure of the spiritual and mystical processes had only been recognised fragmentarily ... All this ... reduced the text to one convenient aspect. (TBI Research Programme 1989:17)

Spirituality is a process of transformation. The 'structural dynamic' approach to spirituality is developing conceptual tools to make possible a longitudinal (diachronic) interpretation which arises out of a (synchronic) cross-section study of the spirituality, to make the dynamic structure of the spirituality visible.

'Structural dynamic' methodology

The problem in any study of spirituality is how to express the experience of the transcendent in a rational way. The strength of the concept of 'structuralism', applied to a mystical text, is that it counteracts distortion of a spirituality. Structuralism is concerned with the phenomenon of the whole outside of which the individual parts have no meaning. Every classical spirituality which has stood the test of time can be said to have an 'inner logic' of its own, its own particular structure, and without that structure it would cease to be that particular form of spirituality.

The metaphor used by the TBI to explain this structure is the architecture of the medieval Gothic churches: 'It does not only consist of pointed arches, crossed vaults and multicoloured stained glass. On the contrary, these characteristics and forms give expression to a particular spirit. It is this spirit that defines the *entirety* of a cathedral or other forms of art' (Waaijman 1991:26). Take away the specific building structure of these buildings and they would no longer be Gothic. In a similar way each spirituality has its own structure and style.

An interdisciplinary approach is necessary to determine this 'inner logic'. For example, tracing through a certain theme in a spirituality is useful, but only when its part within the whole is understood. All spiritualities are transformed by experience and in this way the action of God dynamises the structure, through the person or the group concerned. The structure remains the same but it is transformed by new experiences and cultures. This is called a diachronic (longitudinal) shift.

It was this methodology that enabled me to uncover the charism of Julie Billiart and the unique structure of her spirituality. It is the mystical element that dynamises that structure which enables it to live on in different ages, times and circumstances. I began this search by applying the following methodology to some of Julie's letters. In the process I unearthed the essence of her charism, her special gift, out of which all her spirituality flowed – the *liberty of the children of God*. All led to it and all led from it. It was a charism which could only be lived to the full in a state of continual contemplative prayer.

The important thing about the 'structural dynamic' approach is that it enables the spirituality to be understood as a whole. In this way a religious congregation can rediscover its unique spirit – its charism. It enables all the pieces of the jigsaw to fit together. For example, to trace the themes of *humility, abandonment, simplicity* or *poverty* on their own does not make sense unless the place of these virtues is understood within the whole.

The following is a short account of the five elements of this methodology, a methodology which itself is comparatively new and still in process:

(1) *The synchronic dynamics which operate between elements of the same structural organisation.* The synchronic dimension of spirituality is articulated by opposites which operate simultaneously within the same system, for example, life and death, dark and light, death to self and life-giving. These opposites are part of an on-going process which gives transforming powers in the mystical experience. All these tensions can be found in Julie Billiart's letters, especially in her first letters to Françoise on prayer.

(2) *The diachronic dynamics which operate between consecutive structures.* The diachronic (longitudinal) dimension is articulated by gradually shifting structures within the same system. These shifts occur when the stages of life provoke spiritual development or when cultural changes impose spiritual renewal and adaptation. For example, Françoise made a diachronic shift in her choice to follow Julie, rather than become a Carmelite nun. The shift looks different from the original choice but in fact it is transformed, by the various tensions of choice, within the spirituality.

(3) *The contextual dynamics which operate between the articulated forms of a spirituality and their cultural context.* Every form of spirituality arises out of the historical and personal circumstances of its time – social, economic and cultural. Without that context it would never have been born. For example, Julie Billiart's spirituality was embedded in her experiences of the French Revolution as well as that of a peasant woman of the eighteenth century.

Without those experiences her spirituality would not have taken the form it did.

(4) *The dialogical dynamics which operate between the people and things within the field of their spirituality.* It is articulated by the establishment of relationships, between two human beings, and between the person/s and God. At this level the 'other' becomes a 'thou', a person not an object. The friendship between Julie Billiart and Françoise Blin de Bourdon was crucial as they both grew, in union with God and each other, in a dynamic, mutual, human and spiritual friendship.

(5) *The mystical dynamics which move towards the real encounter of love.* In its mystical dimension spirituality is articulated by the irreducible tension between the person and God. The person is thoroughly transformed in the confrontation with God's overwhelming love, which annihilates the darkness of self-concern in a process of painful self-emptying, de-structuring and de-centring, while being re-structured and concentrated on God alone. This longing for closer union with God arises from Julie's mystical experiences of the 'goodness of God'. It shines through in Julie Billiart's letters and her life. Her intense sufferings are an outward expression of her desires and her letters reveal that no suffering or difficulty is too great in the service of her 'Good God'.

Taking the Gothic church building as a metaphor for Julie's spirituality, the pillars of her spirituality are vision, friendship, the cross and the poor. The spirit which flies between the pillars, the flying buttress, is her charism, *the liberty of the children of God*. It is this that holds all else together and through which the spirituality can be publicly witnessed by those who try to live the charism.

Appendix 2

Glossary of terms

Feminism

The word 'feminist' is a deeply misunderstood and abused word. It is a word which grew in use during the twentieth century to denote reflection on the reality of women, who have been treated as second-class citizens in all areas of life – cultural, religious, political and economic. The gradual development of women's feminist consciousness over long periods of history eventually culminated in the women's movement of the past 150 years.

There is a utopian quality about the many different forms that feminism takes, as it is essentially about a different 'consciousness and vision, a radically changed perspective which calls fundamentally into question many of our social, cultural, political and religious traditions . . . Although it is centrally about women and their experience . . . feminism is therefore fundamentally about men and social change' (King 1989:15–22). Feminists believe that the gradual liberation of women worldwide will change all human relationships and institutions for the better.

Kyriarchy

This term was coined by Elisabeth Schüssler Fiorenza, the American scripture scholar, as she found the term 'patriarchy', understood as generalised 'gender dualism', inadequate to express the interlocking of multiple oppressions – racism, sexism, classism etc. From her vantage point as a scripture scholar she has coined a term from the Greek *kyros* (Lord): 'kyriarchy', the rule of the emperor/master/lord/father/husband over his subordinates. This term interlocks all oppressions and is of particular importance in refining the general concept of women's experience as a source for theology. By focusing on this inter-locking of oppressions women's experience must, at this moment in time, give priority to the experience of the poorest women, especially women of colour. In Fiorenza's own words, 'Until all women are free, no woman is free.'

Patriarchy

The word 'patriarchy' has a long and varied history. The origin of the word, in the sixteenth century, was ecclesiastical: the government of the church by a patriarch. In the seventeenth century, its meaning was enlarged to encompass the prevailing social construction of society: a system of society that was ruled by the father or the eldest male of the family. Today, the word is primarily understood to refer in general terms to gender dualism, 'to male power and property structure in which men are dominant to the detriment of women and one may add largely to the detri-ment of themselves' (King 1989:22). Western civilisation incor-porated a set of unstated assumptions about gender which powerfully affected the development of history and of human thought. It is a worldwide system, dating from classical antiquity, a social, economic, religious and political phenomenon in which a small group of men, mainly white, have dominated and con-trolled all aspects of life. They have dominated not only by laws which favour them, but through the deeply inherited cultural atti-tudes that the male really is superior and the 'norm' of all society. Patriarchy is summed up by Sun Ai Park, the Korean feminist theologian, in a conference paper given at Maryknoll, USA, in 1987: it is 'a system in which a limited number of privileged males have power over women, children and males defined as lesser'. One of the major difficulties facing the eradication of this destructive system is that most religions have adopted it to build a theology and church structures around the system, and thus have perpetuated, and still are perpetuating, 'patriarchy' as though it was 'ordained by God'. It is not surprising, there-fore, that it is a major focus of the feminist critique.

Women's theology

In order to have any understanding of feminist theology, it is important to realise that all theology needs to be modified by an adjective. Pure 'theology' does not exist. Much of inherited theology had a male bias until the explosion of women's theology in the latter part of the twentieth century. Women's theology takes on various hues, according to the experience of the women themselves. Hence, white women's theology, although it has done a great deal to unmask the sexist bias in all theology, has been found wanting by our black sisters and women of colour, because of its lack of understanding of racism and classism. This does not mean that women of different races cannot work together; in fact the dialogues of the Ecumenical Association of Third World Theologians (EATWOT), between women of all races, are some of the most fruitful theological exchanges there are. It means there is no longer one discourse, one way of understanding. Women's theology is always modified by the experience of the women speaking. It is contextual liberation theology from a woman's experience and, as has already been noted, the experience of the poorest of all women should be central to any theological dialogue. More and more women are now beginning to name their own experience and set their own agendas, in church and secular society, in every continent of the world. The following are some examples of women's emerging theology:

African theology: Women in Africa are also naming their own experience and many new forms of women's theology are emerging from this continent. One of the best-known women theologians in Africa is the Ghanaian Mercy Amba Oduyoye. **Mijung** theology is a word used by certain Asian cultures to denote Asian women's experience. Chung Hyun Kyung (Korea), Kwok Pui-Lan (Hong Kong) and Marianne Katteppo (Indonesia) are well known in this field.

Mujerista theology is derived from the experience of women from Latin America. The first publication dealing with Mujerista theology appeared in 1987, edited by A. M. Isasi-Diaz and

Y. Tarango and entitled *Hispanic Women: Prophetic Voice in the Church* (Fortress Press: Minneapolis). Mujerista, because of its newness, is a small daughter born of the hope of Latina women for their liberation and the liberation of all peoples.

Womanist was coined by Alice Walker in her well-known book *In Search of Our Mother's Garden*. Walker defines a 'womanist' as a black feminist or feminist of colour who, among other things, is wilful, serious, loving, and 'committed to survival and wholeness of an entire people, male and female'. It is a theology derived from the experience of black Afro-American women and is deeply critical of some white feminist approaches which reflect white supremacy and neglect a racist and class analysis. It also gives prominence to a reinterpretation of Christology and cross theology.

Suggested reading

Lisa Isherwood and Dorothea McEwan, eds, *An A to Z of Feminist Theology*, Sheffield Academic Press: Sheffield, 1996.

Ursula King, *Women and Spirituality, Voices of Protest and Promise*, Macmillan: London, 1989.

Ursula King, *Feminist Theology from the Third World – A Reader*, SPCK: London, 1994.

Gerda Lerner, *Women And History, Vol. 1 The Creation of Patriarchy. Vol. II The Creation of Feminist Consciousness from the Middle Ages to Eighteen-seventy*, Oxford University Press: Oxford, 1993.

Letty Russell, Kwok-Pui-Lan, Ada Maria Isasi-Diaz and Katie Geneva Cannon, eds, *Inheriting Our Mother's Gardens: Feminist Theology in Third World Perspective*, Westminster Press: Louisville, 1988.

Elisabeth Schüssler Fiorenza, *Jesus, Miriam's Child, Sophia's Prophet*, SCM Press: London, 1994.

Walker, Alice, *In Search of our Mothers' Gardens: Womanist Prose*, Women's Press: London, 1994

Bibliography

Anderson, Bonnie, and Judith P. Zinner, *A History of Their Own: Women in Europe from Prehistory to the Present*, Vol. II, Penguin Books: London, 1988.

Arendt, Hannah, *On Revolution*, Penguin Books: London, 1990.

Baker Miller, Jean, *Toward a New Psychology of Women*, Penguin Books: London, 1988.

Balasuriya, Tissa, OMI, *A third world theology of religious life*, Centre of Concern: Colombo, Sri Lanka, 1985.

Barnard, Howard Clive, *Education and the French Revolution*, Cambridge Texts and Studies in the History Of Education, Cambridge University Press: London, 1969.

Belenky, Mary Field, Blythe McVicker Clinchy, Nancy Rule Golberger and Jill Mattuck Tarule, *Women's Ways of Knowing: The Development of Self, Voice and Mind*, Basic Books: New York, 1986.

Best, G., ed., *The Permanent Revolution 1789–1989*, 2nd edn, Fontana Press: London, 1989.

Book of Instructions of Blessed Mère Julie as preserved in the Mother House of the Sisters of Notre Dame de Namur (undated): the COR Library, British Province Archives.

Borchert, Bruno, *Mysticism, Its History and Challenge*, Samuel Weiser, Inc.: York Beach, Maine, 1994.

Brueggemann, Walter, *The Prophetic Imagination*, Fortress Press: Philadelphia, 1978.

Bynum, Carol Walker, *Jesus as Mother: Studies in the Spirituality of the High Middle Ages*, University of California Press: Berkeley/Los Angeles/London, 1984.

Callahan, Annice, RSCJ, *Karl Rahner's Spirituality of the Pierced Heart: A Re-interpretation of Devotion to the Sacred Heart*, Ph.D. thesis, University Press of America: 1985.

Carlson Brown, Joanne and Carol R. Bohn, eds, *Christianity, Patriarchy and Abuse: A Feminist Critique*, Pilgrim Press: New York, 1989.

Christ, Carol P., *Diving Deep and Surfacing*, Beacon Press: Boston, 1986.

Christ, Carol P. and Judith Plaskow, eds, *Womanspirit Rising*, Harper and Row: San Francisco, 1979.

Chung Hyun Kyung, *Struggle to be the Sun Again: Introducing Asian Women's Theology*, SCM: London, 1990.

Cohen, J. M., trans., *The Life of Teresa of Avila by Herself*, Penguin Books: London, 1957.

Crysdale, Cynthia, sw, *Embracing Travail: Retrieving the Cross Today*, Continuum: New York, 1999.

Daly, Mary, *The Church and the Second Sex*, 3rd edn, Beacon Press: Boston, 1985.

Dictionnaire de Spiritualité Vol. II, Beauchesne: Paris, 1953.

Vol. III, Beauchesne: Paris, 1957, article on the Devil by Stanilas Lyonnet, pp. 142–52.

Vol. V, 17e Siècle, Beauchesne: Paris, 1976.

Vol. IX, Beauchesne: Paris, 1976, Article on Liberty, scripture, by Jacques Guillet, Old Testament pp. 794–810, New Testament, pp. 800–3.

Dictionary of Biblical Theology, ed. Xavier Leon Dufour, 2nd edn, Chapman: London, 1988.

Dorr, Donal, *Option For The Poor: A Hundred Years of Vatican Social Teaching*, Gill and Macmillan: Dublin, 1986.

Dupré, Louis and Don E. Saliers, eds, *Christian Spirituality: Post-Reformation and Modern, Vol. III*, SCM: London, 1990.

Erikson, Victoria L., *Where Silence Speaks: Feminism, Social Theory and Religion*, Fortress Press: Minneapolis, 1993.

Fabella, Virginia, MM and Sergio Torres, eds, *Irruption of The*

Third World: Challenge to Theology, Orbis Books: Maryknoll, New York, 1983.

Fiand, Barbara, SND, *Living the Vision: Religious Vows in an Age of Change*, Crossroad: New York, 1992.

Releasement: Spirituality for Ministry, Crossroad: New York, 1987.

Embraced by Compassion: On Human Longing and Divine Response, Crossroad: New York, 1993.

Wrestling with God: Religious Life in Search of its Soul, Crossroad: New York, 1986.

Fiorenza, Elisabeth Schüssler, *In Memory of Her: A Feminist Theological Reconstruction of Christian Origins*, Crossroad: New York, 1986.

Forrest, Alan, *The French Revolution and the Poor*, St Martins Press: New York, 1981.

Garry, Ann and Marilyn Pearsall, eds, *Women, Knowledge and Reality: Explorations in Feminist Philosophy*, Unwin Hyman Ltd: London, 1989.

Gateley, Edwina, *a warm moist salty God: Women Journeying Towards Wisdom*, Anthony Clarke: Wheathampstead, 1993.

Gibson, Ralph, *A Social History of French Catholicism 1789–1914*, Routledge: London, 1989.

Giles, Mary E., ed., *The Feminist Mystic*, Crossroad: New York, 1986.

Gnanadason, Aruna, *No Longer A Secret: The church and violence against women*, 2nd revd edn, Risk book series no. 58, WCC Publications: Geneva, 1997.

Gnanadason, Aruna, ed., *Living Letters: A Report of Visits to the Churches during the Ecumenical Decade – Churches in Solidarity with Women*, WCC Publications: Geneva, 1997.

Graham, Elaine, *Making The Difference: Gender, Personhood and Theology*, Cassell: London, 1995.

Grant, Jacquelyn, *White Women's Christ and Black Women's Jesus: Feminist Christology and Womanist Response*, Academy Series, Number 64, Scholars Press: Atlanta, 1989.

Grey, M., *Redeeming The Dream: Feminism, Redemption and the Christian Tradition*, SCM: London, 1989.

Gutiérrez, Gustavo, *A Theology of Liberation*, SCM Press: London, 1974.

Harris, Maria, *Dance of the Spirit: The Seven Steps of Women's Spirituality*, Bantum Doubleday Dell: New York, 1991.

Harrison, Beverly Wildung, *Making the Connections: Essays in Feminist Social Ethic*, Beacon Press: Boston, 1985.

Hogan, Linda, *From Women's Experience to Feminist Theology*, Sheffield Academic Press: Sheffield, 1995.

Hopkins, Julie, *Towards a Feminist Christology*, SPCK: London, 1995.

Hufton, Olwen, *The Poor of Eighteenth-Century France*, Oxford University Press: Oxford, 1974.

The Prospect before Her: A History of Women in Western Europe, Vol. One 1500–1800, Fontana Press, Harper Collins: London, 1997.

Huls, Jos and Hein Bloomestijn, *The Simplicity of Love As The Key: Bishop Zwijsen's special emphasis*, SCMM-CMM: s-Hertogenbosch-Tilburg, 1995.

Hunt, Mary E., *Fierce Tenderness: A Feminist Theology of Friendship*, Crossroad: New York, 1991.

Irigaray, Luce, *Speculum of The Other Woman*, trans. Gillian C. Gill, Cornell University Press: Ithaca, 1985.

James, William, *Varieties of Religious Experience*, Fontana: London, 1963 edn.

Jantzen, Grace, *Power, Gender and Christian Mysticism*, Cambridge University Press: Cambridge, 1995.

Keenan, Brian, *An Evil Cradling*, Vintage Press: London, 1992.

Kerns, Vincent, MSFC, *Treatise on the Love of God*, Newman Press: Westminster, Maryland, 1962.

King, Ursula, *Women and Spirituality: Voices of Protest & Promise*, Macmillan: London, 1989.

Knotts, Betty I., trans., *The Imitation of Christ* by Thomas à Kempis, Collins: London, 1963.

Küng, Hans, *Christianity: The Religious Situation of Our Time*, SCM Press: London, 1995.

Laker, Mary Eugenia, SSND, trans., *Aelred of Rievaulx, Spiritual Friendship*, Cistercian Father Series, Number 5, Cistercian Publications: Kalamazoo, Michigan, 1977.

Langlois, Claude, *Le Catholicisme au Féminen: Les Congrégations Françaises supérieure Générale au XIXe Siècle*, Les Editions du Cerf: Paris, 1984.

Leclercq, Jean, *The Love of Learning and the Desire for God*, Fordham University Press: New York, 1962.

Monks and Love in 12th century France, Clarendon Press: London, 1979.

Lerner, Gerda, *The Creation of Feminist Consciousness*, Oxford University Press: Oxford, 1993.

Lipsett, Linda Otto, *Remember Me: Women and Friendship Quilts*, Quilt Digest Press: San Francisco, 1985.

Little, Graham, *Being Ourselves with Others*, The Text Publishing Co.: London, 1993.

Lorde, Audrey, *Sister Outsider: Essays and Speeches*, The Crossing Press: New York, 1984.

McCarthy, John and Jill Morrell, *Some Other Rainbow*, Corgi Books: London, 1994.

McEwan, Dorothea, ed., *Women Experiencing Church*, Gracewing: Leominster, 1991.

McFague, Sallie, *Metaphorical Theology: Models of God in Religious Language*, SCM Press: London, 1982.

McGinn, Bernard, *Mysticism, Origins to the Fifth Century*, Vol. 1, SCM Press: London, 1992.

McManners, John, *The French Revolution and the Church*, SPCK: London, 1969.

Death and Enlightenment: Changing Attitudes Towards Death in Eighteenth Century France, Oxford University Press: Oxford, 1981.

McNamara, Jo Ann Kay, *Sisters in Arms: Catholic Nuns Through Two Millennia*, Harvard University Press: New Haven, 1996.

Martin, Fanny, Dorothea McEwan and Lucy Tatman, eds, *Cymbals and Silences: Echoes from the First European Women's*

Synod: Women for Change in the 21st Century, Sophia Press: London, 1996 (private publication).

Merkle, Judith, *Committed by Choice: Religious Life Today*, Liturgical Press: Minnesota, 1992.

A Different Touch: a study of vows in religious life, Liturgical Press: Minnesota, 1998.

Miles, Margaret, *The Image and Practice of Holiness*, SCM Press: London, 1988.

Miles, Rosalind, *The Women's History of the World*, Paladin, Harper Collins: London, 1989.

Moltmann-Wendel, Elisabeth, *The Women around Jesus: reflections on authentic personhood*, SCM Press: London, 1982.

Moltmann-Wendel, E. and Jürgen Moltmann, *His God and Hers*, SCM Press: London, 1991.

Morton, Nell, *The Journey is Home*, Beacon Press: Boston, 1985.

Murphy, Desmond, *The Death and Rebirth of Religious Life: a landmark in religious life literature*, E. J. Dwyer: Alexandria, Australia, 1995.

Neale, Marie Augusta, SND, *From Nuns to Sisters: An Expanding Vocation*, Twenty-Third Publications: Connecticut, 1990.

The Just Demands of the Poor: Essays in Socio-Theology, Paulist Press: New York, 1987.

Nemeck, Francis, *Receptivity*, Vantage Press Inc.: New York, 1985.

Nemeck, Francis and Teresa Coombs, *Contemplation*, Michael Glaizier Inc.: Delaware, 1982.

Newsom, Carol A. and Sharon H. Ringe, eds, *The Women's Bible Commentary*, SPCK: London, 1992.

O'Murchu, Diarmuid, MSC, *Reframing Religious Life: An Expanded Vision for the Future*, St Pauls: Slough, 1995.

Reclaiming Spirituality: a new spiritual framework for today's world, Gill and Macmillan: Dublin, 1997.

Quantum Theology: Spiritual Implications of the New Physics, Crossroad: New York, 1997.

Orilio, Rodriguez and Kieran Kavanagh OCD, trans., *The Collected Works of Teresa of Avila, Volume II*, ICS Publications: Washington DC, 1980.

Peers, Alison, ed., *The Complete Works of Teresa of Avila, Vol. II*, Sheed and Ward: London, 1972.

Peters, Henriette, *A World in Contemplation*, trans. Helen Butterworth, Gracewing: Leominster, 1991.

Petroff, Elizabeth, *Medieval Women's Visionary Literature*, Oxford University Press: New York, 1986 edn.

Puhl, Louis J., SJ, *The Spiritual Exercises of St. Ignatius*, Loyola University Press: Chicago, 1951.

Purvis, Sally B., *The Power of the Cross: Foundations for a Christian Feminist Ethic of Community*, Abingdon Press: Nashville, 1993.

Quinonez, Lora Ann, CDP, ed., *Starting Points: Six Essays on the Experience of U.S. Women Religious*, Leadership Conference of Women Religious of the USA: Washington, D.C., 1980.

Rahner, Karl, *Theological Investigations Vol. VII, Further Theology of the Spiritual Life*, trans. David Bourke, Darton, Longman and Todd: London, 1971.

Grace and Freedom, trans. Hilda Graef, Herder and Herder: New York, 1969.

Rait, Jill, ed., assisted by Bernard McGinn and John Meyendorff, *Christian Spirituality, High Middle Ages and Reformation, Vol. II*, SCM Press: London, 1996.

Raymond, Janice, *a passion for friends: towards a philosophy of female affection*, The Women's Press: London, 1991 (first published 1986).

Roberts, J. M., *The French Revolution*, Opus Books, Oxford University Press: Oxford, 1978.

Rohr, Richard and Andreas Ebert, *Discovering the Enneagram, An Ancient Tool for a New Spiritual Journey*, Crossroad: New York, 1996.

Rudé, G., *The Crowd in the French Revolution*, Oxford University Press: Oxford, 1959.

Revolutionary Europe 1783–1815, Fontana: London, 1964.

Ruether, Rosemary Radford, *Women-Church, Theology and Practice*, Harper Row: New York, 1985.

Introducing Redemption in Christian Feminism, Sheffield Academic Press: London, 1998.

Ruether, Rosemary Radford, ed., *Religion and Sexism, Images of Woman in the Jewish and Christian Tradition*, Simon and Schuster: New York, 1974.

Ryan, Frances, DC and John E. Rybolt, CM, *Vincent de Paul and Louise De Marillac, Rules, Conferences and Writings*, Paulist Press: New York, 1995.

Jesus, Miriam's Child Sophia's Prophet: Critical Issues in Feminist Christology, SCM Press: London, 1994.

Sheldrake, Philip, *Spirituality and History*, SPCK: London, 1991.

Slee, Nicola, *Easter Garden: A Sequence of Readings on the Resurrection of Hope*, Collins: London, 1990.

Sölle, Dorothee, *Strength of the Weak: Towards a Christian Feminist Identity*, trans. Robert and Rita Kimber, Westminster Press: Philadelphia, 1984.

Spender, Dale, *Women of Ideas and What Men Have Done to Them*, Pandora Press: London, 1982.

Stichele, Caroline Vander, van der Helm, Ad, van Dijk, Bert, Torfs, Rik, Veliscek, Svetko (eds.), *Disciples and Discipline: European Debate on Human Rights in the Roman Catholic Church*, Peeters: Leuven, 1993.

Stuart, Elizabeth, *Just Good Friends: Towards A Lesbian And Gay Theology Of Relationships*, Cassell: London, 1995.

Thistlewaite, Susan, *Sex, Race and God: Christian Feminism in Black and White*, Geoffrey Chapman: London, 1990.

Thompson, W. M., *The Classics of Western Spirituality, Bérulle and the French School: Selected Writings*, Paulist Press: New York, 1989.

Thorold, Algar, *The Self-Abandonment to Divine Providence*, Burns and Oates: London, 1959.

Toril, Moi, *French Feminist Thought, A Reader*, Blackwell: Oxford, 1987.

Townes, Emile M., ed., *A Troubling in my Soul: Womanist*

Perspectives On Evil and Suffering, Orbis Books: Maryknoll, New York, 1993.

Tracy, David, *The Analogical Imagination, Christian Theology and the Culture of Pluralism*, Crossroad: New York, 1981.

Underhill, Evelyn, *Mysticism*, 11th edn, Methuen: London, 1926.

Wadell, Paul J., CP, *Friendship: Pastoral-Liturgical Tradition*, Liturgical Press: Collegeville, 1996.

Ward, Hannah and Jennifer Wild, *Guard the Chaos: Finding Meaning in Change*, Darton, Longman and Todd: London, 1995.

Warner, Marina, *Maidens and Monuments*, Picador Pan Books: London, 1985.

Welch, John, O'Carm., *The Spiritual Pilgrims: Carl Jung & Teresa of Avila*, Paulist Press: New York, 1982.

Welsh, Sharon D., *Communities of Resistance and Solidarity: A Feminist Theology of Liberation*, Orbis Books: New York, 1985.

Wolski, Joanna, ed., *Women's Spirituality: Resources for Christian Development*, Paulist Press: Mahwah, NJ, 1986.

Wright, Wendy M., *An Introduction to the Devout Life and Treatise on the Love of God*, Crossroad: New York, 993.

The Bond of Perfection, Paulist Press: New York, 1985.

Julie Billiart and Françoise Blin de Bourdon

Billiart, Julie, *The Letters of Julie Billiart*, trans. Frances Rosner, SND and Sr Lucy Tinsley, SND, Gregorian Press: Rome, 1974.

Blin de Bourdon, Françoise, *The Memoirs of Frances Blin de Bourdon*, trans. Sister Therese of the Blessed Sacrament Sullivan, SND, Christian Classics: Westminster, Maryland, reprinted 1989.

Clare, James, SJ, ed. and Partridge, Mary Xavier, SND, author *Life of Blessed Julie Balliart*, Sands & Co.: London, 1909.

Linscott, Mary, SND de Namur, *Quiet Revolution: The Edu-*

cational Experience of Blessed Julie and the Sisters of Notre Dame de Namur, Burns and Oates: Glasgow, 1966.

To Heaven on Foot, John S. Burns: Glasgow, 1969.

McCarthy, Esther, 'The French Revolution and its impact on the founding congregation' (unpublished paper given at the Julie Renewal Session of 1992).

Murphy, Roseanne, SND de Namur, *Julie Billiart, Woman of Courage*, Paulist Press: New York, 1995.

SND de Namur, *The Life of Mère St Joseph: Françoise Blin de Bourdon 1756–1838*, Longmans, Green and Co.: London, 1923.

SND de Namur, *Mère St. Joseph*, Sands and Co.: Cambridge, 1964.

Recker, Mary Jo, 'Julie, Françoise And Our Heritage Of Friendship; A Treasure Beyond Price', (unpublished paper) 1997.

Rees, Elizabeth, 'The Influence of Teresa of Avila on Julie Billiart', 1998 (unpublished paper).

Themes and *Extracts from Instructions* given by the Servant of God, Julia Billiart, to the members of the Institute she founded, The Sisters of Notre Dame, Namur USA: Cincinnati, 1905.

Tomme, Sr Frances de Chantal, SND, *Julie Billiart and Her Institute*, Longmans, Green and Co.: London, 1938.

SND de Namur, *The Life of Mère St. Joseph*, Longmans, Green and Co.: London, 1923.

Articles, Journals

Aldrich, J. Ruth, 'Teresa, a Self-Actualised Woman', *Carmelite Studies*, ed. John Sullivan, OCD, ICS Publications: Washington, DC, 1982.

Chittester, Joan, 'Religious Life in Contemporary Society: A Need for the Prophetic Dimension', *Signum*, August 1996.

Fiedler, Maureen, SL, 'New Women, New Church', *Women's Ordination Newsletter*, 1999.

Geels, Antoon, 'Chaos Lives Next to God. Religious Visions and the integration of the Personality', *Pharos: Studies in*

Spirituality, 12/1992, Kok Pharos: Kampen, The Netherlands.

Hughes, C., 'St Julie: a happy saint', *The Month: A Review of Christian Thought and World Affairs* (September/October 1994).

Jantzen, Grace M., 'Feminists, Philosophers, and Mystics', *Hypatia, A Journal Of Feminist Philosophy*, University Press Journals, Indiana, vol. 9, no. 4 (Fall 1994).

John XXIII, Pope, *Pacem in Terris* (Encyclical Letter), London: Catholic Truth Society, 1963.

Miller, Julie B., 'Eroticized Violence in Medieval Women's Mystical Literature, A Call for a Feminist Critique', *Journal of Feminist Studies in Religion*, vol. 15, no. 2 (Fall 1999).

O'Brien, Susan, 'Women Religious: Historical Past – Future Perspective', 1994 (unpublished paper).

Ranft, Patricia, 'A Key to Counter-Reformation Women's Activism: The Confessor-Spiritual Director', *Journal of Feminist Studies in Religion*, vol. 10, no. 2 (Fall 1994).

Tackett, T., 'The West in France in 1789: the religious factor in the origins of the counter-revolution', *Journal of Modern History*, 54 (Dec. 1982).

Waaijman, Kees, 'Spirituality as Transformation demands a structural dynamic approach', *Studies in Spirituality* 1/1991, Kok Pharos: Kampen, The Netherlands.

Williams, Rowan, 'Carmelite Spirituality' (book review), *The Way*, vol. 40, no. 4 (Oct. 2000).

review of Grace Jantzen, *Power, Gender and Christian Mysticism*, *Theology*, vol. C, no. 794 (March/April 1997).

Notes

Introduction

1. These are the famous spiritual exercises of St Ignatius, the founder of the Jesuits in the sixteenth century. On this occasion I made them in full at Guelph, Canada. Here, they last for forty days to allow extra time for reflection. During the latter part of the twentieth century the spirit of these exercises was refound and revived, initially by Paul Kennedy SJ. Since that time the exercises have become one of the most used texts for retreat giving. The main centre in Britain is at St Bueno's, St Asaph, Wales.

2. My Congregation owes much to Sister Mary Linscott for her pioneering work on the Congregation, especially her book *Quiet Revolution* (1966), which concentrates on the educational development of the Sisters of Notre Dame de Namur in many parts of the world, as well as other works by SNDs: Mary Daniel Turner, 'On Becoming Religious' (1980) in *Starting Points: Six Essays on the Experience of U.S. Women Religious*, edited by Lora Ann Quinonez, pp. 45–58; Marie Augusta Neale, *The Just Demands of the Poor* (1987) and *From Nuns to Sister: an Expanding Vocation* (1990); Barbara Fiand, *Releasement* (1987) and *Living The Vision: Religious Vows in an Age of Change* (1992); Judith Merkle, *Committed by Choice* (1992) and *A Different Touch* (1998).

3. The Greek word *charism* means a free gift, a favour. St Paul introduced the term into religious language to curb the many squabbles in the churches he established over which gift was the greatest – especially the members of the church at Corinth, who valued the gift of tongues over all others. For Paul, a charism is a free gift of grace given by God to be used for 'the common good' (1 Cor. 12:7). In 1 Cor. 12:7–11, Paul gives his fullest list of charisms, but he has complementary lists in Rom. 12:6–8, Eph. 4:11–12; 1 Pet. 4:10–11. He insisted that charisms take the form of service to the community, something the Corinthians did not particularly want to

hear. Paul's insistence on service led him to give greater significance to some charisms rather than others – for example, the gift of teaching over the gift of tongues. Chapter 13 of 1 Corinthians, where Paul declares the most 'excellent way' is *love*, as all else will pass away, seems like an intrusion into his arguments about the highest gift. But this chapter paves the way for the answer to the question of the highest gift, charism, of all. And his answer is firmly stated: that the gift which contributes most to the life of the community is *prophecy*: 'the prophet is one who speaks . . . for the . . . upbuilding and encouragement and consolation . . . the one who edifies the church' (1 Cor. 14:3–4).

4. See Appendix 1.

1. Women of Protest

1. Parisian women had introduced the idea of the salon into France by the last quarter of the seventeenth century and they reached their greatest popularity in the eighteenth century. Wealthy hostesses aspired to attract the talented, witty and powerful to their homes. Outside the powerful French court and often opposed to it, these new social circles offered women places of literary and political discussion. The focus of all these salons was attracting influential male guests, people such as Voltaire and the *Encyclopédistes*. It was in these salons that women and men discussed and wrote many of the ideas from which the Revolution was to spring. They were the places where ideas fermented, the power houses of change. Many women writers emerged from them, and despite the male predominance in these salons, commentators 'both French and foreign stressed and even exaggerated the power of female influence' (Anderson and Zinner 1988:103–28; Hufton 1997:428–33).

2. This French warrior became the legendary hero of medieval romances. He took North East Spain from the Moors and invaded Bavaria and Italy. He restored the papacy to Leo III, who then crowned him Emperor. He was also a brilliant administrator and intellectual, who encouraged the arts and codified the law.

3. The saying of the rosary dates back to the time of St Dominic in the 13th century. Using rosary beads to pray to the Virgin Mary became one of the most popular devotions in the Roman Catholic Church. The groups where people met to pray were called confraternities.

4. Langlois 1984:286. He distinguished four groups of women foundresses of religious congregations, in the Third Estate, in the nineteenth century. It is noteworthy that he places Julie Billiart in the second group of these women, 'Artisans aises et notables rurauxs, 'aises' meaning 'well off', in comparison with 'les pauvres' of the time: 1. Aux frontières de la bourgeoisie 2. Artisans aises et notables ruraux 3. Petits artisans et

boutiquiers, petits exploitants 4. Salarié(e)s, domestiques, prolétariat rural et urbain.

5. There was very good communication between women who cared about their beliefs, irrespective of their social strata, because the differences between the sexes overrode all other factors 'in shaping a woman's piety. A pious peasant woman and a pious noblewoman were more like each other in religiosity than either was like the male saint of her social status' (Rait 1996:134).

6. Langlois is very clear on his understanding of the role of these new congregations as 'in parenthesis' and his comments are very important to a further understanding of the rise and decline of these new nineteenth-century congregations in the western world. The following are his exact words: '*Remis en perspective, le temps des congrégations apparait d'une transition. Il correspond, dans l'enseignement, à la longue parenthèse qui s'étend entre le moment où l'Eglise en controllait tous les aspects et celui où l'Etat a revendiqué la totalité de l'héritage. Il correspond aussis au moment où le statut des femmes, tant dans l'Eglise que dans la société, se transforme profondément. Entre la religieuse cloîtrée et la militante laïque se situe la congréganiste, 'fille séculière' qui veut être 'religieuse'; entre la femme de la société traditionelle et celle de la vie moderne accèdant à tous les emplois ne fut-il pas aussi insérer la congréganiste, menant une activité fort séculière selon un mode tout régulier? Les congrégations féminines ont incontestablement leur place dans une histoire de l'Eglise. Elles appartiennent à l'histoire, plus largement*' (Langlois 1984:648).

7. McEwan 1991. This book is divided into six parts and illustrates from women's stories the many sufferings that the official churches have caused them. It contains articles, not only by such well-known writers as Margaret Hebblethwaite ('How I was Arrested for Demonstrating in the Vatican') and Mary Grey ('And He Said to Me'), but also by less well-known but by no means less influential women, such as Nikki Arthy, who later left the RC Church to become a priest in the Anglican Church, ('On Being a Lay Chaplain'), and Penny Toller, on the church as 'The Abusive Parent'. This book is a very good illustration of women's endurance within the various Christian traditions and their different responses to the problems they met.

8. John Hans Wijngaards in May 1999 established a website devoted entirely to establishing the reasons why women should be ordained: *www.womenpriests.org*.

9. For a full account of the lives of these two remarkable early feminists see Dale Spender, *Women Of Ideas And What Men Have Done To Them*, Pandora Press: London, 1982, pp. 270–309.

2. Women of Vision

1. Michel Certeau in *Concilium*, vol. 9, no. 2 (Nov. 1966), p. 4.

2. O'Murchu 1995. The author reflects on the findings of Jung in this regard. For Freud there are basically three states of consciousness: 'conscious' – what I am at present aware of; 'preconscious' – what I can recall from the past; and 'subconscious' – the aggregate of instinctual feelings and emotions that I am consciously aware of but that influences at least 70 per cent of my daily behaviour as a human being (ibid.:137). Chapter 11 is entitled 'Integrating the Shadow' (137–50). Mystics are the 'shadow integrators' of the societies in which they live.

3. The following thought comes from Desmond Murphy 1995, which uses K. Wilber's theory of Transpersonal Psychology (*A Sociable God*, New Science: London, 1983). Levels of consciousness refer to permanent structures of the psyche from which other stages and eventually another consciousness develop. This consciousness is dependent on other stages of awareness being experienced first. As with all theories, there is criticism, especially because of its stages/hierarchical approach (Desmond Murphy 1995, chapter IV, pp. 55–88). However, 'Transpsychology' calls us beyond our more familial pattern of ego awareness, to a critical examination of the very ground from which our behaviour, thoughts and emotions emerge (ibid.:72). One of the strengths of Wilber's approach is the starkness with which the need for transformation is highlighted. In fact mysticism in Wilber's terms can be called a 'transrational epiphany'. I found this book very helpful towards a further understanding of the mystical experience, as well as the death and rebirth of religious life.

4. See Williams 1997:132–3. While affirming the importance of Grace Jantzen's book as the first that has deconstructed the mystical tradition from a gender perspective, Williams takes issue on the association of the *via negativa* with an essentialist masculine perspective. He states that this tradition can also be found among women visionaries such as Marguerite Porete.

5. Geels 1992. This study is based on questionnaires, letters and short biographies written by 92 ordinary Swedish citizens. Most of them had visions of Jesus, or of angels and 'divine light'. Geels chose to describe 35 cases in the form of short biographies. Since more than 90 per cent of all informants mentioned a crisis prior to the religious vision, the author focused his study on the relationship between life-crisis and religious vision. Visions of Jesus or the divine light are symbolic representations of order, as against chaos. In almost all cases the vision brings an end to the life-crisis, ends chaos and establishes order. Such is the case with Julie Billiart.

6. The Compiègne vision is part of the oral tradition of Julie's life. It is not mentioned in the first four biographies. The first account appears in

the *Life of Julie by Père Clair* (1906 edn), and it was from this that Clare SJ ed. and Partridge SND (author) took their account in 1909. It was from the 'depositions' of 1881–2, i.e., the testimony given to the Vatican for Julie's Beatification, that Père Clair based his account of the vision. The complete testimony to the vision can only be found in the Vatican archives which are being worked on at present by Mary Hayes SND. Her findings will be in the new *Life* which she will be publishing by 2004. It could be that Clare and Partridge embellished the facts a little in their flamboyant style, but it is this description of the vision that has fuelled the imagination of the Sisters over the years. NOTE: In the foreword the author is acknowledged in the following way: 'By a member of the same society'. It is now generally accepted that Mary Xavier Partridge SND was the author.

7. 'The Ecstatic Life', March 1814, in *Themes*, Cincinnati edn, 1905, p. 59.

8. Desmond Murphy 1995. Wilber, in describing the development of consciousness, speaks of the 'outward arc'. This is the process of personal ego development from subconsciousness to selfconsciousness. The 'inner arc' is the development from self-consciousness to superconsciousness, with consciousness extending beyond the body–mind into various 'higher' realms, or levels (ibid.:29). Hence the concept of a transpersonal contemplative vision (ibid.:208–10). A transpersonal human being is one whose consciousness is becoming 'more awake, self-realized, enlightened, liberated and whole' (ibid.:77).

9. See for a development of this theme Gerda Lerner, *The Creation of Feminist Consciousness*, Oxford: Oxford University Press, 1993, chapters 4 and 5; Jo Ann Kay McNamara, *Sisters in Arms: Catholic Nuns Through Two Millennia*, London: Harvard University Press, 1996.

10. Ward and Wild 1995. This was written for the latter part of the twentieth century, for women and men who feel they are in 'chaos' and are in this 'liminal' time. They name this time as a 'wilderness experience', a time of 'betwixt and between' in the lives of individuals, societies and institutions. A time not only fraught with risks of chaos and disintegration, but also a time of unparalleled opportunity for creative insight. The authors discuss various images of this 'wilderness' experience including Biblical images. There are also fascinating accounts of how four well-known individuals perceived and coped with this experience: Dorothy L. Sayers, Evelyn Underhill, C. S. Lewis and Charles Williams.

3. Women of Friendship

1. There is an imposing genealogy, from the beginning of Christianity till the present time, of these forms of friendship. The point is well illustrated by the following well-known examples: Jerome and Paula, John

Chrysostom and Olympus, St Lioba and Boniface, Francis and Clare, Diana of Andola and Jordan of Saxony, Catherine of Siena and Dominican Raymond of Capua, Catherine of Genoa and Ettore Vernazzio, not forgetting the three great friendships nearer to Julie's time, John of the Cross (1542–91) and Teresa of Avila (1515–82), Francis de Sales (1567–1622) and Jane Chantal (1572–1641), and Vincent de Paul (1580–1660) and Louise de Marillac (1591–1660).

2. Friendship quilts were a form of folk art that peaked in the 1840s in the USA (see Lipsett 1985). Thousands of these quilts were made in New England, many given to pioneers as they headed West. They were treasured more than the ordinary quilt and often preserved as wall decorations. Each patch was the same shape and size, often containing the address or a message from the person concerned. The most popular designs were the 'Chimney Sweep' and 'Album Patch'.

3. These young people were Aglae and Jeanne du Fos de Mery and Josephine and Gabrielle Doria. It was not long before the group broke up. Lise left to join her married sister in Paris. This sister died soon after, and Lise also died young. Julie acknowledged to Françoise her grief over Lise, as Madame Baudoin had left her in Julie's care.

4. Father Antoine Thomas SJ (1753–1833), Doctor of the Sorbonne, was born in Sotteville, Normandy. He refused to take the oath required by the Civil Constitution of the Clergy and fled from Paris. He was arrested and imprisoned at Arras. His death was delayed due to sickness and he was released after the fall of Robespierre. Though the 'reign of terror' was over, persecution of priests continued. Fr Thomas made his way in disguise to Amiens and eventually sought refuge with Julie and Françoise in Amiens and later at Bettencourt. He remained a constant friend to the two women throughout his life, saying of Julie, 'I know no one to whom I am under greater obligations, and I am praying to God with all my heart to reward her for my sake and that of others who were helped by her wise counsels' (*Memoirs* 288).

5. The very human side of their lives is well illustrated by the marriage of Félicité to a local schoolteacher in Bettencourt. It was with great sadness that Julie parted from her beloved niece, not only because she would miss her a great deal, as she had been with her since she was seven and looked after her so well, but because she always felt that Félicité had a religious vocation. Julie's forebodings were later realised, as the marriage was not a happy one. Félicité suffered considerable poverty, and both she and her husband had early deaths. Chapter seven of the *Memoirs* tells of the last meeting with this beloved niece in 1809. Julie was staying temporarily with an aunt of the Bishop of Ghent, and as Félicité lived nearby Julie sent word to ask her to come and see her, so that she could thank her again for all she had done. Julie noticed with great sadness that Félicité was

'pale, emaciated and poorly clothed, the image of poverty' (*Memoirs* 245). But they talked 'happily – it was the last meeting they were to have, and they seemed to sense it; for they spoke, as it were, heart to heart. Julie strengthened the younger woman against the dangers and miseries that she must inevitably meet, and in this spirit they parted' (ibid.:136).

6. The history of Père Varin (1769–1850) traces a complicated history of three male religious congregations. In 1794, he, with four other seminarians, founded the Fathers of the Sacred Heart, which was to carry on the work of the suppressed Society of Jesus, the Jesuits. In 1797 the Fathers of the Sacred Heart were asked to join forces with another group in Italy, the Fathers of the Faith. The connection with this Society lasted only four years. In 1807 Napoleon dispersed the Society, but after his fall in 1814, the Papacy issued a Bull restoring the Society of Jesus, which Père Varin now joined.

7. Pius VII (reigned 1800–23) had been imprisoned in the castle of Fontainebleau by Napoleon, because he had excommunicated Napoleon, who had confiscated the Vatican States. He also did not accept the civil changes that Napoleon had made in France. In February 1813, Julie went to visit him to ask for his blessing on her new congregation: 'She chose as her companion for the journey, a novice, Madeleine Quequet . . . the two travellers took turns riding on a donkey Julie had borrowed for the forty-five mile trip from Paris to Fontainebleu. She had not explained to Madeleine the purpose of the trip, and when they arrived the novice was told to stay in the courtyard of the palace and mind the donkey. After what seemed to Madeleine a very long time, Julie appeared, her face bathed in tears. She confided to the novice, "My daughter, I have seen the Holy Father; we have wept together over the troubles of the Church". The Pope had given Julie a crucifix which she held reverently throughout the long journey back to Ambleville. She could scarcely speak. Pius VII had been suffering from bitter remorse for having given permission to the bishops to take the oath of loyalty to Napoleon . . . He felt he had betrayed the church' (Roseanne Murphy 1995:162–3).

8. See the chapter by Ida Raming entitled 'Women in the Structures of the Church', in Stichele et al. 1993:53–64.

9. See Adrienne Rich, *Of Woman Born: Motherhood as Experience and Institution*, Norton and Company Ltd.: London, 1986.

4. *Women of a Mystical Text*

1. There is some debate over whether the French School should be called a school or schools. But it is clear there were common elements among all the various mystics who made up this school. Although they all had a slightly different emphasis, they shared a very clear soteriology (the

doctrine of salvation), and a strong Eucharistic and sacramental emphasis.

2. See Callahan 1985. Eudes's devotion to the Sacred Hearts of Jesus and Mary probably grew out of the William Harvey's (d.1657) discovery of the heart's role in the circulation of the blood.

3. The main sources of the thoughts of Julie, besides her letters, are the *Memoirs* of Françoise; the *Dialogue Letters, between Julie Billiart and Françoise Blin de Bourdon, August 10, 1807–February 26, 1809*; and those written by the young women she taught. These thoughts have been collected into small unpublished books known as *Themes* and *Instructions*.

4. I owe thanks for the information on women in Julie's writings to Elizabeth Rees for her unpublished paper on *The Influence of Teresa of Avila on Julie Billiart* (1998).

5. Mary Magdalene de' Pazzi was herself a Carmelite, and Julie's knowledge of Judith no doubt came from the same source, as the reading of the Old Testament was frequent among the Carmelites in Julie's time. Magdalene de' Pazzi is a little-known saint today, who came from a very wealthy Florentine family and was related to the Medici family. She was named after Catherine of Siena, but took the name of Mary Magdalene at her profession in 1584. She had a great love of the Eucharist and made her first holy communion at the age of ten years; at the age of twelve she consecrated her virginity to God and entered the Carmelite monastery in 1584. Her life had certain outward similarities with that of Julie, as she suffered severe bodily sickness throughout her life, and had a life-long love of the poor, and an extraordinary devotion to the Eucharist. See Butler's *Lives of the Saints*, Burns and Oates: London, 1996; and *Maria Magdalena de' Pazzi, selected revelations* (The Classics of Western Spirituality), trans. and introduced by Armando Maggi, Paulist Press: New York, 2000: ix, 386, reviewed by Kevin Alban O'Carm in *The Way*, vol. 40, no. 4, Oct. 2000, pp. 396–7. It is interesting to note that for her to write down her experiences was 'a betrayal of their essentially oral nature. She has a dynamic concept of the Word . . . it is used in every vision: it is her preferred term of addressing Jesus and yet she doubts whether the mystic can express the Word fully in any human language . . . The Word is not one of presence, but of absence . . . Maria shared some of the traits of John of the Cross, she brings some originality to Carmelite spirituality which emphasizes the apophatic stratum in her teaching' (Alban, p. 397).

6. When dealing with women, officialdom used a vocabulary of dismissive derivatives – *femelles, femelettes, bigotes, bêtes, moutons, légumineuses, fanatiques* (females, little women, bigots, beasts, sheep, vegetables, fanatics) (Hufton 1997:482). Julie used the same word of *femelettes*, to point out to her Sisters the dangers of conforming to the way society thought women behaved.

5. Women of Freedom

1. Karl Marx continued in the context of the social question, rather than making the wider application of freedom. For him the surrender of freedom to the state was a necessity and in the *Communist Manifesto* material abundance, not freedom, became the aim of revolution (Arendt 1990:64).

2. Teresa's crystal, rounded, castle is her 'mandala', her image of wholeness, whose centre is dominated by the figure of Christ. Her castle was not one of the normal Castilian castles, which she would have seen all around her, but 'a most beautiful crystal globe like a castle in which there were seven dwelling places, and in the seventh, which was in the centre, the King of Glory dwelt in the greatest splendour. From there He beautified and illumined all those dwelling places to the outer wall. The inhabitants received more light the nearer they were to the centre. Outside of the castle all was darkness, with toads, vipers, and other poisonous vermin' (Orilio and Kavanagh 1980:268 and 482 n. 16). It is also a castle of many sub-divisions, to denote the uniqueness of each individual's journey: 'in each of these there are many others, below and above and to the sides, with lovely gardens and fountains and labyrinths, such delightful things that you would want to be dissolved in praises of the great God who created the soul in His own image and likeness' (ibid.: Epilogue, no. 3).

3. See Aldrich 1982. This article takes the description of the self-actualised person of Abraham Maslow and applies the concepts to Teresa of Avila. The following is his description: 'There are in the world people who are good, strong, triumphant: they are saints, wise men (and women), recognised leaders, winners instead of losers, constructive rather than destructive people' (Abraham Maslow, *Toward a Psychology of Being*, 2nd edn, Van Nostrand: New York, 1968), p. 11. Self-actualised people can live with the tensions produced by having to live between two worlds, heaven and earth, and the anomalies on earth.

4. In spite of the great friendship between Teresa and John of the Cross, she did not think or write in John's categories. Teresa seldom used the expression the 'dark nights', but she was mainly concerned with the second of John's nights (Thomas Dubay, *St. Teresa of Avila, St. John of the Cross, and the Gospel – on Prayer*, Ignatius Press: San Francisco, 1898, p. 171). Teresa spoke in a much more female and non-theological way, for like all women of her time, she had not had the opportunity of the theological education offered to men. Teresa often declared herself 'ignorant', and for her Christ himself became 'her living book' and from these experiences she wrote her many works.

5. Peers 1972, *Interior Castle*, p. 233. St John of the Cross does not refer to this inner turmoil as distractions, but rather 'storms'. Distractions

are more appropriate for the discursive form of meditation, since it implies that our attention is drawn away from a particular trend of thought by someone or something else. However, in contemplation where a soul is lovingly attentive to God without any particular trend of thought, the word 'storm' is a far more accurate description of the turbulence the person is undergoing. Hence Julie's use of the word 'turmoil' (Nemeck and Coombs 1982:92–3).

6. Valerie Saiving, 'The Human Situation', 1960, reprinted in Christ and Plaskow 1979.

7. Elizabeth Johnson, *Friends of God and Prophets: A Feminist Theological Reading of the Communion of Saints*, SCM Press: London, 1998; Katherine Zappone, *Hope for Wholeness: A Spirituality for Feminists*, Twenty Third Publications, Connecticut: 1991.

8. The texts and sources on the victimisation of women by a male-dominated society are too numerous to mention, but suggested readings on this topic include any of the following well-known authors: Mary Daly, Rosemary Radford Ruether, Elisabeth Schüssler Fiorenza, Mary Grey, and, specifically on women of colour, Katie Canon, Susan Thistlewaite, the novels of Alice Walker, and the Asian women's theology of Chung Hyun Kyung. Important reports include that of the United Nations Conference on Women, held in Beijing in September 1995, obtainable from the National Association of Women's Organisations, The Barn, 114 The Street, Ashwell Thorpe, Norwich NR16 1EZ; the resolutions of the First European Synod of Women in Gmunden in July 1996 (Martin et al. 1996: 109–13); and Aruna Gnanadason's two books published by the World Council of Churches, Geneva, *Living Letters to the Churches* (1997) and *No Longer A Secret: The Church and violence against women* (1997).

9. The origin of the word 'perfection' is found in the Hebrew scriptures, expressed mainly in the adjective *tamim*, meaning the integrity of animals destined to be sacrificed (Exod. 12:29; Lev. 1:3). It is also used in the Hebrew scriptures for union with God (Gen. 6:9; Sir. 44:17). In the New Testament text, 'You, therefore, must be perfect, as your heavenly Father is perfect' (Matt. 5:48), the idea of perfection is linked with social justice, including, 'go, sell what you possess and give to the poor ... and come follow me. When the young man heard this he went away sorrowful; for he had great possessions' (Matt. 19:16–23). This form of poverty is known as evangelical poverty and in Matthew this way was recommended only for a few. Traditionally, this ideal has been lived out in the celibate religious life for women and men, and has led to the idea that virginity and perfection were synonymous. This leads to an understanding of a 'state of life' being perfect and, in the Church, the hierarchy of states of life remained until the Second Vatican Council in the 1960s.

10. In the terms of Transpersonal Psychology it is the making of the

transrational identity, the authentic liminal, marginal, person, different from your pre-law and counter-law person. The pre-law person is your 'good religious', your pharisee, who keeps every dot and tittle, but has not understood the spirit of the law. Your counter-law person is one who is unable to discern between good and unjust laws. Your truly humble person can discern between just and unjust laws and ways, and in Transpersonal Psychology is known as the transrational person, someone who fully apprehends the present but sees beyond reason to something greater. In fact it is a characteristic of the prophetic personality: 'Transpersonal Psychology supports Brueggemann (1978) in his characterization of those who channel archetypal values. These people he calls prophets. Transpersonal Psychology calls them people who exhibit trans-law behaviour. The term prophet though revered in christian circles, may not be one that is worn comfortably in this day and age. However, the behaviors as outlined by Brueggemann are the important issue, not the label' (Desmond Murphy 1995:205).

11. The notion of the Devil as an independent power is not to be found in the Old Testament. The move towards an independent tempter was a development of the inter-testamental period, the unwritten time between the Old and New Testaments, where 'the shift in the role of the Devil may have arisen in apocalyptic literature as a way to explain the subjugation of Israel by foreign nations, that is, the rule of evil over the righteous covenant cannot be ruled out' (*Dictionnaire de Spiritualité*, Vol. III, 1957:144). All the features of the Devil in Judaism are present in the New Testament in Beelzebul, prince of demons (Matt. 12:24), 'ruler of this world' (John 12:31; 14:30; 16:11). The Devil brought sin into the world (1 Cor. 11:3). He is a murderer and a liar (John 13:2, 27). Christ came to destroy the works of the Devil (Heb. 2:14–15) and to cast him from heaven (Luke 10:18; Rev. 12). The Devil will intensify his work against humankind and God in the last days (Rev. 12:12), will be hindered by Christ (Rev. 20:2), and be thrown into eternal fire with his angels (Matt. 25:41; Rev. 20:10).

6. Women of the Poor

1. Quoted in Barnard, Howard Clive, *Education and the French Revolution*, Cambridge Text and Studies in the History of Education, Cambridge University Press: London, 1967:67.
2. Rudé George, *Revolutionary Europe 1783–1825*, Fontana Press: London, 1985: 234–235.
3. Hufton 1974:3. 'The Church preached unflinchingly the God-given nature of an unequal social order, it also manifested a visceral distaste for the *making* of large sums of money, and for social mobility: old wealth

was fine, new wealth was suspect' (Gibson 1989:13). The idea, therefore, that some were meant to be born poor and others rich was accepted as a right ordering of society. The concept of *structural sin*, i.e. that the reality of rich and poor that the world has inherited is not the order proposed by God, is of fairly recent origin, and grew for a large part out of the development of Liberation Theology in South America in the 1960s. (See Gutiérrez 1974.)

4. The 1770s, as a result of inquiries into this issue, reached an important watershed through a gradual change in official attitudes. The child gradually became accepted as not the result of a sinful union, but the unfortunate offspring of poverty, and hence received more compassionate treatment (Hufton 1974:350).

5. Pope Pius VII declared 1804 a Jubilee year to celebrate the re-opening of the churches in France. The Fathers of the Faith began a mission in Amiens Cathedral, in April, as a part of their campaign to restore the faith to France. They asked Julie to accompany them to give religious instruction to young girls and women. Julie was taken in a sedan chair to the Cathedral and gave instructions four or five times a week.

6. Louis-Barthélemy Enfantin (1776–?), was born at Eymeux, a village near Valence in the department of La Drôme. He was of farmer stock and used to working in the fields, like Julie. He was a young priest, a member of the Fathers of the Faith, whom Julie met while they both helped in the mission at Amiens Cathedral.

7. I owe these facts about the journeys of Julie mainly to the new research of Mary Hayes SND, who claims that Françoise wrongly calculated the number of journeys made by Julie. Françoise calculated 120, in fact it was 119. Moreover Mary Hayes believes that Julie's journeys could have been as many as 378, if we take into account the numerous times she diverted her travels to cover a wide variety of concerns.

8. Those most at risk were the Sisters living near the battlefield of Waterloo in June 1815 – at Fleurus, Jumet and Gembloux. Although all were in great danger, Gembloux was the most severely attacked: soldiers climbed through windows, destroying everything, and the Sisters were forced to flee the house. However, following the battle of Waterloo it was Namur that felt the brunt of the marauding soldiers, to the point where Julie had to barricade the front door in an attempt to keep them out of the convent. Julie was worn out by the enormous distress of the days of the war and, allowing herself very little sleep, she became very ill shortly after the fighting ended. (See Roseanne Murphy 1995, ch. XII, 'Soldiers Along the Road, 1813–1815', pp. 165–74.)

9. A Vicar General of the Diocese of Amiens under Bishop Demandolx.

7. *Women of the Cross*

1. Most prominent women theologians have written on some aspect of this theme: Rosemary Radford Ruether, Elisabeth Schüssler Fiorenza, Susan Thistlewaite, Katie Cannon, Diane Hayes, Chung Hyun Kyung, Ursula King, Mary Grey, Janet Martin Soskice, to name but a few. All make the connections between the treatment of women as scapegoats for sin, from the inherited tradition that Eve brought sin into the world.

2. Ruether 1998. Ruether has some interesting remarks on this Biblical saying of Paul. Her stance is that Paul accepted this baptism formula from the tradition he had joined, and the part of the formula that interested him was 'the Jew–Greek ethno-religious pair, or as he puts it, "In Christ neither circumcision counts for anything, but only faith working in love"' (Gal. 5:6). This chapter deals with the conflicting paradigms on women in Paul, especially in the Pastoral Epistles. The rest of this book unfolds the continuation of this conflict throughout history to the present day. It was written specifically for students of Feminist Theology and is a very useful summary of the problems inherent in the dominant atonement tradition on Redemption.

3. Fabella and Torres 1983. This book does a survey of all the emerging theologies in a Third World context.

4. Belenky et al. 1986. This is an important book based on research on how women learn. Seven ways of knowing are listed from their research: 1. Silence. 2. Received Knowledge: Listening to the Voices of Others. 3. Subjective Knowledge: The Inner Voice. 4. Subjective Knowledge: The Quest for Self. 5. Procedural Knowledge: The Voice of Reason. 6. Procedural Knowledge: Separate and Connected Knowing. 7. Constructed Knowledge: Integrating the Voices.

5. Townes 1993: see esp. the chapter by Katie Cannon, 'The Wounds of Jesus: Justification of Goodness in the Face of Manifold Evil', pp. 219–31.

6. The words of Sojourner Truth, an African-American woman and former slave who could not read or write, who was addressing a mainly European-American suffrage gathering in the 1840s:

> If the first woman God ever made
> Was strong enough to turn the world
> Upside down, all alone
> Together women ought to be able to turn it
> Rightside up again. (quoted in Schüssler Fiorenza 1994:58)

Bishop de Buoglia became Bishop of Ghent in 1807, replacing Bishop Beaumont.

7. Father Pierre-Charles-Marie Leblanc (1774–1851) was born at Caen, Normandy, of a family of high rank and heir to a large fortune. He distinguished himself as a soldier and joined the Fathers of the Sacred Heart in 1801 and later the Fathers of the Faith. He became one of their most intelligent and esteemed members and in 1814 worked for the re-establishment of the Society of Jesus, of which he became a member.

8. 'Praise, praise, praise to the Lord! An' I begun to feel such a love in my soul as I never felt before – love to all creatures. An' then all of a sudden, it stopped, an' I said, Dar's de white folks that have abused you, an' beat you, an' abused your people – think o' them! But then there came another rush of love, through my soul, an' I cried out loud – "Lord, I can love *even de white folks*!"' (Grant 1989:214)

9. Sambucy was determined to keep Sister Ciska Steenhaut, a seventeen-year-old, in Amiens. He first summoned her to meet Père Cottu, the Vicar General, to tell her of the Bishop's wishes: '"You know Mère Julie is leaving", said the priest. "What do you think of that?" "Father I will go with her" ... "But, child, you will lose your soul. You are on the wrong path; Mère Julie is deluded". "I belong to Mère Julie. I will follow her" ... "Do you know that I may refuse you Communion? You are being disobedient; the bishop does not wish you to leave" ... "I will follow Mère Julie"' (*Memoirs* 104). Ciska was so certain that the right thing to do was to go with Julie, that both Père Cottu and Sambucy were unable to change her mind. In desperation and anger, Sambucy summoned her to meet the Bishop. However, Ciska was undaunted as she knew she was not under vows, and therefore did not have to obey him. No doubt she added salt to the wounded pride of the clerics concerned because before leaving the Bishop she knelt down and asked for his blessing! He refused to give it. Sambucy never gave up. Even then he decided to write to Bishop de Broglie of Ghent, Ciska's own bishop. The lengths to which Sambucy would go knew no bounds and that began to make people suspicious. Bishop de Broglie was now well acquainted with the dealings of Sambucy and Père Varin was also beginning to recognise the error in his judgment of Julie. So Ciska won.

10. Any reader who wants to follow this up can read a full account in Roseanne Murphy 1995, chs 6 and 7.

11. The matter of the relationship between the Bishop of Namur and Napoleon is complex. The rumours that spread against the Bishop were fed by the fact that he had been an appointment of Napoleon. The truth was his appointment had been ratified by Rome in 1804. In the end, the Bishop used his influence to persuade Napoleon's government to give up the idea of the *Universal Catechism*.

12. Lucy Rooney SND, 'The Memoirs Reprinted: The Missing Pages' (unpublished MS, p. 8).

13. The classic feminist text on this question of the female self, and the difference between male sins and female sins, is that written in 1960 by Valerie Saiving entitled 'The Human Situation' and included in *Womanspirit Rising* eds Carol P. Christ and Judith Plaskow (1979), pp. 25–42). In this article she poses the question: 'Are character differences between the sexes the result of heredity or environment, of biology or culture?' She concludes that women are brought up with a sense of worthlessness, as the 'current role of society is to define the male role satisfactorily' (34). Men are not conditioned to think of themselves as worthless and lose a sense of who they really are. Women have to be awakened to their possibilities of growth. Hence the importance of the woman mystic. The modern era, in which Julie and Françoise also lived, can be called the 'masculine age' *par excellence*, which devalued the functions society gave to women and the whole reproductive process (35).

14. In other words, 'they fled when their "immanence" had holes made in it through the experience of transcendence, when their "power of relationship" was put into question' (Moltmann-Wendel and Moltmann 1991:89).

15. Hogan 1995:171. All feminist thought has long talked of the 'underside of history', the 'dangerous memory'. Black women theologians such as Katie Cannon give priority to black women's experience. Her special favourite is the novelist Zora Neale Thurston. She, along with others, often uses black women's literature as sources of women's theology. For black women theologians in the USA, slave literature is often referred to as sacred texts, not only as a historical record. (See Townes 1993, esp. the chapter by Katie Cannon cited in note 5 above.) The question often asked is do they (i.e. black women) have 'epistemological right' over white women's stories? (Hogan 1995:125).

16. Lorde 1984. The essay was first given as an address in 1978.

17. Julia Kristeva is one of the most important and creative thinkers in French feminist and post-modern thought. She critiques and expands Freudian psychoanalytic thought. In Kristeva's thought the symbolic is contrasted with the semiotic, that is, the time before a human being enters the symbolic language system of a given culture. It is pre-linguistic. On entry into the symbolic system the semiotic is submerged into the all-male symbolic symbol system. In Kristeva's analysis, the semiotic is an ongoing part of female reality since we are never able fully to identify with the father, and therefore not with the symbolic system we enter. Furthermore, the semiotic can never be fully controlled by the symbolic. It has a subversive and potentially revolutionary character. It is within the realm of the semiotic that Kristeva locates and discusses *jouissance*. 'The French word *jouissance* can be translated by the English word *joy*. In Kristeva's work it can be translated as "female orgasm". As such it is both intense and

diffuse. She also speaks of it in connection with pregnancy' (Purvis 1993:46).

18. Slee 1990:78. Nicola Slee is one of a new generation of young women poets in Britain. *Easter Garden* came out of her personal sufferings. She writes in her Preface, 'As seeds begin to sprout in darkness, so the beginnings of the anthology took root during a bleak and wintry season of my own life ... I never doubted that God was with me in the struggle, but I had to learn that God would not rescue me from the pain and confusion ... rather the resurrection I was seeking for my own life could only come about by entering into the darkness and submitting to its terror, believing against all hope, that new life could be born from the hidden depths' (9–10). Two books which greatly influenced Nicola at this time were *The Secret Garden* by Frances Hodgson Burnett and Rowan Williams' *Resurrection*.

8. *Women on the Threshold of Change*

1. Margaret Mead, quoted in an unpublished paper by Joan Chittister OSB, 1987.

2. For example, to the best of my knowledge, in the archives of Notre Dame, no Sister appears in any way involved in the suffragette movement of the early twentieth century.

3. In Britain, two events were the catalyst for this change: firstly a weekend given by Rosemary Radford Ruether, often known as the 'mother of feminist theology', at King's College, London, in 1983, and secondly the founding of CWN, Catholic Women's Network, in 1994. This network became the seedbed for change, in Britain, for RC women who were becoming very uneasy with the theology pertaining to women in the Church. It became a vehicle for asking some of the best women theologians in the world to share their theological thoughts. The 1980s and 1990s were a time of great ferment and change. This was coupled with the emergence of the first generation of British feminist theologians. Mary Grey followed Catherine Halkes as Professor of Feminist Theology at Nijmegen, and with other women in Britain, such as Professor Ursula King at Bristol and Dr Grace Jantzen, then at King's College, London, British women's theology began to take on a distinct identity. This was coupled in 1992 with the beginning of BISFT, the British and Irish School of Feminist Theology, together with a *British Feminist Theology Journal* and the later Diploma, which arose from it. The growth of the Women's European Synod movement, in the 1990s, in various countries of the world, is an important development of the growing consciousness of women and some men, that a more meaningful Christianity has to be found for both women and men in all Christian traditions.

4. In the words of Maureen Fiedler, s L, 'the "theological cleansing" of the church of those, men and women, who dared to loyally criticise parts of the inherited tradition' (Fiedler 1999).

5. Hans Küng, in his book *Christianity: The Religious Situation of Our Time*, claims that Christianity has already undergone six such shifts. The first was the early Christian apocalyptic paradigm; the second the Early Church Hellenistic paradigm; the third the Medieval Roman Catholic paradigm; the fourth the Reformation/Protestant paradigm; the fifth the Enlightenment/Modern paradigm; the sixth the Contemporary Ecumenical Paradigm. The earliest of these major shifts was the shift from Jewish to Gentile Christianity.

6. This same thought is also echoed by Desmond Murphy (1995:213), reflecting the ideas of the anthropologist N. Turner in *Which Seeds Will Grow?* (Collins Dove: Melbourne, 1988 p. 206).

7. Although these groups are more numerous in the Western world, there are a growing number of similar groups developing in Africa, Asia and South America.

8. There is a regular group of this kind at the Julie Billiart Centre, Clapham, London, that meets every first Friday, 7.30–10 p.m., for shared liturgy, prepared by a different woman each time. It is run by Catholic Women's Network (CWN), which is a part of the Women-Church movement in Britain. These kinds of groups are springing up in different parts of the world and are crucial, particularly for women, to gain confidence and develop liturgical symbols from women's experience. See also Ward and Wilde 1995, ch. 8, pp. 93–107.

Index

CPSIA information can be obtained
at www.ICGtesting.com
Printed in the USA
FFOW01n1335221116
29679FF